# *P a s s i o n*
## *&*
# *S c a n d a l*

*Great Canadian Love Stories*

## Barbara Smith

## Detselig Enterprises Ltd.

Calgary, Alberta, Canada

Passion and Scandal
© 1997 Barbara Smith

Canadian Cataloguing in Publication Data

Smith, Barbara, 1947-
Passion and scandal

Includes bibliographical references.
ISBN 1-55095-148-7

1. Canada—Biography.  2. Love—Canada—History.  3. Unmarried couples—Canada—History. I. Title.
FC25.S64 1997            920.071            C97-910330-4
F1005.S64 1997


Detselig Enterprises Ltd.
210-1220 Kensington Rd. N.W.
Calgary, Alberta  T2N 3P5

Detselig Enterprises Ltd. appreciates the financial support for our 1994 publishing program, provided by Canadian Heritage and the Alberta Foundation for the Arts, a beneficiary of the Lottery Fund of the Government of Alberta.

Printed in Canada
ISBN 1-55059-148-7
SAN 115-0324

Cover design by Dean Macdonald

Care has been taken to trace the ownership of copyright material used in this book. The author and publisher welcome any information enabling them to rectify any reference or credit in subsequent editions.

*For Dennis Mills, who generously gave me the idea on which this book is based, and, of course, for my husband Bob, the object of my Great Canadian Love Story*

*For my grandsons and their peers — who will need forests as much as books — arrangements have been made to plant a sufficient number of trees to compensate for those used in publishing this volume.*

# Acknowledgements

Many people contributed to this project and I owe a great debt of thanks to all of them. Unfortunately, some of those who offered assistance were anonymous voices at the other end of telephone wires or nameless faces behind counters. As the bulk of people in that category are employed across Canada at our libraries and archives, I shall just say thank you to all Canadian librarians and archivists. Your skills and courtesy made my life much easier.

I also wish to extend my thanks to others who were helpful and certainly not anonymous. The following poor souls have been all too aware of this book over the past few years. Please know your contributions were and are appreciated. Editor Dennis Mills of Toronto, whose creativity conceived of this project and whose generosity allowed me to write it. Sociologist and author Dr. Barrie Robinson of Edmonton, for his patient and skillful editorial guidance. Artist and teacher Bob Dmytruk of Edmonton, for his direction regarding the Tom Thomson story. Debbie Trumbley of Calgary, for her help in obtaining photographs. Denise Lyons of Edmonton, for arranging translation services. Louise Adams of Gibbons, for translating the necessary documents. Ruth Hunter of Toronto, for her generous gifts from my father's library. Nathan Tichenor of North Vancouver, for the generous gift from his library. Gerry Janzen of Edmonton, for her patient and skillful proofreading.

Thanks too to my family and friends who supported and encouraged me every step of the way.

# Table of Contents

# Introduction

People often ask a writer what his or her current project is and my reply for the past few years has been, "an anthology of Canadian love stories." That answer has certainly provoked some interesting replies. Many people were enthusiastic and congratulated me warmly for having conceived of such a unique project. Unfortunately for my ego, I had to tell them it wasn't my idea but rather was given to me by a dear (and very creative) friend. Other people just stared blankly, wondering, I suppose, what choice of words might be construed as a suitable reply to the news of such an off-the-wall project. Still others were very specific in their expressions of doubt about the sanity behind such a venture. "I didn't know Canada had any love stories" was one comment I remember well. My all time favorite response, though, came from my much-adored brother, who pronounced, "That'll be a short book."

With all due respect (and sisterly admiration), I suspected at the time that these comments reflected the respondents' lack of awareness of Canadian social history and not the numbers of interesting love stories buried in the annals of our past. Thankfully, my research bore out my suspicions. Soon after starting to dig for stories, I realized there was such an abundance of potentially good material out there that I would have to weed stories out. As a result, over the years this book has changed form many times. The final idea-editing process was a tough one because, in order to give the volume unity, I was forced to discard some stories that appeared to have great potential. For instance, who can deny the drama of the Pierre and Margaret Trudeau relationship, or the glamor of Hollywood star Janet Jones marrying Canada's greatest gift to hockey, Wayne Gretzky, and then there's the quintessential and enduring Canadian couple Catherine MacKinnon and her husband, Charlie Farquharson's alter ego Don Harron, to say nothing of the quirky pairing that was Harold and Yolanda Ballard. The list went on and on.

Sometimes it seemed that every love story I chose for inclusion suggested another one. Having chosen to include the chronicle of William Lyon Mackenzie King and the women in his life, it was tough to ignore Sir Wilfrid Laurier's long standing affair with his partner's wife, especially as Laurier was King's mentor. I didn't, however, want the book to be filled with stories of politicians and their love lives.

When the sheer numbers of stories available overpowered me and weakened my decision-making powers, I turned to Linda Berry, my editor at Detselig, for direction. As we shared a vision for the finished product, I accepted her input with thanks. A quick scan of the Table of Contents will tell the reader that we have decided to exclude any stories of people still living. The choice was somewhat arbitrary, but certainly had the effect of creating a sort of popular history book rather than one of current affairs (pun intended). This presented some challenges and, in order that readers not misunderstand my motivation and intention as I wrote this book, I offer the following commentary.

History by its very nature invites review, retrospection – hence in any re-telling of historical matters the narrator risks being accused of committing that most dastardly of all sins – creating "revisionist history." I don't think that in writing any of the following stories I have chosen to shine an arbitrarily favorable or sinister light on existing information. If the reader notices a distinct difference in my version of any of the stories, I would ask that he or she keep in mind that my focus throughout has been the love stories entwined around these historical figures. I have, therefore, excluded facets of their lives that would be necessary to a more comprehensive interpretation. Moreover, I have spotlighted other anecdotes and character traits that seem minor except when viewed through the lens of love.

Although each chapter has been carefully researched, as evidenced by the endnotes and bibliography, I have taken creative license and invented dialogue where I thought to do so would make the reading more enjoyable and the characters' motivations more obvious. As it was never my intention to write a scholarly text, I felt no pangs of conscience.

What, then, were my intentions and motivations as I carried out the process that led to this volume? As a self-styled student of social history, I knew there were some Great Canadian Love Stories out there. I simply wanted to share them with others.

# Tom Thomson
# & Winnifred Trainor

Scalding pain. Then nothing. A void – a cold, white void.

"This is the   end, then, is it?"

The lucidity became all-encompassing, a physical quality. What irony – coming now and in this way. It might have been amusing if he'd read it in a novel.

"My final thoughts – how pathetically insignificant," he lamented before releasing his grasp and accepting, even inviting, death.

Feeling an almost startling contentment, he died and the world lost an irreplaceable gift – the burgeoning brilliance of the artist Tom Thomson.

The life that ended so abruptly and mysteriously on July 8, 1917, in Algonquin Park had begun less than 40 years before.

On August 4, 1877, in the village of Claremont, Ontario (roughly between Toronto and Oshawa but north of them both), Margaret Thomson, wife of John Thomson, gave birth for the sixth time.[1] The arrival of this baby temporarily evened the family count to three girls and three boys.

In choosing their children's names, John and Margaret Thomson were not given to flights of fancy. They favored the solid and unadorned. They had chosen George and Henry for their older sons, and they decided to name the tiny squalling infant Thomas, after the children's paternal grandfather.

Within two months of Tom's birth, the family moved to a farm by the town of Leith, near Owen Sound, Ontario.[2] Here the Thomson family grew to a total of 10 siblings. The children's upbringing was unremarkable except that young Tom developed a lung infection and missed a year in school. That year, with freedom from academic structure, Tom explored the natural world around him.

Details of Tom's formal education are sketchy: he may or may not have finished high school.[3] One aspect of his youth, however, has been solidly recorded for posterity. A series of family photographs show that Tom

*Tom Thomson, circa 1904. (F 1066 s. 2794; Archives of Ontario)*

Thomson grew into a handsome young man. In addition to appealing facial features, he was tall, over six feet in height, with a well-developed physique which reflected his interest and ability in sports. As a result, women found Tom extremely attractive.

Thomson may have added to this physical attractiveness by making himself something of an enigma: he left different people with very different impressions. He is variously reported as being "socially inclined";[4] having a "quiet, reserved manner";[5] and being diffident, moody, bashful, reticent, melancholy and "defeated in manner"; congenial, unselfish, kindly, impetuous, easygoing, gregarious;[6] and "as timid as a deer."[7] Thomson has been credited with both a "sunny personality" and a "fierce temper."

These inconsistencies might indicate that Thomson suffered from bouts of depression. This possibility, coupled with an occasional over-indulgence in alcohol, may be behind some of the contradictory impressions left by Tom Thomson.

Like many young men, Tom spent a few directionless years. In 1901, at the age of 24, he followed his older brothers to Seattle, Washington, where they had helped to establish the Acme Business College.[8] Here, Thomson had what may have been his first serious relationship.

Alice Elinor Lambert, a waitress and the daughter of a minister, was only 15 when Tom Thomson proposed marriage to her. She rejected his proposal and Thomson immediately returned to Canada. He never corresponded with the beautiful Miss Lambert again.

What terminated this relationship so quickly and permanently is unclear. The girl may have reacted, understandably, in an unsophisticated way to the suggestion of marriage. If Tom had as sensitive a nature as some say he did, he may have fled, humiliated. There is also some indication that a third party came between the two young lovers.

Whatever the truth, Alice Lambert matured into a pretty and financially independent woman who wrote romance novels. Her books, with provocative titles such as *Lost Fragrance* and *Women Are Like That*, sold well and provided her with a comfortable living.[9] Possibly her writing was an outlet for the melancholy she felt at losing the dashing young Tom.

Harold Town, in his book *The Silence and The Storm*, suggests Thomson "was probably more of a womanizer than he has been given credit for."[10] It is difficult to credit this opinion given the number of references to the artist's reclusive nature. Another Thomson scholar, Joan Murray, implies that by his mid-20s, Thomson was all but inexperienced with women.[11]

This inexperience probably wasn't due to lack of effort on Tom's part, for shortly after he returned to Canada, Thomson began keeping company with another young woman, Elizabeth McCarnen. The reason for the dissolution of this relationship is well documented. One of Miss McCarnen's siblings died, and she abruptly left Toronto to live in Phelpston, Ontario, and care for the newly orphaned children.[12] The questions of why the children could not have been brought to Toronto or, alternatively, why Thomson could not have relocated to Phelpston, were apparently never addressed.

If Tom's love life hadn't settled down by his early 30s, at least his career had. After holding a number of short-term positions, Thomson took a job with Grip Limited, a well-respected photo-engraving firm in Toronto. The pool of talent at Grip during the time Tom was with the firm was nothing short of amazing.[13] He worked alongside J.E.H. MacDonald, Fred Varley, a very young Franklin Carmichael, Arthur Lismer and others. The studios of Grip Limited effectively served as the birthing room for the Group of Seven, which was eventually created in 1920.

Evidently, the talented Grip employees longed to express their creativity in ways not available to commercial artists, and loosely-structured groups of artists began to make weekend jaunts to the countryside.

Always a great outdoorsman, Tom enjoyed the trips with their inherent camaraderie and opportunities to become re-acquainted with rural Ontario's rugged geography. His colleagues were encouraging about Tom's painting ability, and their comments evidently influenced the young man. The excursions, which had begun only as day trips, had, by 1912, extended into outings of several days duration in the wilds of Algonquin Park. As history soon proved, Tom Thomson was in his element. He began spending as much time as he could in his beloved Park.

It is said that Tom inherited his father's tremendous ability to concentrate. That skill, combined with his latent artistic talents, allowed Tom Thomson, the artist, to progress quickly from being merely an awkward replicator to the genius originator whose work is now recognized in a glance.

Working for a living cut a wide swath in the time Tom had available to paint. In the fall of 1913, Dr. James MacCallum, an oculist (forerunner of today's optometrist) with a profitable practice and a great affinity for northern Ontario, saw the work Thomson was producing and he offered to cover the painter's expenses if Thomson would devote himself to serious painting on a full-time basis.

Initially, whether out of shyness or lack of confidence, Tom declined the offer. Fortunately for Canadian art, Tom stayed up too late one night, improving a sketch he'd brought back to Toronto with him. The next morning he was late for work, and someone in authority pointedly looked at the wall clock as the young artist arrived at his desk. This implied criticism was enough for Tom: he immediately quit his commercial art job and accepted Dr. McCallum's patronage. Except for occasional positions as a guide or a fire ranger in Algonquin Park, Thomson never sought paid employment again.

His art and his life, for they were inseparable at that point, flourished. His former co-workers continued to join the artist in the Park when they could. Soon Tom had made other friends and acquaintances as well.

When the weather was too harsh for camping, Tom stayed at Mowat Lodge, owned by Shannon and Annie Fraser. The couple was glad of the business. Their lodge had been named for the nearby town of Mowat, a place for which prosperity had once been predicted. Sadly, the railway route, that was to bring the boom with it, was re-designed. The new plan meant the train tracks came nowhere near Mowat, and the place dwindled into a virtual ghost town.

The Frasers stayed on, providing the bypassed community with post-office facilities, lodging for visitors and a meeting place. People in the area, both year-round residents and visitors, thought highly of Annie Fraser, and sought her warmth and hospitality. Most folks liked Annie so well that they charitably overlooked her husband's considerably less appealing personality.

When Shannon Fraser drank, and many said that happened far too frequently, he became antagonistic. Periodically, that hostility was seen to be directed at Tom Thomson. Over the years Tom spent in the Park, Shannon Fraser vacillated between displays of open affection and outright malevolence towards Tom.

Typical of those in any tightly knit community, the people living in and around Mowat Lodge enjoyed a bit of gossip now and again.

"Thomson 'had a thing' going with Shan's wife, there's no doubt," suggested one who thought he knew for sure.[14]

Little hard evidence exists to back this premise, but it doesn't take too great a stretch of imagination to build such a case. Annie Fraser, a robust young Irish immigrant, cloistered in the wilds of northern Ontario, was struggling to preserve Mowat Lodge. She was uneducated, unsophisticated, overworked and under-appreciated. Ottelyn Addison, park ranger Mark Robinson's daughter, wrote in her book, *Tom Thomson, The*

*Algonquin Years:* "Mrs. Fraser appeared to do most of the work while her husband looked after the horses."[15]

Annie Fraser's parents lived with the couple. While this may have provided some degree of companionship for Annie, it might just as easily have provided increased feelings of confinement. Instead of being answerable only to her husband's demands, she may also have felt obligated to honor her parents' requests.

Into the scenario entered the handsome, talented, free-spirit of Tom Thomson. Only an unimaginative prude would deny the volatile possibilities. Tom and Annie could well have been involved in a clandestine love affair. Conversely, they may never have laid a hand on one another. Even if their behavior remained circumspect, Tom may still have been a serious point of contention in the Frasers' seemingly less-than-idyllic marriage.

The mere thought that his wife might have been looking approvingly at another man may have incited jealous rages in Shannon Fraser. Residents in the Canoe Lake area knew to avoid Fraser when he was provoked. The force of the man's temper and his fondness for brew were both common knowledge.

If the flames needed to be fanned further, Thomson was also known to imbibe to excess on occasion. In addition, there were frequent business dealings between Thomson and Fraser. Thomson cared little for money and kept poor track of it. Almost all the potential ingredients necessary for a major conflict were at hand.

Whether or not Annie Fraser and Tom Thomson were involved romantically is mere conjecture. Tom's all-consuming devotion to his art, however, is not. Re-creating the rugged landscapes of Algonquin Park was, by then, the man's *raison d'être*. No woman could ever hope to distract him from his quest.

Today it's almost impossible to imagine that someone might not appreciate the importance of Thomson's art. During his lifetime, however, he was not widely recognized or respected. His early painting expeditions, his activities with easels and sketches, were even viewed with skepticism verging on suspicion. In 1912, Mark Robinson, the Park ranger, who eventually became Thomson's closest friend, listened when advised that the artist's behavior might bear close watching. Sitting in the bush at an easel for hours, and even for days, seemed a decidedly questionable activity. A contradiction like this – between the community's attitude to his work and Thomson's own attitude – would not make fertile soil for love.

Conversely, it is easy to imagine that a man so obsessed by his art would be attracted to a woman able to appreciate it. This thesis gives credence to the possibility of a love affair between Tom Thomson and Frances McGillvray. In 1917 Thomson was 39 years old. He was at the height of his creativity, both qualitatively and quantitatively. He had little time for anything except his passion for painting. Enter 50-year-old Frances McGillvray – a vivacious, intelligent and, most importantly, an interested and knowledgeable woman.

She visited Tom at his Toronto studio during the winter of 1916-17, and then in the spring of 1917 she travelled to Canoe Lake to be with him.

"Of all who know my work, only Frances immediately grasped what I'm trying to achieve," Thomson stated.[16]

Did Tom Thomson have an affair with this older woman? He may have, but she may only have been a treasured friend, a supportive critic who, "liked Thomson's work and gave him courage and confidence to press on with it."[17]

Despite the man's devotion to his art work, he lived with another, even stronger obsession. Tom Thomson loved to fish. One of his earliest paintings, "Sufficiency," is of a young man fishing from a dock. In her book, *Tom Thomson: The Last Spring*, Joan Murray implies that the choice of title indicated Thomson's attitude toward fishing. He was telling the world that there was nothing, other than fishing, sufficient for a whole and satisfying life. Murray further points out that Thomson used the image more than once, indicating, to her, that he was pleased with it.[18] Such indications of pleasure or pride connected with Thomson's art are sparse.

"Tom was never very proud of his painting," J.E.H. Macdonald wrote, "but he was cocky about his fishing."[19]

When informed of the sale of one of his early paintings, Thomson reportedly asked, "What damn fool picked that?"[20]

And that certainly wasn't an isolated incident, merely reflecting a day's sour mood. If anyone admired a painting Thomson was working on, he would give it to them. When artists with more business sense took over the responsibility of selling his work, Thomson recommended that they try to get $10 or $15 for a piece, but added, ". . . if they don't care to put in so much, let it go for what they will give."[21]

However, he took tremendous pride in his prowess as a fisherman. Many photographs remain to back this claim. Thomson often had his photo taken with his day's catch. He also took his own pictures of a day's catch fanned out like so many trophies. One photo shows a fish baking under a reflector. There is even a photo of the reflector by itself. This seems a strange picture for anyone to take, especially for a man with an eye for natural beauty.

Friends referred to Thomson's "uncanny ability to catch fish."[22] His passion for fishing was so intense, especially when compared to the off-hand way he treated his paintings, that it seemed his hobby and his vocation were reversed in his mind. Perhaps then, Tom could only love a woman as devoted to fishing as he was.

Enter Winnifred Trainor. (Her first name has been variously recorded as Winnifred and Winifred. I use Winnifred, the spelling used more frequently by Thomson's biographers.)

Winnie's father, Hugh, was a foreman at a lumber mill in nearby Huntsville and her family owned a summer cottage on Canoe Lake. Winnie was at home in the outdoors, she loved to fish, and perhaps Tom loved Winnie for that alone. She certainly fit with his history of being attracted to strong-willed women such as Alice Lambert and Elizabeth McCarnen.

Algonquin Park was a virtual wilderness in the early 1900s. City slickers would have found it a difficult place to stay for more than a day or two. To the outdoor enthusiast, however, it was a veritable paradise.

Winnie Trainor's parents placed great value on natural surroundings. They shared their deep appreciation for nature with their daughters, Winnifred and Marie. Winnie was especially receptive to their efforts. She left the nearby town of Huntsville as often as she could in order to spend time at Canoe Lake, hiking, fishing and just enjoying being in the wilds of Algonquin Park.

The building that served as the Trainor's cottage had once been a shelter hut for lumberjacks working for the local lumber company. With tongue in cheek, the men used to refer to the building as "The Manse." Today it would be considered too "rustic" for all but the hardiest cottager, but it suited the Trainor family's needs well. They delighted in any opportunity to retreat to the tranquility of the Park.

As early as the spring of 1914, Winnie Trainor, a 30-year-old spinster, had an additional reason to visit the former "manse." A handsome, eligible man had begun to frequent the area around her parents' summer home. Tom Thomson was his name, and he was an artist!

"I can't hold that against him, though," Winnie decided. "He may be a bit quirky but he certainly has a magical way of catching fish. Just to watch that man cast is a privilege – a perfect figure eight every time."

And Thomson's handmade lures and flies, how she admired the artistry that went into those.

Although Winnie was not a pretty young woman in a conventional sense, she didn't need to go out of her way to catch the eye of a healthy young man. Thomson passed by the Trainor's cottage several times a week. Occasionally he waved or called a greeting, but never anything more – until one Saturday afternoon early in the summer of 1914.

A loosely structured group had gathered at the cottage next to the Trainors'. Mr. and Mrs. Bletcher, an American couple of German extraction, owned the place. This weekend neither of the elder Bletchers had made the trip to the lake. Only their adult children, Martin and Bessie, were there.

Returning from a lengthy hike in the woods, Winnie Trainor intended to go straight home and fix herself a long-overdue meal. However, the sounds of laughter and raised voices distracted her. As she approached the two side-by-side cottages, "Come join us!" young Bessie Bletcher called out enthusiastically.

"Well, I suppose," Winnie answered, somewhat hesitantly. She'd never been in the Bletcher home. It wasn't that the two families disliked one another. They simply didn't know one another.

Winnie joined the periphery of the group in the yard, and within minutes she was mixing easily with them. Then, someone introduced her to Tom Thomson, the man she'd been admiring from afar.

"You two have a lot in common," the man making the introductions assured both Tom and Winnie before abruptly leaving to continue a conversation he'd been engaged in previously.

Both Winnie and Tom were initially reserved, perhaps intimidated by their noisy surroundings. Fortunately, their mutual friend's comment implying shared interests served its purpose – it inspired a lighthearted conversation.

"I wonder what he could have meant by that?" Tom asked while trying not to stare at Winnie.

"I can't imagine," she replied, with only a hint of dishonesty. "I've heard you're an artist and I'm afraid I know nothing about art. Perhaps you enjoy the out-of-doors? Or maybe you like to fish?"

"Oh, yes," Tom responded, flicking an errant lock of dark hair from his eyes.

"Which is it then?" Winnie asked, "fishing or being outdoors?"

"Oh, both," Tom said, not wanting to pick one over the other in case he chose the one she was less interested in.

"Me too," Winnie said. "I've just come from a hike over toward the Tea Lake Dam. Tomorrow morning I'm going to try out a new lure. I think the trout will love it."

For Thomson, Winnie had just uttered magic words.

The balance of the afternoon flew by for the newly introduced pair. Oblivious to the crowd around them, they set about getting to know one another better. The more they found out, the more they liked. By dusk, Tom Thomson and Winnie Trainor were both very happy people.

They were also grateful that they had met near the beginning of the summer. Even so, their time together would be limited. Winnie's job as the bookkeeper at the lumbermill in Huntsville meant she was only free to be at Canoe Lake on weekends. Between painting and fishing expeditions, Thomson supplemented his income – Dr. MacCallum's annuity –

by guiding or by doing odd jobs. At the end of summer, the Trainors would leave the area for winter and Thomson would return to Toronto.

Despite their schedules, Tom and Winnie still managed to see each other frequently during that summer. As autumn approached, the Trainors prepared to close "The Manse" until the following May and Tom began to pack his sketches for the train trip back to Toronto.

"My parents want to know if you could join us for the Thanksgiving weekend," Winnie told Tom as she waited with him on the platform at the train station in Huntsville.

Thomson was silent for a moment. Was there an implication included in the invitation? Probably, he decided, but looking at Winnie standing there beside him, he realized he didn't mind the implication at all. As a matter of fact it pleased him enormously.

"That would be nice. Please thank them for me," Thomson answered just as a noisy, dirty, steam engine came into view.

Winnie turned toward the sound of the train. The long, lonely, boring weeks ahead, keeping accounts straight for a lumber company and living in her parents' home, didn't bode well when compared with the past months of summer.

The platform was crowded by the time the train hissed to a stop, and since neither Tom nor Winnie were given to public displays of affection, he boarded the train after they exchanged simple "good-byes" and chose a seat on the far side of the coach. He did not want to endure waving to Winnie as the train pulled out. He needn't have bothered. Winnie had left the station and was striding toward Huntsville's main street by the time Tom was settled in his seat.

But Winnie knew she couldn't face going home. It was Saturday morning, so she had the option of spending a few hours poring over the company records, but Winnie couldn't face that either.

There was only one place where she could find the solitude she needed – the old graveyard at the edge of town. Sweeping her skirt up above her ankles, Winnie hurried toward the cemetery gate. The tears she'd fought so hard to control spilled onto her cheeks before she found the seclusion she sought. Finally, hidden among the tombstones, Winnie let both the love and the sorrow flow out in shuddering sobs.

Before long, the all-consuming urge to cry gratified, Winnie unwound from her hunched position between the marble markers. Like many urgent needs, once satisfied, her overpowering sorrow now seemed somehow foolish. Winnie wiped her eyes, brushed off her clothing and, with as much dignity as she could muster, strolled back along the path to the cemetery's entrance.

Once out on Main Street again, Winnie began to accept the reality that would be hers, at least until next spring when she and Tom could be together again in the place they both loved. Besides, they'd write to one another and he'd be up to see her at Thanksgiving and that was only a few weeks away.

Once the train left the station, Tom, however, had left the summer well behind him. He had dozens of incomplete sketches in his case. These had to be finished over the coming winter. He would be busy night and day, but before he even got to those he'd have to do something to make the shack habitable.

A small smile spread across Tom's face as he thought of his shack nestled in Toronto's Rosedale Valley. Even though it was in the heart of the city, he loved the place. His friends' studio was close at hand, and the artists visited one another frequently. As a matter of fact, it was Lawren Harris and Dr. MacCallum who'd originally found this place for Thomson. Now all he had to do was build himself a bunk, and seal a few cracks in the walls. Once winter came he could snowshoe for miles up the valley.

Less than a week after he'd left Huntsville, Tom had turned the shack into what he considered quite adequate accommodation. What was most important was the light. It was bright, and would be marvelously conducive to finishing his sketches.

He set to work right away. Many of his friends, including Dr. MacCallum, his patron, some of Tom's brothers and even a brother-in-law, stopped by to visit Thomson now that he was back in the city. These

*Tom Thomson Shack: The original Shack was acquired by Robert and Signe McMichael, and was moved from Toronto's Rosedale Ravine to its present site in 1962. It was restored in 1989.*

people all felt somewhat protective toward the artist. His friends received and distributed his mail; his family occasionally chided him over his self-imposed isolation; and MacCallum paid Tom's bills.

Lawren Harris delivered the first letter from Winnie while Thomson was away on a day-long hike north and east of Toronto. Upon his return, the envelope lay on a shelf unopened and unnoticed.

When her second letter arrived some days later, Harris brought it over to Tom's home with a stack of other correspondence, some of which were bills.

"Shall I look after these for you, then?" asked Harris, who was well aware of Thomson's disregard for financial matters.

"Yes, yes please. There's money in my account, I know. Dr. MacCallum's just made a deposit to it," Thomson replied, barely looking up from his easel.

"All right then," Harris agreed. "You'll want to look after this yourself, though, I'm sure."

Thomson looked up from his work and saw the envelope in Harris's outstretched hand. Both men smiled broadly, having correctly guessed from the stylized handwriting that the letter was from a woman.

Although Harris had intended to suggest the two take a break for a drink and a smoke, he saw his friend was anxious to read his mail.

"I must be going now, Tom," Harris considerately lied before showing himself out.

Tom grinned as he read Winnie's long, friendly letter. He was delighted to hear from her and enjoyed every word she'd taken the time to write. One paragraph puzzled him slightly: she made some off-hand reference to a previous letter. That struck Tom as being strange: he thought this was the first one.

For a few minutes after reading Winnie's letter, Tom wasn't able to get his mind back on his work. He paced the length of the shack several times before some unseen force stopped him.

"I know what I'll do," he shouted to the otherwise empty building. "I'll finish this painting and take it to Winnie when I visit next month."

Smiling broadly and singing quietly in his lilting tenor voice, Tom Thomson happily returned to his painting.

At first, Winnie Trainor checked at the Huntsville post office every day. She told the post mistress that her mother was expecting some important news from relatives in the States.

"A likely story, that one," assessed the woman behind the counter after being a part of the charade for several weeks. "It's got more to do with that artist fellow than any American relatives, I'd hazard to guess."

Correctly suspecting the burgeoning wave of gossip about her, Winnie eventually let her mother resume her own mail-checking duties. By the beginning of October, when Winnie hadn't heard a word from Tom, the nearly heartbroken woman wrote a third letter.

Trying to keep her anxiety out of the tone of the letter, Winnie kept to topics of very general interest, and closed by saying, "Please let me know if anything will be interfering with your upcoming visit."

Tom received the letter with delight. He failed to notice its reserved tone and didn't feel compelled to answer with a return note of any sort. After all, Winnie only asked him to let her know if there'd been any change in his plans. There hadn't. He was greatly looking forward to his trip to Huntsville and to seeing Winnie once again. Why even the painting he'd earmarked as a gift to her had turned out well. He smiled with barely concealed anticipation each time he thought of watching her reaction to it.

Even better, two of his friends from the city, Alex (A.Y.) Jackson and Jim (J.E.H.) MacDonald, would be joining him for the trip. They all agreed the opportunity to view the park in the fall was too good to miss. Thomson would stay with the others at Mowat Lodge until Monday, when he'd make his way to see Winnie at the Trainor's home in nearby Huntsville.

"Winnifred, whatever is the matter with you these days?" Hugh Trainor finally asked his sulking daughter. "You're certainly not yourself at work, and when you get home you barely say a word to Marie or your mother. Thanksgiving is only a few days away. Can't you find anything in your life to be grateful for?"

Winnie knew she'd been acting poorly. Having her father mention it only added shame to an already hefty stack of negative feelings.

"I'm sorry," she muttered with quiet sincerity, and vowed to put on a better show in the future. Who did Tom Thomson think he was anyway? Certainly no one she couldn't live without. She'd approach middle age without him just fine. She supposed one summer's romance shouldn't be allowed to interfere with her mundane existence.

Still, though, as the Friday night of Thanksgiving weekend neared she couldn't deny the anticipation she felt. Taking the long route home from work that evening, Winnie stopped by the train station. The express from Toronto was due on time – at seven o'clock.

Should she stay to meet the train or should she wait at home? Picturing herself waiting on the platform embarrassed her. She didn't want to appear that eager to see the man she used to think of as her lover. But then again, letting Tom get off the train at an empty platform seemed inhospitable.

In the end, Winnie Trainor arranged to be strolling toward a nearby group of stores when the train arrived. The platform was empty as the train slowed, but Winnie judged she could make her way to it in less than two minutes, after she saw Tom step down from the coach.

Fifteen minutes later, Winnie remained where she'd stood. There'd been no need to hurry to the station. Tom had not alighted from the train. No one had. The stationmaster had loaded some bags of mail aboard and then signaled the engineer to continue his northbound route. Only a tiny puff of smoke on the horizon remained as proof the train had even made an appearance.

A few miles away, Tom, oblivious to the distress he'd caused, sat with his friends at Mowat Lodge. They'd arrived by train the day before and had spent the day happily smoking, gossiping and drinking from a bottle of Irish whiskey. The next day they'd all head out into the bush where they'd spend the weekend fishing and painting and enjoying themselves. All except Tom, that is. Tom intended to leave the others after Sunday night for dinner the next day with Winnie and her parents.

At noon on Monday, Winnie joined her mother in the kitchen and debated the best way to suggest canceling the planned Thanksgiving dinner. There wasn't much point in proceeding as though they'd be enjoying company, when it had become quite evident to Winnie that Tom would not be joining them.

"Mother," she began before being interrupted by noises coming from the front of the house.

"Well, well, Tom my boy," Winnie heard her father exclaim. "We've all been looking forward to seeing you again."

"Wouldn't have missed the visit for the world, Mr. Trainor," Winnie heard Tom reply.

"Winnifred, Winnifred," her father called from the hall. "Come and see who's here."

Winnie swung quickly toward the direction of her father's voice. She tried to call an answer, but merely staying vertical took every bit of her strength. It took several moments before she was able to make her way to the parlor, to Tom Thomson, the man she loved.

"I'm glad you like it," Tom was saying to Winnifred's father as she approached the doorway. "I brought it for you and your family, as a gift."

Mustering as much dignity and courage as she could, Winnie Trainor entered the family's parlor and calmly said, "Hello, Tom."

Both men jumped to their feet.

"Winnie," Tom exclaimed eagerly. "It's good to see you again. I received your letters. That was thoughtful of you to take the time to write, even though you knew I'd be here for this visit."

The best Winnie could manage in response to all the enthusiasm in the room was a half-hearted smile.

"Hugh," her mother called from the kitchen. "Perhaps you could come here and give me a hand for a moment."

The older man nodded self-consciously as he left the room. How transparent could his wife be? He wasn't completely insensitive. He'd intended to leave the room in just a moment. His wife's ruse was amusingly obvious and entirely unnecessary, but, of course, he'd never tell her that.

"Coming dear," he replied, excusing himself from the living room.

As soon as he did, Tom moved toward Winnie wanting to give her a hug and a kiss in greeting, but she pulled away.

"How could you, Tom?" she implored.

"Could I what?" he asked, confused.

"What do you mean, 'could you what?' You know perfectly well what I mean. I thought this past summer had meant as much to you, as it did to me. Then you leave here weeks ago, and I never hear a word from you until you suddenly show up today."

The color drained from Tom's face.

"Isn't today the day you invited me for supper?" he asked hesitantly.

"Yes, of course it is, silly," Winnie assured him.

A pregnant silence hung between them and remained there until Winnie broke into a fit of laughter. For a moment Tom nearly panicked. He thought the woman was crying. When he realized his mistake, he too began to laugh. With the laughter, the awkwardness vanished.

"Let's go for a walk, shall we?" Winnie suggested.

Relieved to have an apparent problem cleared up so easily, Tom agreed wholeheartedly.

"Mother," she called into the hallway. "We're going for a walk. We won't be long, I promise."

"Yes yes, dear, you two run along, but be back for dinner by five," the older woman admonished.

They walked along in silence for several blocks.

"I'm sorry that I haven't written to you, Winnie. I see now that I should have, but the days go by so quickly, and really, Winnie, I'm not much of a one for letter writing. It doesn't mean I don't think of you because I do, honestly." Tom's words tumbled out, almost in disarray.

His honesty melted any last resentments Winnifred might have held. She reached for his hand and squeezed it to tell him all was well. When she went to release her squeeze she found that Tom held her hand tightly in his. They walked along happily holding hands until they reached the end of the residential section.

"Maybe we should get back now," Tom suggested. "Dinner may be ready, and besides, I want you to see the painting I brought for you and your family. Maybe then you'll understand how my time in Toronto is spent."

The Thanksgiving dinner was as enjoyable as any at the small dining-room table could remember. The food was delicious, and everyone enjoyed everyone else's company. As Tom Thomson and Hugh Trainor were tucking into their second brandy after dessert, Winnie and her mother cleared away the dinner dishes.

"Will you be able to stay for a few days, Tom?" the older man inquired.

"No, I'm afraid not, sir. I have a ticket on this evening's train for Toronto."

"You have to be back in the city so soon?" Hugh Trainor asked.

"I do, unfortunately," Thomson confirmed. "I still have a great deal of work ahead of me. Dr. MacCallum's offer of support won't extend forever, I'm sure, and I have to accomplish as much as I can while his generosity holds."

"Commendable, Tom, most commendable," Trainor acknowledged.

"Perhaps I should say good-bye and thank you to your wife and daughters now," Tom suggested, standing. "It's getting on toward train time."

"I suppose it is. Perhaps I could give you a lift to the station?"

"No, that's fine sir, the walk will do me good after that big meal."

As the two men approached the entranceway to the kitchen Trainor suggested, "I'll bet Winnie would enjoy a brisk walk now as well."

Both Winnie and Tom blushed at the man's poorly hidden attempt to give them a few last private moments. Despite their embarrassment, they appreciated his intentions and, indeed, the time alone to say their good-byes.

As the train approached the station, Tom and Winnie both steeled themselves against the pain of parting. Before boarding, Tom promised to write. The lump in Winnie's throat prevented her from promising anything or even from replying.

He kissed her lightly on the cheek, got on the train and was gone. As she watched the caboose disappear into the horizon, Winnie made herself a promise. This time she wouldn't allow herself to write to Tom until he had first written to her. That pledge meant that she and the man she loved had no further contact until the summer of 1915.

When the weeks without letters from Tom had built into months, Winnifred Trainor became resigned to having lost the only man she'd ever loved. Right up until the previous spring there had still been a few interested suitors in town, but none compared to Tom. Since the artist's arrival in her life, the others had given up their attempts to call on Winnifred. She clearly wasn't the least bit interested in them.

In keeping with tradition, the Trainors spent the first weekend in June opening their summer home. All of them, and Winnie especially, were looking forward to another season in Algonquin Park.

She hoped the summer would provide an opportunity for nature to heal the pain of Tom's silence. She hadn't heard either from him or about him and Winnie presumed she'd never see Tom Thomson again. She was just coming to terms with that thought when she accompanied her parents on their drive to the cottage. Hours later, she was face to face with the man she thought she'd loved and lost.

The strength of her anger was matched only by the depth of his confusion.

"Why are you so angry, Winnie? I told you how busy I was. You knew we'd see each other again here, this summer," Tom implored.

"You said you'd write and you didn't." Winnie's anger seethed. She was barely able to speak. "And now you show up here, as though nothing were wrong. How insensitive can you be, Tom Thomson?"

"No, Winnie, it's not me who suddenly showed up here. It's you. I've been here since May. I've been painting and fishing and waiting for you."

Winnie stomped the ground in frustration, then turned and walked away from the angry, hurt and confused man. The following day she returned to Huntsville and threw herself into her job with a fervor she hadn't realized was possible.

Tom released his feelings somewhat differently. Although he, too, attacked his work with an energy borne of pain, Tom's reaction also took the form of moodiness and frequent drinking bouts. He would disappear for days and not let people know where he was going. Or he'd sit drinking silently and steadily in a room full of jovial people. At first, his friends found this habit considerably unnerving, but by the end of the summer they were quite used to Tom's behavior.

There were times when Thomson was the life of the party, whether there was a party in progress or not. And he was certainly turning out some remarkable paintings. The only projects to suffer were the ones he attempted when his art supplies were growing low. Then he had to use poorer quality paints, and the results reflected the inferior goods.

Dr. MacCallum continued his financial gifts, but Tom handled those so poorly that he kept running into trouble. Thomson's colleagues noted early on in their relationship with the painter that any deterioration in his work was always the direct result of his inability to organize his finances. With Tom's blessing, they took over complete control of his finances.

Only Tom, however, could control his work habits. He'd spend several days lazing around Mowat Lodge, drinking with his friends, or taking groups on guided fishing expeditions. When it was the latter, he claimed to need the extra money, but then, as often as not, he gave away the money he'd earned.

Despite his erratic work schedule, by the fall of 1915, when Tom Thomson headed back to his shack in the Rosedale Ravine, he had a substantial number of paintings started. He and Winnie, however, had not seen one another over the summer, a situation that left both of them confused and hurt.

Neither Tom nor Winnie said anything to anyone about either their relationship or how they were feeling. Perhaps this was something too personal to be shared. Each dealt with the pain in their own way. Those around them may have noticed changes, but no one had any idea that the loss of that relationship was the cause.

By the spring of 1916, both Tom and Winnie had become accustomed to living without the other. They each buried their passion deeply, hoping it would never surface again. And it didn't – until the Victoria Day weekend. That was when they met, by chance, at Mowat Lodge.

Winnie walked into the Lodge intent on delivering a message from her father to Shannon. Thoughts of Tom Thomson were far from her mind. She was just inside the doorway when she saw him standing there, leaning up against the counter, smoking his pipe. The draught from the open door blew his pipe smoke back in his face. Thomson looked up and directly into the face of the woman he loved.

For a moment Winnie considered turning around and walking right back out but it was too late. He'd seen her and was striding purposefully across the room to greet her.

"Winnie," he said quietly, "How have you been? You look wonderful. May I buy you a drink?"

"Oh, Tom," she muttered. "Can't we just leave well enough alone?"

"Could we at least talk before we decide what to do?" Tom asked. "Come on, let's go for a walk. We need to be outside, you and I."

Winnie hesitated only a few seconds before accepting Tom's arm. The sunlight seemed brighter than usual somehow, especially to Tom who'd been sitting in the darkened Lodge slowly recovering from the previous evening's drinking bout.

In unspoken agreement, the two walked toward the woods they loved so well. When they were well hidden from any curious eyes, they slowed their pace. Tom reached down and took Winnie's hand.

"I've missed you," Tom told her simply.

"Then why didn't you write, or call, or come to see me? Was I supposed to guess how you were feeling?"

"That's not fair, Winnie. You didn't call or write to me either."

Another silence. Tom broke this one, too.

"Let's not fight, Winnie. Not now that we're finally together again. I'll be here in the Park until fall. We can sort things out over time."

Winnie smiled. "I've been unhappy all winter. It doesn't make any sense to still be unhappy now that I'm here with you."

The two hugged quickly and then both began talking at once. They each had a year's news to catch the other one up on. Laughing and holding hands, Tom Thomson and Winnifred Trainor strolled toward a secluded spot they both knew well. That meeting set a pattern they would happily and intimately keep for the next five months.

Winnie never learned to like Tom's unpredictable behavior. She soon came to realize that when his artist-friends from Toronto came to the Park she'd see little of him until they were gone. And, occasionally, he'd just disappear by himself for several days at a time, not letting anyone know where he'd be or when he'd be back.

There were times, too, when Winnie chose not to see Tom. Sometimes that man could get downright ornery. It often happened when he and his friends from the Park would get together over a few drinks. When they did that, Tom's pleasant temperament went right down the drain, and Winnie had no interest in being anywhere around him. He'd pick a fight with anyone and that included Winnie herself. The worst, though, was when he was with that Bletcher fellow from the cottage next door to her parents'.

"How those two hate each other," she often thought.

Winnie felt sorry for Martin Bletcher. He'd always been courteous to Winnie and her parents, but many around the lake spoke disparagingly about him and did everything they could to avoid him.

Winnie couldn't help but smile when she thought of Bessie, Martin's young sister. The girl clearly had a crush on Tom. She was sure he would have been flattered if he hadn't been too wrapped up in his work or his fishing to notice.

At times, Tom was aware of how distracted and aloof he was. But it was his painting, damn it, that was doing this. When the art was going well, he needed to be by himself. He had to paint what needed to get painted. Then there were times when he couldn't paint. Just couldn't.

Nothing would work. He needed to be by himself during those times, too.

It wasn't that he wasn't grateful for his friends. He was – profoundly so. But his work had to come first, and those around him had to understand that. For this reason, he appreciated Winnie's independent spirit. He couldn't fragment himself, not at this point in his career. When he could paint, he had to, and when he couldn't, others were just as well to leave him alone.

Winnie developed a wonderful ability to know when he needed solitude and yet be there for him at the same time. Thomson smiled every time he thought of the woman he loved. There was little about their relationship he would change. Her passion for fishing very nearly equaled his. Their hours alone together on the lake, looking for the perfect spot to cast, were some of his fondest memories. Recently they had even become lovers.

By the end of August there was a definite hint of frost in the air. The changing colors on the larch and maple trees filled Tom with an overpowering sense of urgency. He wanted to record each day's unique display. Then, during the dreary winter months in his shack in Toronto, he could complete the paintings and get them ready for MacCallum or one of the others to show.

For Winnie, the fall was a melancholy time. She knew that in a few weeks Tom would be gone, her parents would close up the cottage and the magical summer would be over. The chill in the air seemed to portend the months of painful loneliness ahead. Tom had promised this year would be different and, perhaps because Winnifred was so deeply in love with him, she believed him wholeheartedly.

"I'll come up to visit you often, Winnie," Tom declared the day before he was due to leave. "This won't be like last year. This year we both know how we feel and where we stand with one another. Maybe you could even take the train down to see me in the city a few times before spring."

"Oh, Tom, I couldn't and you know it. For one thing, what would I tell my parents? Certainly not the truth. They could never accept such a thing and even if they could, I've never been to Toronto in my life. I'd be terrified. No, Tom, you come to see me in Huntsville and then, in spring, we'll be back together again here."

"All right, Winnie," Tom agreed. "But please tell me you'll write. Not hearing from you all of last winter was nearly more than I could bear."

"Of course I'll write, silly," she teased. "I'll write every time I receive a letter from you."

They both laughed at her good-natured kidding, knowing full well that Tom would likely never write even as much as a note to Winnifred, in spite of his affection for her. The man whose feelings found expression in oil paints was completely at a loss with a pen in his hand.

True to her word, Winnifred Trainor frequently wrote letters to Tom during that winter. Tom also kept his word. Every few months he took the train north. Usually he combined a bit of painting or guiding or visiting friends with seeing Winnie.

If any of their mutual friends suspected there was anything more than a friendship between the two, they kept the thought to themselves. Winnie's co-workers weren't sure what had caused the change in the woman's disposition; they only knew they liked the result.

Early in 1917, Hugh Trainor had some news for his wife and daughters. The lumber company was sending him into the woods, and so for the next few months he'd be staying at "the Manse." He hoped the ladies would join him as soon as the warmer weather came. While he was gone he'd leave the family's motor car for their use. Then, when spring came, they would re-locate for the season.

Neither of Winnie's parents realized why the idea pleased her so much. They didn't know that even the thought of being closer to Tom each spring evening would give the young woman such a boost. Her father was just pleased that the change in his work pattern was met so positively by at least one other member of his family. His wife's life, of course, remained pretty much the same, no matter whether she was in their home in Huntsville or at their cottage on Canoe Lake.

In the spring of 1917, Tom arrived back up at Algonquin Park even before all the ice was fully off the lakes. His winter's work had been satisfying, and now he wanted to collect more daily records of the harshly beautiful area. From the moment of his arrival, he acted like a man possessed, paddling from spot to spot and painting at a feverish pace.

When he and Winnie first saw each other that spring there was not even a word of greeting. They ran together to the shore where Tom's battered grey canoe was beached and paddled strongly, in unison, to a small, uninhabited island some distance out.

Presently, their passion temporarily spent, the lovers lay side by side, in a blissfully self-centered world.

"I can feel it, Win, this is my summer, my chance to make my name known," Thomson told the woman lying at his side. "I won't be doing any guiding this season. Alex said he'd be up, and maybe some of the others. If I'm not holding a paint brush this summer, I'll be holding a fishing rod or a paddle."

Winnie smiled fondly at her lover's impassioned talk. She wondered, somewhat prophetically, whether he'd find time in the next few weeks to hold her. Not wanting to spoil the moment, Winnifred Trainor kept her fears to herself and merely listened.

"You know, Winnie, even last year I wasn't sure I could make this work, but now my paintings are selling. Can you believe that? People are even buying my sketches. God bless Dr. MacCallum. Not only does he pay all my bills but now he's even overseeing sales. He got more than $200 just for one board. The man's not an oculist, he's a born salesman."

"Your work, though, Tom, has something to do with it too," Winnie pointed out.

"Do you think so, Winnie? That's an odd thought to me. All I do is try to transfer what I see onto a board. Maybe you're right. All I know with any certainty is that I have to keep at this as long as I can."

Again Winnie wondered where she'd fit into the equation. Did Tom Thomson know that – 'with any certainty'?

They made love again, more leisurely this time.

With that need looked after, another surfaced.

"I'm hungry, are you?" Tom asked.

Winnie nodded her assent. They dressed quickly and pushed Tom's canoe into the water. Winnie caught the first fish – a 12-pound trout.

"Thanks for dinner." Tom's teasing had the distinct sound of pride in it. "Let's go back to my camp with that. I want to take a photograph of you with your catch."

Quickly synchronizing their strokes, the two paddled toward the white speck on the far shore – Tom's tent.

"How good it is to see you settled back out here again, Tom," Winnie said quietly.

When the man, just a few feet away from her in the back of the canoe, didn't answer her Winnie twirled around, nearly upsetting canoe.

"What are you doing?" Tom demanded. "You nearly tipped us. You know better than that, Winnie, this is a canoe not an ocean liner."

Stabbed by Tom's angry words, Winnie said nothing. It took all her energy just to maintain her composure.

Oblivious to the pain he'd caused, Tom jumped out of the canoe and pulled it to within a few feet of the shoreline in front of his tent. Winnie stepped out carefully, holding her skirt up with one hand, her shoes in the other.

"Look, someone's left a note. It's pinned to the tent flap," Tom announced, hurrying past Winnie and tugging the sheet of paper. "It's from Shan. A group is getting together up at the Lodge and he's invited us."

"Us?" questioned Winnie.

"Of course, 'us,'" Tom proclaimed. "Annie'll be there, and there's another couple staying for the summer – the Crombies. She's fun, you'll like her. Daphne's her name."

Winnie smiled weakly. She'd so counted on spending most of the day and the evening alone with Tom. She knew what would happen once he got with his friends at the Lodge; he'd forget she even existed and for three days after he wouldn't be worth talking to. Knowing that voicing her opinion would only worsen an already doomed situation, Winnie remained silent.

"Wait, Winnie," Tom called as he brushed by the tent's flap. "I'm getting my camera. I want that picture of you with your catch, remember?"

Winnie's warmed in spite of her disappointment at the turn of events. "At least he remembered my fish."

Winnie and Tom stood side by side at the doorway to the Lodge's main room. Smoke hung thickly, darkening the air. As soon as her eyes had adjusted to the lack of light, Winnie saw about a dozen men standing about, most of them smoking cigarettes or pipes. Smoldering ashes in the fieldstone fireplace added to both the heat and the smoke in the room.

"I'll be on the verandah," Winnie started to tell Tom, but he was well into the room by now, greeting his friends.

For a moment, Winnie considered just leaving and going home, but she didn't want to risk offending Annie Fraser. The woman may have seen Winnie coming toward the Lodge with Tom and be expecting her to stop for a chat. Annie was such a dear person. Winnie felt uncomfortable enough with Tom's behavior. She wouldn't add her moodiness to the day's agenda.

Annie introduced Winnie to Mrs. Crombie and the three chatted pleasantly about nothing until Winnie felt she could politely excuse herself. She had no desire to be at Mowat Lodge right then, and besides, she'd been hungry several hours ago and still hadn't eaten. It was time to go home.

As she'd guessed she would, Winnie returned to Huntsville for her week's work without seeing Tom again. The fact annoyed her, but not as much as it would have if she'd been feeling better. She really felt quite poorly, nauseated and a bit light headed. Probably a bit of the stomach flu.

By the following weekend Winnie was feeling a bit better and looking forward to leaving Huntsville right after work at noon on Saturday. Her parents and her sister were already out at the lake. She'd enjoyed the week's solitude but now she looked forward to being with her family – and, of course, Tom. She certainly couldn't deny that he was who she wanted to see most.

Unfortunately, Winnie didn't see Tom that Saturday afternoon, nor for the rest of the weekend. In anger, she stayed in town the following weekend. When her parents questioned their daughter's decision, she explained that there were some long-neglected chores she needed to do. What she really wanted to accomplish was to teach Tom Thomson a lesson: let him worry about where she might be for a change.

If Tom had been either in his camp or at Mowat Lodge, Winnie's weekend in town might have accomplished its purpose. As it was, Tom Thomson and Alex Jackson were camped near Tea Lake Dam, aware of nothing beyond their immediate surroundings.

By the following Friday, Winnie's co-workers had noticed a real change in the woman. Not only was she pale and looking tired, she was cranky and short tempered with everyone. On Friday Winnie left work early – as soon as she had the payroll done.

She slept fitfully that night, dreaming of a lovely, delicious-looking trout swimming just below the lake's surface. No matter what lure she used or how she cast, the fish merely swam sleekly about, ignoring the temptation just inches before its eyes.

The next morning she drove directly out to Canoe Lake without bothering to let the lumberyard manager know she wouldn't be in for the expected Saturday morning shift.

"Leaving early the day before should tell them I'm not feeling well," she rationalized.

Winnifred Trainor drove slowly. Not only was she still not feeling well, but she needed time to think. At 33 years of age Winnie had very little appreciation for any part of the world she hadn't personally experienced. And she hadn't personally experienced very much outside Huntsville and Algonquin Park.

There was one thing, however, that Winnie knew for certain. She loved Tom Thomson.

The strength of that thought caused her stomach to lurch. She slowed the car to almost a crawl. For a moment she thought she'd have to stop and get out. She still had this darned nausea and had already vomited once this morning. Illness is just a sign of weakness her mother always said, and so it pleased Winnie when she realized she regained control of her body, at least this time.

By the time the road turned to a dirt path and she was only minutes away from her parents' summer home, Winnie felt as right as rain.

"Maybe it's finally over," she thought with relief before greeting her mother with sincere pleasure.

"Come around front," the older woman said. "Your father's there with Tom. They've been having a great old chat. But I'm sure they'll both be happy to be interrupted by you."

"Oh, mother, you're a tease, but it's so good to see you again. I've missed you," Winnie said, linking arms with the smiling woman.

"And it's wonderful to have you here again. The evenings are awfully long when you're not around."

Winnie's reply was cut off by greetings from both her father and Tom. There were polite inquiries about health, with hugs and questions all around. The afternoon passed quickly. Friends dropped around and left again, but by evening Tom had made no attempt to leave, and Winnie was as happy as she had been that afternoon on the island.

By nightfall Thomson left after promising to visit Winnie again before she drove into town for another week's work.

As it turned out, Winnie and Tom did see one another the next day, but not under the circumstances they'd anticipated. They met quite by accident just past Bletcher's place, on the path to the lake. Winnie was out for a morning stroll, hoping to settle her stomach. From the supplies he was carrying it was clear Tom was heading out to paint.

"Hello," he said distractedly as they nearly bumped into each other on the narrow path.

Winnie was too taken aback to say anything. She stopped walking and watched in disbelief as the man who'd made passionate love to her some weeks ago and spent the entire day yesterday with her and her parents receded into the distance. Hours later, as hurt and confused as she could ever remember being, she left the cottage and drove back into town.

The week passed quickly for Winnie, probably because she finally felt somewhat better. At least physically. It was a good thing, too. Her desk was stacked high with matters she'd neglected the previous week.

She worked quickly, concentrating on the papers before her as a way of avoiding thinking about Tom. She knew she'd be joining her parents at the cottage this weekend. It was the first long weekend of summer, Dominion Day, the day that traditionally marked the beginning of her annual vacation. Two glorious weeks in Algonquin Park. With or without thoughts of seeing Tom, the anticipation was enticing.

As usual Winnie's parents greeted her warmly. They also expressed concern. Had she been getting enough sleep through the week? She looked awfully tired. Winnie had to admit she did feel totally exhausted. In response to her parents' concerns, she retired just after 9:00 that night and immediately fell fast asleep.

When their daughter wasn't up at her normal early hour to go fishing, Mr. and Mrs. Trainor told each other they'd definitely been right. Their child was truly tired. By 8:30, when she'd been asleep almost around the clock, they decided to go into her room to check.

The small creaking sound the door made as they opened it was enough to disturb Winnie's sleep. She rubbed her eyes and made some small effort to sit up in bed. A wave of dizziness forced her head back to the comfort of the pillow.

"Good morning," she said from the safety of her prone position.

Hugh Trainor retreated to the living room. Now that he could see his daughter was all right, he felt distinctly uncomfortable being at her bedroom doorway.

"Good morning, dear," her mother answered as she approached the woman's bed. "We were a little worried about you. It's not like you to sleep this long. Are you feeling all right?"

"Yes, mother, I'm fine," Winnie assured the woman. "I've had a bit of an upset stomach for a few days and I've been busy at work getting caught up so I could take my time off, here with you."

"Let me spoil you then, this morning, dear. Stay where you are and I'll bring you a cup of tea to enjoy in bed."

Winnie smiled.

"I'd like that, mother. Thank you. A piece of dry toast with it would be nice."

The kindly and concerned smile that had spread across the older woman's face disappeared with her daughter's words. She could remember wanting dry toast in the morning twice in her life. Both times more than 30 years ago.

Tom's days were frantically busy. He worked as though propelled by an intense hunger. He painted even when he didn't have proper supplies.[23] Making a visual record of all he saw seemed to be the motivating force behind Tom Thomson's almost manic output.

It would be romantic to surmise that he somehow knew his days were numbered and that this awareness prompted his tremendous productivity. Unfortunately, this theory really can't be supported. Many of his works from this period are repetitive. In keeping with previous years, these would probably have been taken back to Toronto with him to be re-worked or re-assessed through the fall and winter of 1917-18.

It is more likely that Thomson was on a precipice of a transformation in his art, that he was preparing to take a dramatic step in his work. Whatever the instigation, the result was a veritable outpouring of art. He did little else other than paint, and was frequently gone for days on end.

Thomson's absence was noted by his friends in the Park when they found themselves together.

"Has anyone seen Tom?" one asked.

"Not for days," replied Shannon Fraser. "Last time I saw him I gave him the final payment for the canoes I bought from him early in the season. He was so distracted by something that he didn't even thank me for the money. He barely acknowledged it at all. Now that I think of it, he barely acknowledged me either."

"I saw him briefly," added ranger Mark Robinson with a chuckle. "He came tearing into my cabin asking to put all his sketches around the room. He wanted to see them together. I think he thought that viewing them as a group might tell him something that wasn't there individually."

"Who knows with Tom and his painting," Fraser added shaking his head. "But I don't have a patron like Tom, so I have work to do. I'll see you later."

"Will we see you next Saturday evening at Rowe's?" Robinson called after the retreating lodge owner.

Shannon Fraser stopped and turned back toward his friend.

"Yes, I think so. Thanks for reminding me. Martin Bletcher's going to be there. We've all been pretty rough on the guy, what with the war and him being German and not joining up and all. Really the whole thing's got nothing to do with him personally, does it?" Fraser said before re-confirming that he'd be at the planned get-together in guide George Rowe's cabin.

"See you there," called Robinson before the two continued on their opposite ways.

Winnie Trainor walked purposefully to Tom's tent at the side of the lake. He might not be there, but she'd prepared for that eventuality with a painstakingly composed note. She'd driven to the nearby town of Dwight where no one knew her. There a kindly young doctor confirmed her worst fears – her child, hers and Tom Thomson's – would be born this coming February.

Writing the note made Winnie aware of just how little she really knew of Tom. She had no idea if he liked children, or even if he could see himself as a husband. She penned the note with great care, not wanting to let her growing panic show lest Thomson feel cornered and flee like a threatened animal.

Finding no signs of life in or around his tent Winnie merely pinned the note to the outside of the tent flap. Before she left she looked around the place which her future husband called home.

"I can live with this man," she decided and then left.

Had Winnie waited briefly she would have been able to give Tom the news of the impending event herself. He returned from an expedition of several days just minutes after she'd left.

The note caught his eye immediately as it fluttered in the breeze, mildly fighting the pin Winnie had used to attach it. After his third reading, the news the brief letter contained finally sunk in.

"My god. My painting. How will I ever keep up with my painting when I have a wife and a child to support?" he moaned. He thought briefly of his friend Frank Carmichael, whose work Thomson greatly admired. The younger man had married recently and his domestic obligations allowed him very little time for painting.

"What choice do I have, though? I clearly have an obligation. I shall make the arrangements at once."

Leaving the arm-load of sketches leaning precariously up against the outside of the tent, Tom Thomson sat down to write one of the brief letters which were so typical of him.

Dear Mrs. Brooks

I wish to make a reservation for two at your lodge on Bella Lake. Please get back to me if you're not able to accommodate this request for the dates August 25-31.

With thanks,

Tom Thomson

Tom left immediately to mail the letter at Mowat Lodge. As he walked up hill he glanced back. The stack of sketches he'd piled against the tent caught his eye, and he turned around to put them safely inside before proceeding further. It seemed a lifetime ago that he'd propped his week's work there. He wondered now if he'd have to give up painting entirely. The mere thought brought on a blinding headache, but he stumbled on toward Shan Fraser's place just the same.

"Heavens, Tom, whatever's the matter with you?" Annie Fraser shouted when she saw the artist approaching. His awkward gait made him look drunk, but it was caused solely by the intense headache.

"I'll be all right, Annie. I just need to post this letter and see Shan for a moment," he replied.

"Shannon's not here right now, Tom. Do you want me to give him a message for you?"

"That would be fine, Annie, thank you," Thomson told the woman. "I can't wait around for him right now, I have a bad headache. Just tell him I need the money he owes me for that last canoe."

Not wanting to interfere with something she knew little about, Annie made no reply, and as a result, the parting was an awkward, silent one. Oddly, Annie commented later, she thought Tom might have mumbled something about buying a suit.

That taken care of, Tom returned to his tent to treat his headache. It was nothing that a few straight shots of rye whiskey couldn't cure, he was sure. The next morning when he awoke with the first rays of dawn, he still had a headache, but at least now it was a more familiar type of headache – a hangover headache, the kind a swim across the lake always cured.

Stripped down to his shorts, Thomson dove into the chilly waters and, with a strong crawl stroke, headed for the opposite shore, a mile away. He arrived feeling only somewhat better. Fortunately, the swim across the lake meant a swim back, and he knew from experience that, by the time the second crossing was complete, his hangover would be gone and he'd be ready to catch his breakfast. During the return trip, the reason for the drinking escapade came back to him.

"I'll go get Winnie. I can tell her of the honeymoon arrangements I've made while we fish together," he decided and then spent the rest of the swim debating whether or not one should propose to a woman if one's actions had already predetermined the marriage.

Hundreds of strong, effortless strokes later, Thomson's hand grazed the lake bottom. He had swum to within a few feet of his tent. Thomson stood up, smiling, walked out of the water and toward his tent. He hummed happily to himself, anticipating the day ahead.

"I suppose marriage was inevitable," he pronounced out loud. "And I guess I'd never find a finer woman than Winnie. She can cast a lure like few others I've ever seen."

Pushing his battered grey canoe off the beach, Tom prepared to catch his breakfast of lake trout. For the first time in a little over six weeks, no part of the artist's mind was on his painting. There was just no room there right now for any thought that didn't revolve around fishing or Winnie.

"Wait'll I tell the others!" he chortled. "That damn Shan better make good the money he owes me. I can hardly be at my wedding in these grubby old clothes."

Singing and talking out loud to himself, to the fish and to the lake, Tom Thomson spent a eminently satisfying hour planning his future as a married man. Three respectable-sized fish later he beached his canoe at its accustomed spot just a few yards from his tent.

"A husband!" he cupped his hands around his mouth and yelled to the woods, "I'm going to be a husband. I'm getting married."

With the last celebratory holler, Tom Thomson stood completely still. He held the pose until an involuntary shudder ran the length of his agile body. His knees began to shake and to his surprise he found himself suddenly sitting on a washed-up log.

"A father. I'm going to be a father, too."

A wave of nausea momentarily wrenched his gut. Once it passed, Thomson stood up and, in keeping with many a man's reaction when coming to grips with this particular reality, grinned from ear to ear. He sealed the fish in the reflector-cum-baking oven he'd devised and left the camp to find Winnie.

"I shall ask her to join me for breakfast, and then we can make our wedding plans," he thought grandly as he strode toward "The Manse."

"Hello!" he called out as soon as he was in sight of the wooden structure.

When his greeting wasn't returned, he repeated himself. Seconds later, Hugh Trainor appeared on the verandah, wiping his hands on his trousers.

"Tom, hello, we thought it might be you calling. How are you?"

Winnie's father was walking quickly down the verandah steps to meet the visitor. The two men met at the bottom step.

"Tom," the man began awkwardly. "I don't think it's a good idea for you to go in there."

"Why?" asked Tom too loudly, incredulous that his jovial mood wasn't reciprocated.

"Well, I don't know, Tom," the man stumbled apologetically. "You know how it is, women stuff and all, I think. I mean I'm not exactly sure what's behind it all but Winnie and her mother, well, frankly there's quite a fight going on in there and . . ."

He let the sentence hang incomplete, but gestured as though engaging in a play fight.

"Oh, I see," said Tom, although in fact he had no idea what the older man meant or what Winnie and her mother could possibly be fighting about. He even wondered momentarily if the two women were actually having a physical fight and then realized that they were probably arguing.

"I see," he repeated, this time with some honesty.

Tom had been raised with sisters and recalled that they, periodically, would go head to head with his mother over one subject or another. Those incidents always puzzled him. His mother was a dear woman who did the best she could for all of them. How any of his sisters could not have seen that was beyond him.

"All right then, sir," Tom said, the disappointment he felt evident in his voice. "Please tell Winnie I'd really like to see her this morning or this afternoon if she has time. I won't be far from my tent till evening I'm sure. I've been away painting so much this spring, and the old campsite is sure showing signs of disrepair. I want to get those looked after before I head out again next week."

"Sure, Tom. I'll tell Winnifred you'd like to see her, but if not, everyone's been invited to the party at George's this evening."

Wondering exactly who "everyone" would comprise, Tom looked toward the Bletcher cabin. There were no signs of life.

"I don't think we're going to see much of Mr. & Mrs. Bletcher this season, but Martin and Bessie are here for the weekend. Martin says they'll be going tonight, and I think to be neighborly, we should all make an effort to see they feel welcome. I suspect there's bad feelings about this community in that family, and you can hardly blame them. No one's been what you'd call warm to any of them."

Tom stiffened at the news. There was certainly no love lost between himself and Martin Bletcher. He always suspected it wouldn't take much for Martin to begin pursuing Winnie, if she'd ever give him half a chance. And the odd time he'd been with the man's sister, Bessie, he'd felt distinctly uncomfortable. If spending the evening in the Bletcher's company was the only way he'd get to see Winnie today then he'd have to put up with it.

Considerably less buoyant than when he had headed out, Tom returned to his camp. He rekindled his fire pit, and when the embers glowed he put the largest of the freshly caught fish on to bake.

"There'll be more than enough for us both," he thought, sure that Winnie would be along in plenty of time for them to enjoy their favorite breakfast together.

By the time the fish was ready Tom was still alone. He ate his meal slowly, contemplating the unfamiliar feeling he was experiencing. He could not identify it correctly, although it was simply loneliness.

Instead, he thought perhaps he was hungry. It had been almost 24 hours since he'd eaten. Oddly, though, Tom felt worse after he'd eaten. The jubilation and exhilaration he'd felt after his swim this morning was now replaced with lethargy and melancholy. The housekeeping chores he'd said he was intent on doing suddenly seemed overwhelming.

He glanced toward his tent. The flap was still open from when he'd climbed out of his bedroll just a few hours before. His eye fell on a book his sister Margaret had sent him. It arrived with a letter from her husband, Tom Harkness. Thinking of the obvious respect and affection between those two usually made Tom smile to himself. This morning, the thought only added to his pain. Still though, the book might serve exactly the purpose he needed. Reading it would give him something to do until either Winnie came by or it was time to leave for Rowe's cottage.

Tom was very aware that he had inherited his father's ability to concentrate. Neither man had ever made any effort to develop this power, but they hadn't had to. The ability to focus completely on whatever they were doing, despite anything going on around them, was merely a genetic gift passed on by John Thomson to his artistic son.

Hours later Tom put the book down. He'd read it right through.

"Margaret was right, E.M. Forster is truly a craftsman of words. *Howard's End* was an even better book than *Where Angels Fear To Tread*. I must remember to thank her for sending it along with Harkness's letter," Tom thought.

His mind now on the plot of the book he'd just read rather than the complications developing in his life, Tom Thomson attended, with quiet efficiency, to what had to be done in and around his tent.

This morning, little else beyond Winnie Trainor had been on his mind. If she'd chosen this moment to visit Tom, she'd have startled him completely. Once he'd mentally worked his way through parts of the book a few more times, his thoughts moved to the future of his painting.

"Maybe I should go west. Alex Jackson said he'd go back in a minute. I'll talk to him. Maybe we can spend next spring together in the Rockies."

Tom looked around the patch of lakefront property he'd claimed for his campsite. He enjoyed an undeniable feeling of satisfaction as he perused his little section of the world.

"It looks so good I don't want to mess it up even to cook myself some dinner. I'll go to the Lodge and see what Annie's serving the guests tonight. It's time I treated myself to a meal someone cooked for me," Tom decided and headed up the inclining path, away from the lake and toward Mowat Lodge.

As soon as the stark-looking building came in sight, Thomson remembered his morning's resolution to ask Shannon for the money owing on those canoes. Measurable seconds later, he remembered why his need for the money was somewhat urgent now.

"Winnie," he realized. "Winnie never came to see me. I wonder what kept her?"

Tom made his way into the darkened main room of the Lodge. He could hear noises coming from someone working in the adjacent kitchen.

"Hello," he called. "Annie, is that you?"

"In here," the familiar lilting voice answered.

Tom swung open the door to the huge, brightly lit kitchen. It took his eyes, which had just become adjusted to the dimness of the living room after the brightness of outside, time to re-adjust.

"Hello to you too, Tom," the pretty young woman greeted her visitor.

Had Annie Fraser been a different sort of woman she might have felt embarrassed at being alone with a single man, considering the condition she was in. Her apron was askew, her hair was coming untied, and her face was lightly powdered – with flour, not face powder. But such thoughts would never trouble Annie's mind. She was the most unself-conscious person most people would ever meet. Indeed, the total lack of self-awareness contributed greatly to her charm.

Tom smiled in appreciation of the natural beauty he saw before him.

"Annie, does that skallywag of a husband of yours have any appreciation for the woman he has?" Tom asked in a teasing that was based on honesty.

"Oh, away wit' ya," Annie teased back. "What can we do for you this day? If it's Shan you're looking for, he ate early and headed out."

"I was, yes, I was looking for Shannon but he can wait. I also thought I'd treat myself to a meal here at the Lodge if I may be so bold as to join your other guests. I'll pay you for it, of course, Annie," Thomson added quickly.

Annie grinned warmly.

"You'll be my guest, this evening, Mr. Thomson," she replied with mock formality. "It'll be half an hour till it's ready. Go on into the post office there and get your mail. I sorted it all at lunch time. That magazine you like so much came for you."

Tom didn't even reply. He knew she meant *The Compleat Angler* and he was anxious to get at it.

Half an hour later the sound of Annie ringing the oversized brass bell at the end of the verandah jarred him from the article he'd been reading on lures. A most enjoyable piece. The writer concurred with absolutely all of Tom's philosophies on what will work and why. Clearly written by an astute fisherman, Tom decided before putting aside the periodical and joining the group gathering at Annie Fraser's well-stocked dinner table.

Tom enjoyed himself and the meal tremendously. He kibitzed back and forth with Annie's father, much to the delight of Annie, her mother and the other guests staying at the lodge.

"You two young people run along," Annie's mother suggested at the end of the meal. "Go and join that rascal Shan over at George Rowe's. Your father and I'll do the fixing up tonight, won't we dear?"

Annie jumped up, bussed her mother quickly on the cheek, and grabbed Tom's arm. He'd been sitting there quite unaware. He wasn't used to comments prefaced with 'young people' being addressed to him. Before he knew it, he was outside, walking along with Shannon Fraser's wife.

"Life's ironies," he thought philosophically, remembering his mission for this evening was to propose marriage to the woman who was already carrying his child. And here he was walking with a married woman, who, Tom speculated, might be interested in an occasional journey beyond the boundaries of matrimony.

When they reached Rowe's cabin, Annie and Tom were greeted warmly. The place was crowded with park rangers, guides and residents of nearby cottages.

Martin Bletcher was one of the first to greet the newest arrivals. Tom found Martin's sudden friendliness slightly unnerving. The last time the two men had seen one another, they'd argued heatedly about the way the war was going. If Mark Robinson hadn't intervened, they probably would have come to blows. Now Martin stood, extending his hand to shake Tom's.

Tom returned the handshake but didn't follow Annie inside to join the dozen others in the cabin's main room.

"I don't think I'll come in just yet, Martin. I think I'll just drop around the Trainor's first. There's a message I must give to Winnifred," Tom explained.

"You won't have much luck there, chum," Martin declared in a poorly executed stage whisper. "Winnie's gone. She left this afternoon."

"Gone? Gone where?" Tom demanded, confused.

"I'm not absolutely positive, you know, but I think she's gone back to their home in town. There was quite a carry-on for nearly an hour over there," Bletcher continued with an air of confidentiality. "Lots of shouting – all four of them – Winnie, Marie and their parents. If you ask me there's a problem brewing in that family."

Thomson swore under his breath and allowed himself to be escorted into the warm, smokey cottage.

"I'll have a drink first and then I'll go and see if what Bletcher's said is true," Tom thought.

Winnie had used the time driving from the lake back to town to calm herself. Just being alone had helped enormously.

"If I'd stayed in that cabin listening to all of them at me with their accusations and innuendoes, I'd have torn my hair out," she told herself.

"I'll not tell my mother what she wants to know. I'm 33 years old. I don't want their advice and I don't need it. Tom will simply have to marry me, that's all there is to it."

Tom's first drink was strong and good. He felt it warming his insides as it went down. Most people were milling around the room, drinks in hand. There was almost nowhere to sit, just a few uninviting-looking deck chairs scattered about. The only sofa in the room contained the unconscious form of Shannon Fraser.

"Would ya look at him?" Annie suggested rhetorically to any and all within earshot.

Only Bessie Bletcher and Daphne Crombie responded.

"I'd just leave him if I was you," Bessie advised and Daphne nodded her head in obvious agreement. "He got tight right quick, and then even a little pugnacious before George laid him out there. He'll come up swinging if you disturb him before he's slept it off."

"That man," Annie sighed with disgust verging on loathing, audible to all who cared to listen.

Apparently forgetful of how badly he'd felt when he first woke up this morning and why, Tom Thomson proceeded to pour himself a second, equally strong drink. He drank this one as quickly as the first and then prepared to visit the Trainor's cabin.

Daphne Crombie, whose husband, Robin, was an invalid convalescing at Mowat Lodge, was also getting ready to leave the party. She looked at Tom and was shocked by the condition he'd gotten himself into so quickly.

"Tom," she said quietly as they made their way together down the front steps of George Rowe's cottage.

Hearing his name jolted Tom out of a reverie. He apparently hadn't even been aware that he was walking down the stairs with anyone, let alone a pretty young woman.

"Yes?" he said suddenly.

"Tom, I really don't know you well. Certainly not well enough to speak candidly to you, but still I feel I should. I heard all the screaming from the Trainors' cottage this afternoon. I think if you go over there you're making a big mistake, especially right now. It's not long after, and if you don't mind my saying so, Tom, you're already half on your way to being as tight as poor Shannon. Why don't you just go back in and enjoy the party as best you can and deal with anything else tomorrow?"

With that, Daphne Crombie turned and fled toward Mowat Lodge. She could hardly believe that she, a married woman, had spoken so openly to a single man and an attractive, eccentric, inebriated one at that.

Tom sat down on the step massaging his temples. Moments later he got up, swore loudly, kicked the door frame and swaggered back into the cabin. He poured himself a third stiff shot of whiskey, this time neglecting the token splash of water he customarily added to his drinks. He was vaguely aware that many of the eyes in the room were on him, but he didn't care. The only person he cared about right now was that lout Shannon Fraser sleeping stupidly on the chesterfield.

Thomson approached the prone figure and shook him, spilling the few drops left in his glass as he did.

"Please, Tom, just leave him." It was Annie, suddenly between Tom and her sleeping husband. "He'll only make trouble if you wake him. Why spoil everyone's evening?"

"Guess you're right," Tom concurred with alcohol-thickened speech. "He's not worth it anyway, except that he owes me money and I need it."

"Does he, Tom?" Annie asked with concern.

"Yeah, for the canoes," Tom explained.

"He told me he'd paid you. If it's to be over money, then this really isn't a good time to get into it. Let him sleep. I promise I'll look into it for you in the morning, Tom."

He stared blankly at Annie for a minute and then back at the prone figure of her husband before he walked away from them both.

"Howdy, Mark!" he greeted his good friend with sudden good cheer.

"Tom, you're already drunk!" Robinson kidded the artist.

"Nothing to what I will be, Mark my boy," he assured his friend. "You're the park ranger. What are you going to do about it?"

"Not a thing, Tom. Not a thing," Robinson wisely replied.

Shortly after, Mark Robinson offered to walk a distinctly uncomfortable looking Annie Fraser home. By now, Annie was the only woman left in the cabin. Martin Bletcher had seen his sister, Bessie, home just after Tom had attempted to awaken Shannon Fraser. There was no telling what might develop. Annie gratefully accepted Mark's offer, as Bessie had her brother's just a few minutes before.

Moments later the two men returned. Now, in addition to their host, George Rowe, only Shannon Fraser, Martin Bletcher, Mark Robinson, and Tom Thomson remained in the living room of the Rowe's cottage.

Perhaps if the women had stayed, all that followed might have been prevented. Tom had been looking for a fight all evening long. Now that there were no women to offend, he poured himself another strong drink and began to give the still unconscious Shannon Fraser a piece of his mind. Finding that arguing with an unresponsive opponent was extremely unsatisfying, Thomson once again started in at Martin Bletcher and his lack of support for the Allies' war effort.

As they'd done when this conversation had occurred before, Tom's friends Mark and George separated the two just moments before the argument became physical. Because Martin Bletcher's cottage was considerably closer than Tom Thomson's tent was, the two peacemakers chose Bletcher to escort out the door.

Although complaining drunkenly about the injustice of it all, Bletcher left with only verbal protest. Even inebriated, Martin Bletcher knew he was no match for either Mark Robinson or George Rowe, let alone both of them. Still, he had his pride to defend.

"Don't get in my way if you know what's good for you!"[24] Bletcher threatened Thomson from the safety of his escorts.

He made his way an additional 50 yards before muttering the further insults and threats he wished to register.

"You're not worthy of the ground my sister walks on, you cad. If you had a brain you would have seen what a fine woman Bessie is and left Winnifred Trainor for me!"

❦   ❦   ❦

Dawn the next morning, Sunday, July 8, 1917, was gray and drizzly. Tom Thomson may or may not have met the day. Some say guests sitting on the verandah of Mowat Lodge saw him paddling with strong, sure strokes on Canoe Lake. Others reported observing Tom talking to Shannon Fraser and they agreed the time was early in the afternoon on the rainy Sunday.[25]

Tom's good friend Mark Robinson claimed he'd seen the artist talking to Shan, although he did not speak to either man. The sighting was from a distance, but it is unlikely Robinson would mistake his friend for another. And he had no reason to lie. Others who were there believe Tom Thomson had been dead for 12 hours by that time.

In retrospect, all believed Thomson was dead by nightfall.

At the time, however, none of his friends were at all concerned about the man's absence. Over the years they'd become familiar with Tom's habits of solitary fishing and painting expeditions lasting anywhere from a few days to a week or more.

At mid-afternoon that day, Martin Bletcher and his sister, Bessie, paddled in their canoe to fish at Tea Lake.

The next day they casually mentioned to others in the area that they had seen an empty canoe floating on Canoe Lake. Although they were unsure whether the vessel was overturned or upright when they spotted it, they thought it might have been Tom Thomson's canoe.

Mark Robinson immediately organized a search. It was assumed that Thomson had met with some minor misfortune and was stranded somewhere. After several days of fruitless searching, their concern turned to serious worry.

When Thomson's canoe was examined after being towed to shore, the painter's favorite paddle was missing. His portaging paddle was there but it was lashed sloppily – not in keeping with Tom's habits.

Mark Robinson contacted the Thomson family. Tom's brother-in-law Tom Harkness arrived to join the searchers.

They concentrated their investigation around places Thomson was known to frequent, fully expecting to find the missing man either injured or marooned. Despite knowledge of Tom's habits and the area, they found nothing.

Harkness left the following day, taking many of Tom's paintings with him.

Dread hung over the small community. Shannon Fraser suggested dragging Canoe Lake.

The procedure was never carried out. On July 16, 1917, Dr. Goldwin W. Howland, a neurologist vacationing with his family in the Park, spotted an object floating in Canoe Lake. Apprehensive about what he'd seen, the doctor contacted the staff at Mowat Lodge. The search for Tom Thomson was over. Hours later, two guides pulled his body to shore. There was a large laceration above the right eye of the corpse, and evidence of a severe earbleed.

Shannon Fraser sent a telegram to Tom's family. From a perspective of nearly 80 years hence, the wording seems cruelly ambiguous: "Found Tom this morning."[26]

The question of what happened on Canoe Lake that wet Sunday in July has reverberated throughout Canada and the art world ever since. It has never been answered with any authority. The more one delves into the Tom Thomson legend the more intriguing and, indeed, downright puzzling, it becomes.

The easiest theory to debunk is that Tom Thomson drowned accidently while standing up in his canoe to relieve himself. Statistics show that the majority of people who drown as a result of boating accidents are male, and the majority of those are found with their flies open, but those statistics do not have credibility in this case. Not only was Thomson too experienced an outdoorsman to ever attempt such folly, no mention was ever made of his fly being open when he was found.

Shannon Fraser, the first to imply that Thomson may have drowned, staunchly maintained the artist killed himself.[27] He backed this theory by saying that he knew Winnifred Trainor was pushing for marriage, and the pressure caused the man to panic.

While Thomson had seen his friend Franklin Carmichael's freedom severely curtailed by the burdens of marriage and parenthood, booking a honeymoon cabin at Bella Lake effectively defeats that theory. In addition, the day before his disappearance, Thomson wrote and mailed a letter to his patron, Dr. MacCallum. As with all Thomson's correspondences, this letter was brief; however, in reference to his painting, Thomson assured the doctor that he had "every intention of making some more."[28]

Shannon Fraser went on to destroy most of his own credibility by coldly offering some of Thomson's personal possessions, including the artist's shoes, for sale.

If the death was neither the result of accident or suicide, was he murdered? And if so, by whom? And why?

Murder, perhaps, is too strong a word, at least murder in any sort of a premeditated sense. Manslaughter might be closer to being accurate, because it's possible that whoever swung the blow that caused the gash above Tom Thomson's right eye hadn't intended to kill the man.

Two prominent suspects exist: Martin Bletcher and Shannon Fraser. It was generally acknowledged by those who knew them that Tom Thomson and Martin Bletcher were enemies. Did Bletcher strike the fatal blow? If he did, his reasons for doing so have become unclear with the passage of years. Did the two argue once again about the war effort? Was Bletcher secretly in love with Winnie Trainor and therefore jealous of Thomson's relationship with her? It has also been suggested that Bessie Bletcher may have been in love with Thomson and that the artist had rebuffed her. Just days before, friends had defused what could easily have become a fist fight between the two men, so the premise of a disagreement is reasonable.

There is also, however, strong evidence pointing to Shannon Fraser rather than Martin Bletcher as the perpetrator. Even if Fraser hadn't suspected that his wife and Thomson were having an affair, both men were known to drink to excess and were involved in financial dealings, an area in which Thomson was notoriously irresponsible. In addition, it is known that on the evening of Saturday, July 7, the two men were together and neither was sober. A quarrel over money therefore becomes a distinct possibility.

In the late 1970s, Daphne Crombie, who was at the Park when Thomson disappeared, came forward with an apparently credible version of the events that weekend in July, 1917. By the time her story was listened to (she'd told it to Dr. MacCallum in 1917, but was disregarded), Mrs. Crombie was an elderly woman and both Bletcher and Fraser had died.

Like Mark Robinson, Daphne Crombie would have had no reason to lie, especially 50 years after the fact. It is known that Mrs. Crombie and Annie Fraser became friends during the time Robin and Daphne Crombie were staying at the Lodge in the spring of 1917.

Mrs. Crombie maintained that Annie Fraser had confided an exact description of the events surrounding Tom Thomson's death. According to this account, Shannon and Tom quarreled over money, the argument became physical, Shannon pushed Tom and the artist fell into a fireplace grate. Terrified that he'd killed the man, Shannon ran to Mowat Lodge to enlist Annie's help. They tied a weight to Thomson's leg, rowed the body some distance away from shore and threw it overboard. Once back at the shore they launched the dead man's canoe and left it to drift aimlessly.

It's hard to imagine that Annie Fraser would tell her friend such a horrific story if it were not so and certainly Daphne Crombie would have had no reason for concocting such a tale. However, if this is indeed what happened, then who did Mark Robinson see talking to Shannon Fraser that Sunday, July 8, in the early afternoon?

It's also possible that Hugh Trainor returned to Canoe Lake once he'd understood the reason for the argument between his wife and older daughter. Might he have been angry enough to have killed the man responsible for Winnie's out-of-wedlock pregnancy?

There are more points of contradiction surrounding the artist's death than there are of agreement. Whatever became of Thomson's much-cherished paddle? It was never found. Could this, and not the fireplace grate, have been the murder weapon? The only crueller choice might have been one of the boards on which the artist painted.

Now, one can only theorize, impotently, about any of the possibilities.

Winnie Trainor's actions following Tom's death, and indeed until her own death some 45 years later, strongly indicate that she was pregnant with Thomson's progeny. The grieving woman left the area immediately and stayed with a friend until the end of the summer. In September her mother, Maud, joined her. The two women left on an extended vacation, first in northern Ontario and then in the United States.

When they returned, around Easter in 1918, Winnie Trainor was a changed woman. Her experiences, from the early summer of 1917 until her return to her hometown nearly a year later, had apparently aged and embittered the woman. She returned to her job as bookkeeper for the local lumbermill, where she worked until her retirement many years later. Although she lived to be over 80 years of age, Winnifred Trainor never married.[29]

A weak argument against the pregnancy theory can be made by pointing out that no child has ever surfaced. If Winnie was pregnant when Thomson died, then she would have delivered the child sometime in February, 1918, while visiting in Philadelphia. It is safe to assume that the delivery was a straightforward one, that the child was immediately put up for adoption and never told the truth about its heritage. It is also possible that Tom Thomson's only child died at, or soon after, birth. Either possibility would most effectively explain the absence of a child.

Several weeks after Thomson's body had been buried near the shore of his beloved Canoe Lake, his parents asked that the coffin be moved to the family plot near Leith, Ontario. Workers were sent to execute the move, but even this simple removal is clouded with mystery. Many believe Thomson's body was never moved, but remains in its original location at Canoe Lake. Winnie Trainor's actions lend credence to this theory: She kept the grave site at Canoe Lake immaculate and was known to become highly agitated by people visiting the grave or inquiring about the artist.

Further, in 1956 "four of his former cronies"[30] became curious about whether the removal at the Thomson family request had actually been made. They decided to dig up the Canoe Lake grave site once again. It took the group three tries to locate the grave and there are legitimate questions as to whether it was Thomson's remains they found.

The skeleton they found did not, in any way, match Tom Thomson. The crumbling remains of the coffin offered no identification, only the hauntingly ironic words, "Rest In Peace."[31] One can only hope Thomson's soul was resting in greater peace than his possible grave sites were.

Throughout all the intrigue, one unquestionable love affair has persisted – Canada's love for one of its few, legitimate heroes. If, as according to literary tradition, a romantic hero must be handsome, tragic and inaccessible, Thomson was certainly "all of the above."

Considering the recorded tamperings with Thomson's "final" resting place, Tom Thomson even comes very close to replicating the qualifications of a mythical hero. Tom Thomson was certainly of ordinary birth but, in keeping with the requisites for a mythical hero, he did die young. Further, interring and exhuming his body, first shortly after his death and then again years later, makes an interesting parallel to the mythical hero's requisite visit to and return from the underworld.

A provocative ending to a very Canadian love story.

## *Endnotes*

[1]The date of Tom Thomson's birth is variously reported as either August 4, 1877 (Harold Town and David P. Silcox, *Tom Thomson: The Silence and The Storm*, McClelland and Stewart Limited, 1977, Toronto, page 49) or August 5, 1877 (*Tom Thomson: The Algonquin Years*, Ottelyn Addison and Elizabeth Harwood, Ryerson Press, Toronto, 1969, page 2, and *Tom Thomson: The Last Spring*, Joan Murray, Dundurn Press, 1994, Toronto, page 12).

[2]*The Best of Tom Thomson*, Joan Murray, Hurtig Publishers, Edmonton, 1986, page 4.

[3]*Tom Thomson: The Silence and the Storm*, page 50, says yes; *Tom Thomson: The Last Spring*, page 17, says no.

[4]"The Canoe Lake Mystery," Dr. Noble Sharpe, B.A., M.B., *Canadian Journal of Forensic Science*, Volume III, Number 2, June 30, 1970, pages 34-40.

[5]*Tom Thomson: The Algonquin Years*, page 3.

[6]*Tom Thomson: The Silence and The Storm*, pages 53, 54.

[7]"The Rebel Painter of the Pine Woods," Trent Frayne, *Maclean's Magazine*, July 1, 1953, pages 16, 17, 30, 31, 32, 33.

[8]*Tom Thomson: The Silence and The Storm*, page 51.

[9]*Tom Thomson: The Last Spring*, page 25.

[10]*Tom Thomson:The Silence and The Storm*, page 52.

[11]*Tom Thomson: The Last Spring*, page 25.

[12] *The Best of Tom Thomson*, page 16.

[13] About 1908, according to *Tom Thomson: The Algonquin Years*, page 5.

[14] *The Best of Tom Thomson*, page 18.

[15] *Tom Thomson: The Algonquin Years*, page 65.

[16] *Tom Thomson: The Silence and The Storm*, page 204.

[17] Ibid.

[18] *Tom Thomson: The Last Spring*, page 5.

[19] *Tom Thomson: The Silence and The Storm*, page 56.

[20] "The Rebel Painter of The Pine Woods," page 16.

[21] *Tom Thomson: The Algonquin Years*, page 35.

[22] *Tom Thomson: The Last Spring*, page 65.

[23] Ibid., page 7.

[24] *The Tom Thomson Mystery*, William T. Little, McGraw-Hill Ryerson, Toronto, 1970, page 40.

[25] "The Canoe Lake Mystery," page 34, gives the date as July 6, 1917. It is possibly a typographical error.

[26] *Tom Thomson: The Last Spring*, page 80.

[27] Ibid., page 80.

[28] *Tom Thomson: The Silence and The Storm*, page 224.

[29] *Shorelines*, by Roy MacGregor, McClelland and Stewart, 1980, Toronto, pages 297-8. "After Thomson's tragic death his fiancee did leave the area in the early fall of 1917, first on a long journey to northern Ontario and then, early in November, to Philadelphia with her mother, where they remained until Easter of 1918."

[30] "The Canoe Lake Mystery," page 35.

[31] Ibid., page 36.

# Mary Pickford
## & Douglas Fairbanks

On April 9, 1893, Gladys Marie Smith came into the world in her parents' home at 211 University Avenue in Toronto.[1] John and Charlotte Smith stared in awe at their firstborn as she wailed and squirmed, protesting her sudden arrival into the harsh new environment.

The new mother's sister, Elizabeth, was there to witness the joyous occasion, but other than those who were actually in the bedroom, Gladys's birth went virtually unnoticed. The Smiths didn't bother to register the child's birth with the provincial government and they certainly couldn't afford to put a birth announcement in the *Globe and Mail*.

When little Gladys was about one year old, John and Charlotte welcomed a second daughter, Lottie, to their family. The couple's only son Jack was born three years after that.

When the baby boy was only a few months old, the fates, which had not ever been overly kind to the little group, dealt a life-altering blow to the Smiths. Their breadwinner, Gladys's beloved father, was killed in an accident. The family never had any real hope of enjoying life's luxuries and this last blow appeared to have doomed them to a life of destitution.[2]

Gladys was a high-strung and empathetic child. In addition to her own intense grief for her father and some very real worries about the family's financial survival, the child took on her mother's pain as well. Never a robust child, little Gladys was often seriously ill. As a result her early school attendance was sporadic at best. The few months that she was in class were frightening to the child and after less than a year in the school system, the family's doctor recommended that Gladys be educated at home.

During one of those periods of illness, the doctor, also named Smith but no relation to Gladys's family, offered to adopt the pretty little girl. Charlotte Smith felt that was a decision that Gladys should make for herself. The little girl's sense of family loyalty made her decline the physician's kind offer. That decision, made by a sickly, five-year-old child, effectively restricted her future to one of bare survival.

Given this disadvantaged start, followed by the rejection of an offer of better things, it's not much of a surprise that the name Gladys Smith is not a household word. The surprise is that this anonymous little Canadian waif, Gladys Smith, became "America's Sweetheart," Mary Pickford, and journeyed from her parents' working-class home at 211 University Avenue, to Pickfair, the glamorous Beverly Hills mansion at 1143 Summit Drive. The path between those two addresses includes one of the most famous love stories of all time.

❦ ❦ ❦

Charlotte Smith was devastated by the loss of her husband. She had adored the handsome, dashing and fun-loving Jack Smith.[3] Now a widow in her early 20s, the woman had her invalid mother and three children to support. If she had any hope of keeping her family together, Charlotte knew she'd have to find some way of making ends meet. The available options were severely limited, but she would try.

First the widow opened a candy counter in a local grocery store. She tended business while five-year-old Gladys looked after the two smaller children. Predictably, the revenue from penny candies was not enough to keep the family going. Charlotte began to supplement her daily earnings by taking in sewing, which she worked on in the evenings.

*Sculpture of Mary Pickford, which stands near the site of her childhood home in Toronto. (photo courtesy of Barry Hunter)*

When those incomes also proved inadequate, Charlotte resorted to renting out some of the rooms in her house. Initially she only rented to single women, but when a married couple asked to rent the largest bedroom at an enticing weekly rental, the widow agreed. By now she and the three children were all sleeping in one downstairs room of the house, but that didn't matter to any of them. They were adequately fed and most importantly, they were staying together.

Charlotte was even willing to overlook the fact that the couple now occupying the room she and Jack once shared so happily was involved in the theatre. The injection of their board money eased the Smith family's plight considerably. That couple also proved to be the catalyst for a change so dramatic that it has fairy tale-like qualities.

The Smiths pathetic financial situation was, of course, apparent to all their boarders. When the newest renters needed additional child actors in their production of *The Silver King*, they immediately thought of their landlady's daughters.

Initially, Charlotte was horrified at even the thought of such an offer. She held people associated with the stage in poor regard. It was bad enough that she'd been forced, by finances, to rent a room to people earning a living through the theatre, but she was certainly not going to allow her daughters to become involved with such an immoral aspect of life. However, when Charlotte heard that each girl would earn $10 a week, she agreed to at least meet with the cast of the melodrama and decide whether or not they were suitable company for her children. Apparently those unsuspecting folks passed the test they didn't know they were taking, for Gladys Smith and her younger sister, Lottie, made their theatrical debut just a few days later.

The name of the man who introduced Gladys Smith to the stage has, unfortunately, been lost. Of course, no one knew at the time that his choice of children to play two small roles in a Henry Arthur Jones' melodrama would affect the very evolution of North American entertainment. We're left knowing only that he was the stage manager for a company called the Cummings Stock Company.[4]

Right from her modest debut Gladys showed a flair for the dramatic. Many years later, she credited this natural ability to talents apparent for at least two previous generations on her mother's side of the family. In her autobiography, *Sunshine and Shadow*, she explains, "Grandma Hennessey was the pride of the Faeleys in the vaunted Irish art of twisting a commonplace into a humourous tale. She had a fabulous memory and was a sidesplitting mimic. These talents she passed on to Mother, who possessed a remarkable gift for dramatizing a triviality and finding a suitable saying for every situation."[5]

And so, in 1898, apparently predisposed to acting and certainly highly motivated, Gladys Smith began her career. There would be no looking back for anyone in the small and once-destitute family.

Charlotte Smith continued to suppress her negative attitude toward theatre people when it was in her children's best interest. She also learned how to negotiate contracts. By the earliest days of this century, she had discovered that if producers wanted Gladys badly enough they were willing to hire the rest of the family for smaller roles. This served the dual purpose of increasing the family's income and guaranteeing that they would be together.

Charlotte sold the house on University Avenue. The Smiths were travelling so much that they were rarely in Toronto and, if by chance they were there for a few days, it was infinitely easier just to rent rooms. Ironically their previous tenant, the stage manager and his wife, had originally offered the acting role to help the family keep their home. He could never have guessed that this initial opportunity would turn out so well that within a few months the Smiths no longer needed the house.

From Toronto, the family followed their stage parts to Buffalo, New York, and from there to New York City. It was a grueling life. Directly after the day's last performance, Charlotte would escort her children to a hotel room where the little ones would fall into bed, exhausted. She couldn't allow herself the luxury of sleep until she had made sure the children's clothes were ready for the next day's performances. When everything was in order for another day, Charlotte would set an alarm clock, often for the middle of the night. They needed to be in the next town ready to rehearse by early morning.

Gladys's popularity and ability as a child actress were both increasing. Johnny and Lottie, her younger brother and sister, were still restricted to lesser roles, but Gladys's presence in a play was becoming many a show's main draw. In just months she had progressed from bit parts to starring roles. While this provided good leverage for Charlotte when she was negotiating a salary agreement with a producer, it also necessitated that, occasionally, the family be separated.

As the demand and appreciation for her acting abilities increased, so did Gladys's capacity to manage her life in an adult world. Before her 13th birthday the girl who was billed as "Baby Gladys" was able to check herself and her sister in and out of hotel rooms and travel between cities without supervision when the need arose. This was a considerable accomplishment, especially considering the era.

Charlotte's abilities as a business manager had also increased. She'd become a 'pro' at negotiating salary agreements between her daughter and whatever acting troupe wanted the child's services. As a result the Smiths were enjoying a considerably higher income than ever before.

Their years of financial hardship, however, had left permanent scars on the family. None of them, especially Gladys and Charlotte, could take this sudden infusion of funds lightly. They hoarded all they were able to, often at the expense of their own comfort. In order to save spending a nickel to ride the streetcar, Gladys made it a point to walk to and from the theatre in whatever town she was performing. This meant up to four trips a day between the hotel and the stage and therefore the saving of a dollar a week. It was deemed significant. She was earning $25 a week at this time.

By 1909 that figure had increased to a sizable $30 a week. David Belasco, the day's most renowned producer, had spotted the child-actress and knew that offering Gladys that inflated amount to join his acting company would be a wise investment. For this price he was guaranteed the girl's loyalty and affections. The salary also, apparently, earned Belasco the right to change Gladys Smith's name and from then on the child prodigy became known to the world as "Mary Pickford."

In her autobiography, Mary Pickford explains that the new name came from a combination of family names. She also shares an anecdote about the only other person she knew of with the name.

> . . . a little Eskimo boy . . . was evidently given the name in confusion resulting from the male role I played in *Little Lord Fauntleroy*. The story was told to me by a friend of mine who had traveled extensively in the Far North. One day as he was passing an Eskimo hut, a boy of three, giggling merrily and naked as the day he was born, dashed through an open doorway into the lane outside. An anxious mother followed in hot pursuit. My friend watched in amusement till he heard the Eskimo mother scream out a name. In utter disbelief he listened again, and once more the name rang out in the crisp morning air, 'Mary Pickford!'[6]

Charlotte, Lottie and Johnny Smith were all so impressed with the new name their family star had adopted that they also dropped "Smith" in favor of the more exotic moniker, "Pickford."

In 1909, Mary made her debut on the silver screen in a single scene of a seven-minute-long "flick" called, *Her First Biscuits*. An admittedly inauspicious start but, as history bears out, it was obviously an adequate one. Even in that very small part, Mary Pickford stole the show and therefore set a valuable precedent. And so began the long and profitable partnership between the actress and producer David Wark Griffith of Biograph Studios.

The success also cemented Mary's subordinate relationship with her mother, as it was only at the older woman's insistence that Mary agreed to apply for work in the new and untried field of moving pictures. Despite this initial reluctance, Mary took to the "flicks" like she'd been born to the medium. She was highly photogenic, an elusive quality, but one that a screen star could hardly succeed without. This, coupled with her tremendous work ethic, created dynamite potential for fame and fortune. Movies were distributed all over the country and so, rather than just being able to perform to one audience each night, hundreds and thousands of moviegoers could now enjoy Mary Pickford's talents and stage presence.

She had been virtually on her own in New York City. Her sister, brother and mother came and went, but frequently the Pickfords were more scattered than they wished to be. Rather than pine for her family, Mary used what little free time she had wisely. She toured the city, making a point to pass by as many movie houses as possible on her route.

On her mother's next visit, Mary explained the information she'd turned up on these patrols.

"When I pass a theatre showing one of my films there are always line-ups at the door. But if I pass the same theatre, on the same day, the following week and they're showing someone else's films the sidewalks in front of the entrance are bare," she began. "Obviously the theatres are making more money when they show my films. I'll bet Biograph knows that and charges the movie houses more for a picture that I'm in."

She was hurt and insulted by what she considered Biograph's unfair treatment of her, but she was also just plain angry about not receiving her monetary due. Even though they were living on a comfortable income by now, none of the family had ever forgotten the early days of poverty. Charlotte immediately grasped Mary's message of missed profits and vowed to correct the situation. Soon Mary Pickford was earning an astounding 100 dollars a week.

The film industry was beginning to make rapid gains in a pretty little west coast community – Hollywood, California, by name. When Biograph Studios decided to try their operations at this new site, Mary went with them. Her brother, Johnny, made the trip as well. En route, Johnny Pickford the stage actor disappeared – it was Jack Pickford the movie actor who arrived in Hollywood. He and Mary worked diligently and when they rejoined Lottie and Charlotte three months later, they were able to present their mother with an impressive nest egg: $1200.

Mary was undeniably happy to have the family back together, but there was someone else she was even more anxious to see. Some months before, David Griffith, Biograph's director, had ordered Mary to practise a love scene with a handsome young actor named Owen Moore. The rehearsal was the closest Mary, then about 16, had ever had to a sexual experience. She must have enjoyed the encounter, for after that she sought Owen out.

He was 23 years old, tall, well-built, a tasteful dresser with a persuasive way with words. What young girl could resist? Not Mary, that was evident. She took him home to meet her mother. Charlotte looked at her daughter's beau and saw something completely different. She saw a five-dollar-a-day actor with questionable ability and a penchant for alcohol. What worried the older woman the most though, was his irresistible grey bedroom eyes and her daughter's reaction to them. Cognizant of the risk she was taking, Charlotte ensured that the visit was a short one and immediately after Owen had left, abruptly spoke her mind.

"He's no good for you, Mary. I don't ever want you to see him again," she announced, leaving no room for negotiation.

Mary pouted, realizing that her mother's conviction was unalterable and that she, Mary, could not risk losing the maternal approval she'd sought and basked in for years. For the first time in her life, however, she also knew she could not abide by her mother's decision.

Finding the compromise that young lovers have been finding for years, Mary began to see Owen secretly. The relationship may have been hidden from Mary's mother, but the couple's fellow employees at Biograph were well aware of the romance. For awhile it was even rumored that Mary was pregnant. If the gossip was accurate, the pregnancy terminated or was terminated long before the time a child would have been born.

By mid-1910 Moore proposed to Mary. She knew that accepting his offer of marriage would mean damaging her relationship with her mother, perhaps irreparably. The mere thought of losing her mother's love and protection was more than Mary could bear. When she turned down Owen's proposal, he countered with an ultimatum of his own.

"If you don't marry me I'll leave and you'll never see me again," he threatened.[7]

She didn't reply – she couldn't. Rather than giving her strength and confidence, the years of working so hard to, initially, just avoid abject poverty, and then to accumulate a financial cushion, had not provided Mary Pickford with any sense of security. She remained terrified of losing anything or even of losing an opportunity to have anything.

Marrying Owen Moore, a five-dollar-a-day actor with a drinking problem, doesn't sound like much of a boost to someone of Mary's ever-increasing stature, but her thoughts didn't follow that path. If she didn't take Owen up on his offer of marriage, she'd be turning something down. The former Gladys Smith wasn't in the habit of turning down any opportunity. In addition, the situation came uncomfortably close to a parallel with an earlier watershed in her life. Her dearly beloved father had left and never returned. She'd lost him and agonized over the loss ever since. And so, in a secret ceremony a few months before her 18th birthday, Mary Pickford and Owen Moore exchanged marriage vows.

Although it was probably a bad match to begin with, two influences doomed the union beyond redemption. The first and most significant being Mary's mother. The second was Owen's drinking. A review of the years the two were married indicates that the first frequently caused the second.

Despite these difficulties, Owen and Mary did not divorce. Over the years, the couple rarely lived together but they would still, occasionally, go out socially as a couple. And so it was that in the autumn of 1915, Mary Pickford and Owen Moore accepted an invitation to a party given by the well-known actress, Elsie Janis. Beth and Douglas Fairbanks also attended.

Any gathering that included the athletic Douglas Fairbanks was bound to be a very physical event.

"Come on you lot!" he called to the cluster of guests gathered around the bar. "Let's go exploring this beautiful property. We'll see what mischief we can get ourselves into, shall we? Who's game for some fun? Will I have any companions on my adventure or will you slugs just stand around and discuss the dismal state of films and film-makers?"

His admonishment succeeded in thinning out the bar crowd considerably. Mary and Owen joined him, laughing appreciatively at his good natured cajoling. Beth Fairbanks and about half a dozen others, including Elsie Janis, their hostess, also put down their drinks and tagged along.

By the time the game of "follow Douglas Fairbanks" had climbed its second fence, the group's numbers had dwindled considerably. Owen Moore decided that chatting and drinking were more his speed. Several of the other adventurers, including Beth Fairbanks, went back with him. By the time they reached the stream running through the Janis's property, the group could more accurately be called a trio – a trio consisting of Elsie Janis, Douglas Fairbanks and Mary Pickford.

Elsie, of course, was well used to the water patterns on her property and quickly followed Doug. Mary set out bravely, but just at the middle of the stream she momentarily lost her foothold and nearly slipped into the icy current.

Waiting on the opposite bank, Doug noticed her distress and immediately went to her aid. Just as he would have in any role either of them might perform, Douglas Fairbanks swept Mary Pickford up in his arms and carried her to safety. What a textbook perfect start to a romance! Two glamorous and popular movie stars playing perfectly crafted roles.

If the romance had started with that incident, one might even believe, as Mary did, in predestiny. It didn't, however; the physical intimacy brought about by the heroine's distress and the hero's gallantry, in real life, only started a friendship.

As a friendship it was an obvious one. Mary was 22 years old, 10 years younger than Doug, but both were veterans and pioneers in the film industry. Doug relished the fact that Mary enjoyed his physical prowess. As she did most of her own movie stunts, she appreciated his abilities in that area. That was a direct contradiction to Beth Fairbanks' attitude. She thought of all his climbing and jumping as merely proof that her husband was one of the many cases of arrested development that the moving picture shows tended to breed.

Doug admired Mary's accomplishments, too. Unlike Owen, who constantly belittled her career, Doug appreciated just how much Mary had achieved. He spoke often and sincerely of his admiration for her work and her ability. They would each have been surprised by how important their admiration for one another was, for, despite the undeniable successes each one had earned, neither had much self-confidence. Both fretted that their popularity might suddenly leave them and neither star-ego could bear such a thought.

Doug coped with this lack of security by surrounding himself day and night with adoring others. "Does Fairbanks go to the toilet by himself?" became the question of the day for those who knew the star's patterns.

Mary's response to the insecurity was very different. She made sure she worked harder and longer than anyone else, so she could be sure to be on top of all she needed to be. As a result Mary was very much a loner.

They each kept themselves informed of the progress of the other and when they met at yet another party, there was much the two screen idols wanted to discuss with one another. Meaning to pay Mary a compliment, Doug compared her acting skill to that of the very successful Charlie Chaplin. He couldn't have known Mary detested everything about the pantomimist. Her feelings may only have been motivated by professional jealousy, because Chaplin had been even more successful than Mary. Whatever the cause, she disliked everything about the man. Her feelings were so intense that she, uncharacteristically, turned down an opportunity to make a film with "*The Little Tramp*," an opportunity that would, no doubt, have been very profitable for both of them.

As Mary had been known to lose her temper over less, it is noteworthy (and fortunate) that the ill-taken compliment didn't drive Mary to sulk in a corner of the party room. Instead, the two spent a great deal of time together that evening, chatting and dancing. It must all have been discreet because, although Mary's husband was out of town for the soiree, Doug's wife was in attendance. Beth Fairbanks didn't seem offended by the evening's events.

By May of 1915, Doug and Mary were working on opposite coasts, he in Hollywood and she in New York. Mary's approximate yearly salary at the time was an astounding $100 000 – considerably more money than the President of the United States earned. Fun-loving Douglas Fairbanks might not have come near that astronomical figure, but he was, nonetheless, a well-known, well-respected, wealthy actor. And Mary Pickford was certainly one of his biggest fans. She admired everything she knew about him and the more she knew, the more she admired.

While Owen Moore was well-liked by others, the way he treated his wife showed an aspect of his personality that no one could have enjoyed. He was consistently critical and negative toward Mary. This left a void in her life that Doug's heartfelt admiration filled beautifully.

Fairbanks wasn't kind to Mary Pickford because he wanted to benefit from associating himself with her either professionally or personally. He sincerely admired the accomplishments of others. There was nothing self-serving about Douglas Fairbanks' benevolence, even where Mary wasn't involved. He was merely a good-hearted and considerate man. For instance, at the close of filming a cowboy movie, the producers hosted a party for the actors and the crew. Many of those who had played bit parts were actually cowboys, not actors at all. When it came time to sit down at a dinner table with Hollywood stars, producers and directors, these cowboys were understandably apprehensive. Doug soon put them at their ease by adopting their table customs. He propped his elbows on the table, attacked his food with great gusto and when he was done, mopped his plate with bread. The cowboys followed suit and thoroughly enjoyed what was likely the only meal they ever shared with a movie star.

Mary's feelings for Fairbanks terrified her and she made a valiant attempt to suppress them. After all, they were both married – to others. Doug even had a child. In matters of the heart, however, Mary's usually superhuman self-control apparently failed her. A comment in her autobiography, *Sunshine and Shadow*, reveals she felt uncharacteristically powerless about the situation. "I don't think either of us realized, after that second encounter, that we were falling in love."[8]

Resisting the inevitable or not, Mary was clearly enjoying herself and anyone who has ever delighted in those halcyon early moments of a romance will be able to understand Mary's comment: "I hugged the echo of his words for days . . ."[9]

All of this was more than just a chemical reaction between two physically attractive people. Many years later, Mary struggled to reveal the essence of the man and to explain why she felt the way she did about Doug. "How can I possibly convey the impact of this man's personality, the terrific vitality, the completely childlike enthusiasm? One would have had to know Douglas personally to realize the overwhelming dynamism of the man."[10]

Truly the words of a woman in love.

The young lovers' actions spoke even more strongly of their feelings for one another. Each was inordinately fond of, and affected by, their mother. Not long after Mary and Doug met, they introduced these two important women to one another and reveled in the fact that their two mothers plainly enjoyed each other's company. Their mothers seemed to approve of the potential union despite the distinctly immoral overtones.

Mary thought the elder Mrs. Fairbanks was wonderful and often sought the woman out when she could not be with Doug. "The sound of her voice, or the look on her face, which so vividly reminded me of him, would somehow ease my pain," explained the young, smitten woman.[11]

Doug's enthusiasm for Mary's mother stopped well short of that point. He wisely tolerated, humored and even indulged the woman, but only because of her importance in Mary's life, a fact readily evident to even the most casual observer. At this point, little beyond toleration was really called for. After all, this was only a friendship. Wasn't it? Even if they had recognized or acknowledged their feelings, there were much larger concerns to be dealt with than just the potential for tensions between Douglas Fairbanks and Mary Pickford's mother.

Mary's public persona depended heavily upon her being known as "Little Mary." Those with vested interests in her career knew the importance of maintaining that image. Once when she was fidgeting with a lipstick during an interview, the tube was taken away from her for fear someone might think it was a cigarette.

Publicly, her marriage to Owen Moore was never promoted. The line of reasoning went that if Mary Pickford was married, then she must be an adult, and not therefore "Little Mary." Carrying that theory a little further, it's not difficult to imagine how potentially damaging a divorce and re-marriage might be to her career.

Fairbanks had many of the same concerns. He was worshipped as the epitome of the clean living, upstanding, all-American man. He had written a book entitled *Laugh and Live*, in which he declared rather pompously, "If a man is a manly man, he should marry early and remain faithful to the bride of his youth."[12]

For Douglas Fairbanks and Mary Pickford, the road to romance may have been pre-destined, as Mary was convinced it was, but it would not be smooth. For now they would merely have to get on with their lives and careers, Doug in California and Mary back in New York.

Then on December 23, 1916, Ella Fairbanks, Doug's mother, died. He was devastated, especially that he'd not been with her at the end. The grief-stricken man withdrew emotionally from all around him, arranging and attending the funeral in a nearly robotic trance. Days later word of Mrs. Fairbanks' death reached Mary when she returned to California. She wrote him a letter of condolence, for who, after all, could better understand just how crushed he must be by the loss of his mother?

Doug responded to her note by asking to see her. The next day, in the back of Mary's chauffeured limousine, the two went for a long drive. Her empathy sparked the emotional freedom he needed and Douglas Fairbanks, the great swashbuckling star, sobbed uncontrollably into Mary Pickford's famous blonde ringlets. When he recovered his composure, both he and Mary noticed that the clock in the back of the huge car had stopped. So had their friendship. They could no longer deny that they were in love.

Now they would have to prepare for the complications those deeper feelings were bound to bring into both of their lives. The affair contradicted both their public and self-images. Mary saw herself as always in control, focused, productive and above all, moral. Her adoring public saw her as a sweet, innocent young lady. To his fans and to himself, Douglas Fairbanks epitomized clean living. There was certainly no room here for adultery or divorce. The situation seemed to be an insurmountable dilemma. They loved each other and yet they also each loved their careers. Satisfying their great craving for one another could destroy their status as idolized icons of perfection.

Mary, especially, was tormented and at one point in the early days of 1917 she telephoned her mother, sobbing uncontrollably.

"Mama, please come quickly," she pleaded.

Charlotte Pickford arrived at the apartment just in time to prevent her suicide attempt. A doctor was called. Although 'Mama' was no doubt fully aware of what had caused her daughter's melancholy, it is doubtful that either woman would have shared the information with an outsider like the doctor. It is probably just a good coincidence, then, that he recommended Mary Pickford treat herself to a trip away from New York.

When Doug heard that his secret beloved was leaving once again, he hosted a good-bye party for her. On Saturday, February 3, 1917, the Fairbanks' suite in the Algonquin apartment house in New York began to fill up with the day's luminaries. This was an occasion. Those who knew Mary would understand the implication of her expensive new dress. Mary Pickford, the practical, sensible, almost miserly millionaire, purchased a "new frock," as the press reported it, specifically for the occasion.

Although she was leaving Doug behind in New York, she was also, at least temporarily, leaving Owen. One unhappy factor balanced out a happy one and the worshipping crowds of fans that came to bid her a safe journey and watch her train chug out of Grand Central Station must have tipped the scales to a positive balance.

If Mary's doctor thought getting away from New York would mean Mary would be getting away from work he was sadly mistaken. The train she was on was headed for Los Angeles where crowds of fans waited on the train station platform to greet Mary. A limousine whisked her away to the luxurious Alexandria Hotel, where she was the guest of honor at an elegant soiree.

The next day, in typical Pickford style, Mary began filming another movie. The torments of being married to a man she'd never loved and being in love with a man she couldn't marry would not stop her. Personal problems must never be allowed to interfere with professional productivity. This assignment actually offered Mary an advantage she rarely enjoyed. Aside from her mother, Mary only had one friend, script writer Frances Marion. Although Frances was already back in New York, she had also worked on the movie and both she and Mary were delighted with the results. They felt confident it would be an unqualified success. Once the movie was 'in the can,' everyone, including the leading lady, had a two week break before shooting for the next one would begin. Mary phoned her friend Frances.

"I'm going to come to New York. We can go to the movie's opening together and then I can get some spring shopping done before I have to be back on the lot again," she informed Frances.

"Really?" her friend responded, somewhat surprised.

This meant that Mary would be riding a train, first in one direction and then the other, across the entire breadth of the United States. The train trips alone would consume 10 of the 14 free days she had between films. Given that Mary's lack of interest in adding to her wardrobe was well-known, Frances's reaction was understandable.

During the train ride east Mary agonized, as she always did, over the film she'd just finished. She was sure it would be awful, that the public would hate it and she'd be finished, washed up, never able to make another movie again.

As planned, Mary and Frances attended *The Poor Little Rich Girl's* opening night together, with Mary disguised by hiding her trademark curls under a large hat and wearing oversized sunglasses. The ruse worked until the closing credits were shown. The audience loved the movie and especially enjoyed Mary Pickford's performance. As the lights in the theatre came back on, one by one scattered members of the audience recognized Mary. Within minutes management at the Strand Theatre had to call in police officers to help regain order. By the time she was escorted out of the theatre, Mary's fur coat was in tatters from fans grabbing at her. Her nerves were equally damaged, but at least she knew for certain that her fans still appreciated her talents.

Doug sent his congratulations and the further message that he'd be leaving shortly to make a film in Los Angeles. As Mary was also heading back to Hollywood immediately, that news must have delighted her. Once again she'd be near her love. Any reservations Mary might have had about the wisdom of an affair with Douglas Fairbanks were swept away on a wave of excitement and anticipation. The world's most popular screen idols were truly in love with each other.

Mary's work, first on stage and then in the movies, had always been good. She certainly began with a natural talent for acting, but her work ethic and determination saw any innate abilities enhanced to produce unequaled performances. No one in the business could compete with her, even at the worst of times. Now, she was virtually unstoppable, for these were the best of times. She was young, beautiful, wealthy beyond her wildest dreams and she was in love with the man thousands considered the most handsome in the world.

Doug and Mary saw each other daily as they came and went from their individual movie sets. They were even doing some travelling together, promoting the sale of Liberty Bonds to aid America's war effort. Then, in the hours after their obligations were fulfilled, carefully disguised, they would slip away together. Neither took any steps toward divorcing their spouse and the affair proceeded for the first few weeks of 1917 as just that, an affair.

During this time Beth Fairbanks, Douglas's wife, became ill. Perhaps as part of the subterfuge necessary to carry out an extra-marital affair or perhaps because her conscience was troubling her, Mary frequently went to the hospital to see the woman. When visiting hours ended, she would then go for long, clandestine drives with the ailing woman's husband.

This sort of an arrangement would be difficult for any two people to maintain. For two of the most famous people in the world, it was, of course, impossible. As Beth Fairbanks convalesced, she realized what was happening. Any other cuckolded wife might have confronted the love birds, but Beth was not just 'any' woman. She called a press conference.

To gasps of horror Mrs. Fairbanks explained, in agonizing detail, exactly what was going on between two of the world's most famous stars. Although she possibly relished naming 'America's Sweetheart' as the 'other woman,' the revelation didn't have all the effect she'd hoped for. The press was too shocked to name Mary Pickford in their reports. Their articles only referred to 'an actress.'[13]

Not to be outdone by his wife, Douglas Fairbanks called his own press conference.

"Mr. Fairbanks," a reporter asked, "is there any truth to the announcement your wife made just days ago?"

"The story is false," Fairbanks assured them. "It is a piece of German propaganda!"[14]

When the reporters approached Mary for a comment, she denied everything. "If Mr. and Mrs. Fairbanks have separated it is no concern of mine or of any other person but themselves as far as I can see. We are simply associated together in business. And now we're working together to help put over the Liberty Loan," she asserted with equal doses of self-righteousness and dishonesty.

All of this may have satisfied the press, who desperately wanted the information to be wrong, but it didn't do too much for either Doug's wife or Mary's husband. Owen Moore learned of his wife's infidelities via the Biograph studio grapevine. He was no more pleased with the situation than was Beth Fairbanks.

Moore must have liked the press conference approach, because he called one too. He began by explaining that he was making the announcement on behalf of his wife. This is highly unlikely as she hadn't yet been named in the press. After Moore's carefully worded announcement, however, the corners of the love triangle had been identified to all the world.

"The 'other woman,' is now ill and under great nervous stress . . . I feel it obligatory upon myself to save her the humiliation of making a public statement."

Next he choose another tactic. In the time-honored tradition of wronged husbands before and since, Owen Moore began issuing vague threats against Fairbanks. He assured anyone who would listen that he was ready to 'take action.'[15] When he was drinking, which was a good percentage of the time, he clarified what action he intended to take. He would shoot his wife's lover.[16] If Owen Moore hoped these threats would be taken seriously, he must have been disappointed, because whenever Doug referred to Owen, he did so with a smirk.

Mary, however, was afraid. She was very afraid that she couldn't have the man she loved without sacrificing her career, a totally unacceptable, even unthinkable, loss.

While she and Doug certainly weren't free to live together, they were, at least, working together. Not only were they among the stage and screen stars travelling throughout the U.S. giving "Buy Liberty Bond" pep talks, but they had begun a business partnership. Mary Pickford, Douglas Fairbanks, Charlie Chaplin and David Griffith had created the movie production company, United Artists. (The inception of the business caused one movie mogul to comment, "So the lunatics have taken over the asylum.")[17]

The opinions of others aside, Mary was happier than she could ever remember. Initially Doug was satisfied too, but, as the weeks turned to months with no indication from Mary that she was preparing to divorce Moore, Doug became less and less content with the arrangement. America's Sweetheart,' the woman virtually every man in world dreamed about, had been in love with him for two years. He didn't want to pretend it was a secret any longer, he wanted to tell the world.

He began to pressure Mary. Beth had already divorced him and was remarried by now. Finally he issued the ultimatum that she'd heard once before, "Marry me or I'll leave forever."

Mary responded by arranging for a quick, but very expensive, divorce from Owen. Buying him off was rumored to have cost her nearly $100 000 – a substantial figure even today but far more so in 1920. The dissolution of the marriage had some very questionable legal qualities to it. Not content with the money he'd gained, Owen made sure the press fully understood that his ex-wife hadn't met the residency requirement that was a prerequisite for a divorce in Nevada.

Due in large part to his excessive drinking, Owen Moore's influence in the acting community had steadily decreased over the years. By now only the fact that he had once been "Mr. Mary Pickford" differentiated him from hundreds of other drunken Hollywood 'has-beens.' Despite this, Mary issued her own statement protesting Owen's. In it she made the very puzzling assertion that she would never marry again. And yet, on March 28, 1920, Mary Pickford became the second Mrs. Douglas Fairbanks.

For Mary it was the second time she had married in a secret ceremony. She was becoming more and more superstitious and repeating the clandestine circumstances of her first wedding made her feel extremely uncomfortable. She might as well have enjoyed a public ceremony, because a secret like two of the biggest stars in Hollywood marrying could not be kept under wraps for long.

They hoped the news would break while they were away on their honeymoon and would have died down before their return. Unfortunately, as Doug had long suspected might happen, Mary's mother interfered with their plans. The older woman became ill and the honeymoon had to be postponed for two months.

This may have been Doug's first experience with not being able to control and manipulate whatever he needed to in order to accomplish his own ends. Up until now, his talent, his looks, his popularity and, of course, his money had bought him just about anything he wanted.

Even reality could be, and frequently was, altered to meet Douglas Fairbanks's needs. Although he was undeniably athletic and capable of performing his own stunts, the stage hands routinely made furniture and other obstacles, which the star had to jump over, just a bit smaller than normal. This way not only could he leap over them, but he could do so with amazing ease.

For a man with this kind of manipulative power, it must difficult to accept that his mother-in-law could now control where he went and when. It wasn't, however, a surprise to him. Mary's family was well known around the movie industry. When they were being kind, studio executives referred to Charlotte Pickford as 'formidable.' Doug himself had told a friend that even though he loved Mary deeply he still found her family hard to bear. By way of an explanation for his attitude, he added that, "They were all alcoholics."

Doug also resented Jack Pickford's success. The young man had done well even though he'd been considerably more serious about partying than about working. For the industrious, abstaining Douglas Fairbanks, this was easy to resent. Mary's sister, Lottie, enjoyed very few redeeming qualities in Doug's eyes. He considered her merely an untalented hanger-on with offensively low moral standards and the poor reputation she deserved.[18]

If Doug knew just how significant a role the other Pickfords would play throughout his marriage, he probably wouldn't have been the least bit surprised when his mother-in-law accompanied the newlyweds on the first leg of their honeymoon. The trio reach New York on May 19, 1920, at which point Charlotte became ill once again and Mary refused to travel. It was not until May 29, more than two months after their wedding, that Mr. & Mrs. Fairbanks boarded a ship to sail to Europe. The sight of Charlotte on the wharf waving good-bye as the ship left the harbor must have warmed Doug's heart.

Their trip abroad did more than just provide the couple with the privacy they'd been denied for so long. It reassured them both of their international popularity. Because silent films had no language barrier, both Mary and Doug were as well known in Europe as they were in North America. Not only did the censure they had both feared as a result of their marriage not materialize but, judging by the adoring crowds that met them everywhere they went, fans heartily endorsed the relationship.

In show business, as in life, timing is everything and the timing of their marriage couldn't have been better. The First World War was over and the flu epidemic that had ravaged the world had run its course. People were eager to replace those years of horror with as much happiness as possible. The Roaring Twenties had begun and almost anything that was fun suddenly became acceptable. The definition of 'anything' included divorces and remarriages, especially if that remarriage created 'the most popular couple the world has known.'

During their European honeymoon, both Mary and Doug revealed aspects of their personalities that the other may, until then, only have suspected. Mary, with her phenomenal work ethic, managed to do an impressive amount of business during the trip and Doug began to disclose the extent of his jealous nature.

In an ambiguously worded request, Doug explained to Mary that he would not stand for her 'twosing'[19] with anyone else. Mary agreed. When she accepted another man's invitation to dance, however, she soon discovered how narrowly Doug was defining 'twosing.' He did a slow burn for the rest of the evening and then, when they were back to their quarters, he exploded in a jealous rage. Mary learned her lesson so well that in later years she declined the Duke of York's invitation to join him on the dance floor by explaining the promise she'd made to her husband.[20] Clearly she thought rebuffing royalty was a small price to pay to ensure Douglas's peace of mind and therefore prevent a further temper tantrum.

The crowds that had greeted the couple at every stop during their travels in Europe duplicated themselves upon their return to the States. America had their very own King and Queen. (The fact that Gladys Smith was actually a Canadian had been, by now, conveniently forgotten.)

And where else could reigning monarchs live but in a palace? In anticipation of that residential requirement, Doug purchased a hunting lodge on 18 acres of land. From its location in Beverly Hills, the site afforded an unobstructed view of the Pacific Ocean. Extensive and expensive renovations later it became the exquisite mansion, Pickfair, as close to a palace as America had ever seen. In retrospect it is worth noting that, in naming the enormous house, the abbreviation of Mary's name came ahead of Doug's. When the couple entertained, she was always seated at the head of the dinner table. Small points, admittedly, but viewed through the advantages of hindsight, they may be significant.

At that time, however, events obviously couldn't be seen in perspective. There was only the happy, if vague, sense that the glory years had begun. Invitations to Pickfair for one or more of the lavish soirees the Fairbanks hosted not only served to acknowledge a guest's social standing but actually increased it. This truism is extremely revealing, considering the average guest lists for Pickfair included America's most influential business magnates, like Henry Ford, sports heroes like Babe Ruth, ruling world monarchs, the brilliant scientist Albert Einstein and of course other movie stars. (Although Mary had never warmed to him, Charlie Chaplin had become Doug's dear friend. As the "little tramp" lived nearby, he frequently took advantage of his open invitation to Pickfair.)

These 'dos' were reported to be great fun, which isn't surprising with Douglas Fairbanks and his childish sense of enthusiasm involved. Guests were treated to games of tennis, frolics in the swimming pool and Fairbanks' endless silly pranks, which Mary tolerated with mild irritation.

Despite implications to the contrary, all this unabashed frivolity took place in an atmosphere of total abstinence. Alcohol was never served at a Fairbanks' party. Doug had promised his mother that he would not take a drink of spirits until he was fully 40 years of age and he intended to keep his word. Besides, to Doug Fairbanks his body was a temple and it would be blasphemy to pollute it. (He did smoke fairly heavily, however; in that era smoking was actually viewed as a positive influence on a person's health.)

Further, if either Mary or Doug had to work the following day the guests understood that while they may have been welcome to arrive early, they must also leave early. All of this, the happiness at being together, the sensible routine and their enormous popularity both as a couple and individually, built on itself. They made better and better films, became happier and happier and wealthier and wealthier.

Mary and Doug were rarely alone together except to sleep. Even if company wasn't expected for dinner, places would be set in case anyone dropped in unexpectedly. And many people did. Because Doug was so extroverted he had many more friends than Mary did. Frequently she would be the only woman at the dinner table.

At formal dinners where the guest list was created in advance, the gender equation would be balanced. It would also be spectacular. The world's most beautiful and powerful people aspired to break bread at Pickfair – and they did. Robert Windeler, in his book *Sweetheart, The Story of Mary Pickford*, puts it succinctly in two paragraphs that are well worth quoting verbatim.

A typical formal dinner for a dozen at Pickfair might include the King and Queen of Siam, Babe Ruth, a well-known publisher, [an] opera singer, [a] feminist, the Duke and Duchess of Albania, an inventor, or a violinist. Any celebrity, particularly royalty or athletes, was fair game for Douglas, whether he knew them previously or not. And celebrities visiting Los Angeles always wheedled invitations to Pickfair, and a dinner or a whole weekend soon became an important part of any distinguished visitor's stay in the Hollywood area.

In the 1920s whenever any foreign notables came to the United States, the first place they wanted to go was Hollywood, and the three people in America they most wanted to see were Mary Pickford, Douglas Fairbanks and Charlie Chaplin. . . . The guest list at Pickfair reads like a Who's Who of the World. The Crown Prince of Japan, Alfonso XIII, [the] ex-King of Spain, Marconi, Lindbergh, Einstein, Amelia Earhart, Sir Austen Chamberlain, Crown Princess Frederica of Prussia, the glamorous Lord and Lady Mountbatten, who spent part of their honeymoon visiting Pickfair. The great authors, painters, politicians, all found their way to the hill.[21]

Despite this stellar line-up, Mary especially never forgot her humble beginnings. The King and Queen of Siam were avid tennis players. During a match on the courts at Pickfair, the Queen slipped on a patch of wet ground. She needed to wash and so Mary showed her to the bathroom. While the queen rinsed clean the results of the royal spill, Mary sighed and pondered the twists her life had taken. Here she was, poor little Gladys Smith, born into poverty on University Avenue in Toronto, waiting while the Queen of Siam bathed in her tub![22]

Interestingly, Mary writes very little about this period in her autobiography, *Sunshine and Shadow*. Perhaps she eventually learned to take it all in her stride, or perhaps, in hindsight, it was just a period she didn't want to dwell on.

During this time both Mary's and Doug's careers were extremely demanding. Their filming schedules, combined with entertaining at Pickfair, severely limited the opportunity for intimate moments between husband and wife. That was not a situation Doug would tolerate for long. He bought a small place in Santa Monica[23] so he and Mary would have a private retreat. Ironically, they soon found it too small to comfortably accommodate the number of people constantly congregated around them. Not long after taking possession of the "hideaway," Doug had a sizable addition built on to the new place. He also installed a swimming pool to which he regularly invited dozens of friends, thus effectively defeating the entire point of the second home.

Whether a Fairbanks' get-together was held in the opulence of Pickfair or at the smaller, less formal 'hideaway,' guests could still count on spending a short and sober evening. Visitors from out of town often stayed overnight. Now that Mary's and Doug's love affair had been legally sanctioned into a marriage, they each re-discovered their holier-than-thou attitudes to sex. Displaying either a fair degree of hypocrisy or astoundingly short memories regarding their own previously clandestine relationship, they adopted a firm rule at Pickfair – if you weren't married, you didn't sleep together.

Even if you could circumvent Doug and Mary, it wouldn't have been wise to attend a Pickfair party with anyone but your own partner. Cameras were everywhere and frequently the photographs showed up the following day in any number of publications. Poses were continually struck and shots snapped, many of them capturing Doug especially, engaging in his much loved hijinks. Mary tolerated the carry-on only because Doug loved silliness and she loved Doug.

There is little question that, at that time, Mary and Doug were good for one another. Within days of each other, they enjoyed the opening nights of movies that became brilliant successes. Crowds gathered to attend the first showing of Fairbanks' newest movie. As Mary and Doug made their way to the theatre, the throng of fans began pressing in on them. Police had to be called to control the growing mob and escort the idols to the safety of the theatre. Even with police protection, the crowd swarmed frighteningly. Doug hoisted Mary up on his shoulders and, to the delight of those gathered, carried his wife the rest of the way.

Mary's movie, *Little Lord Fauntleroy*, opened a few days later to even greater crowds. It was the most demanding film she'd made so far. For some time now, Mary had wanted to shed the "Little Mary" roles and widen her horizons. Here was a real opportunity to show the world the extent of her talent, for not only was she not playing the little girl that the world had come to know and love, but she was playing a dual role – the title role as a boy and that of Little Lord Fauntleroy's mother.

Mary's perfectionism and work ethic deserve much of the credit for the film's artistry and success. Because she played both leading roles, she appeared in virtually every scene. Often her two characters were in scenes together, once they kissed – no simple feat in those pre-computer-enhancement days. That movie and those involved in making it were the pioneers of today's "special effects." All her life Mary remained justifiably proud of that project.

The glory days of Mary's much-heralded cinematic accomplishment coincided with the earliest days of changes that would, in time, prove to be the eventual undoing of 'the most popular couple the world has known.' The silent film era was drawing to a close. Production crews and actors were having to adjust their methods to accommodate the burgeoning technology. Actors from New York's live theatres were making their way to the west coast to cash in on an art form in which they were already proficient.

This infusion of talent brought many implications with it, including a residential construction boom. As a result, Pickfair, once isolated in the Beverly Hills, became surrounded by like mansions as the wealth of the movie industry built on itself logarithmically. The world around them was changing and to a large degree this pleased Mary.

Good clean living can only slow the ravages of time; it can do nothing to prevent technological progress. At 30 she had absolutely shed the "Little Mary" image, but a major change in her art form, such as these newfangled "talkies," represented was quite another matter. She couldn't see that the fad would last, but as always where Mary's career was concerned, she was as aggressive and flexible as she needed to be.

Mary's last silent film, *My Best Girl*, was released late in 1927. Critics and audiences were aligned in their praise. This was Mary's best film, a significant achievement for the woman who had made hundreds of flicks. Mary's co-star in *My Best Girl* was also significant. He was the handsome young actor Buddy Rogers – an inexperienced 22-year-old whose acting ability was exceeded only by "his incredible good looks."[24]

Mary's dearly beloved Douglas was not faring quite as well. He was now 40 years old and although he was still in good physical condition, he was certainly no longer a young man. He responded to this natural and inevitable progression as though it were a personal attempt at intimidation. Fairbanks challenged the inevitable ravages of time, and himself, by making an even bigger and more spectacular movie – *The Three Musketeers*.

Whenever he could, Doug visited the set where his wife was making her movie. *My Best Girl* included some pretty racy scenes for that era and Doug had a vested interest in watching that they were carried out with dignity and decorum. Presumably everything met with Fairbanks' approval, because the movie was completed, apparently without incident.

In the spring of 1926, Mary's success turned against her in the form of a serious threat against her life. Information leaked to the local police department indicated there was a plot to kidnap Mary Pickford. The authorities knew many details of the abduction scheme. So that the criminals would not suspect their cover had been partially blown, the police asked both Doug and Mary to maintain their regular schedules. One nerve-wracking week later, the would-be abductors were caught, but from then on Pickfair was always guarded. Doug could not live with the possibility that someone might have access their home and therefore the potential to harm Mary.

Through all their years as a married couple and individual stars, Mary and Doug had never attempted what seemed to be the obvious – they had never made a film together. When the idea finally occurred to them, they were understandably choosy about what the film might be. After much deliberation they decided to do *The Taming of the Shrew*. Making the movie was pivotal, not only to the Fairbanks as stars, but also to them as a couple.

Like the choice of the story itself, Mary and Doug demanded that everything concerning the movie be of the highest possible quality. Because the film was being made by United Artists, their own company, no one could argue with them. They were effectively spending their own money. Mary had never lost her respect for the value of a dollar and while she would happily spend money to ensure a superior product – that she rightly considered an investment, she could not abide waste of any sort.

In order to be financially viable, Doug's and Mary's first joint venture had to be efficient. From the first day of shooting, Doug balked at the attempt to control his life. He rebelled by extending his daily workout schedule into filming time and when he finally did arrive on the set he was ill-prepared for the day's shooting. The film that was to cement their status, both as a couple and as stars, proved to be their demise.

Before making *Taming of the Shrew*, Doug was already suffering. His always-precarious ego certainly wasn't handling the aging process well. It may not have been such an issue if his son, Douglas Fairbanks Junior, who was both taller and more handsome than his father, had not begun to make motion pictures himself. Father and son had never been close and now Doug Junior was in a position, not only to compete with his father, but also to confirm that Fairbanks Senior could not be any younger than middle age by now. Filming *Shrew* and doing it right could have provided Doug with an opportunity to show his fans something different, but equally appealing – a newly developed maturity. This would also have assured him of Mary's respect but, with his flagrant disregard for production schedules, Fairbanks destroyed that potential as surely as he could. Shooting the movie and the movie itself were equal disasters.

Mary commented later, "The making of that film was my finish. My confidence was completely shattered, and I was never again at ease before the camera or microphone."[25]

Their careers and their marriage were effectively over.

It is a given, however, that actors are able to pretend and Mary Pickford and Douglas Fairbanks were nothing if not two of the greatest pretenders. Doug's "business" trips to Europe became more frequent and, in a short time, clouded with gossip. He was rumored to be seeing a far greater number of women than movie industry executives while he was abroad. As early as 1931, Doug's name was linked with the beautiful Sylvia Hawkes, who preferred to be known as Lady Ashley, a title she gained by virtue of the fact she had once been married to Lord Ashley.

About this time retrospective rumors about Mary's association with Buddy Rogers, her handsome young co-star in *My Best Girl*, her last successful film, began to float through Hollywood's rumor mill.

Who committed the first adultery, or when, became purely academic questions. The World's Most Popular Couple[26] had been driven apart. All Mary ever wanted to do was work and, increasingly, all Doug wanted to do was play. Still, they had their roles to act out. In 1932 the Olympics were held in Los Angeles. Pickfair was ablaze with international guests. Doug and Mary were once again the perfect hosts.

When the sporting events were over, Doug left to go travelling once again. Although the trip was ostensibly a golfing expedition in England, he certainly found time between rounds for a fair amount of marital infidelity. Despite this, Doug and Mary spent Christmas that year – together, once again at Pickfair.

In the next 12 months the two saw less and less of one another, although those close to them say there were many signs that they were still deeply in love. The following Christmas, miscommunication, not desire, deemed that they would spend it apart. The separation tarnished their public image and Mary did not improve the situation when she chose to "confide" her concerns about Doug's infidelities to gossip columnist Louella Parsons. An overindulgence in alcohol may have been a factor in her verbal indiscretion, but Parsons was taking no prisoners. After all, a gossip columnist's job is to share all the sordid details she's aware of with the widest possible audience.

Throughout their 15-year marriage, Mary Pickford's and Douglas Fairbanks' attitudes to drinking caused numerous problems in their relationship. He would not have liquor at Pickfair and this frequently embarrassed Mary when she entertained. Had Mary solely been a social drinker, though, Doug's prohibitive attitudes might not have been an issue. An examination of her life indicates that Mary Pickford had, early on, developed a serious drinking problem. Chuck Lewis, one of Doug's many friends, may have poignantly summed the situation up with the statement, "All Doug ever wanted was a sober Mary."[27]

Mary's family was another negative pressure on the marriage and one that could not be completely separated from the drinking issue. All the Pickfords drank excessively and all, of course, suffered the ravages of overindulgence.

Even if they'd all been as sober as judges, however, Doug would likely still have been resentful of them. Not only did they compete against him for Mary's affections and time, in Doug's opinion they were nothing more than "hangers-on" who rode, undeservedly, on his wife's coat-tail. To a large degree his assessment was correct, but while her family were dependents, Mary Pickford did not consider them liabilities, because in a very different way she was equally dependent on them.

What the causes for the marriage break-up finally were could be debated extensively without ever reaching a resolution. The sad and unarguable fact remained – the love between the most loved couple in the world had died. They divorced early in 1936. Doug gave up his interest in Pickfair, reasoning that the house had been his wedding present to Mary Pickford and he was not about to rescind his generosity.

Despite this show of fondness and caring, Douglas Fairbanks married for a third time just three months after the divorce. Mary Pickford was not far behind him in re-issuing her vows. She and Buddy Rogers married in June of the following year.

Because they were still partners in United Artists, the two continued to see one another. Many years after their divorce and re-marriages, Mary and Doug attended a business meeting together where someone rudely disagreed with a point Mary had been making. Doug angrily exclaimed, "How dare you speak to my wife like that."[28]

Perhaps the outburst reflected that Doug felt, as many of their fans did, that he and Mary Pickford would forever be a couple. The romantics of the world, Douglas Fairbanks included, had to accept that their futures would be very separate and, as history proves, very different. Their popularity began to wane, but that probably would have happened even if their personal circumstances had been better and they'd stayed happily married. Their time as stars was simply drawing to an end.

On June 12, 1939, when a friend informed Mary that Owen Moore, her first husband, had died, she accepted the news with a nod. When exactly six months later, on what would have been Owen's birthday, her second husband Douglas Fairbanks died, Mary Pickford was considerably more distressed.[29] Buddy Rogers consoled Mary as best he was able, but then gave her the privacy she needed to mourn the man who had meant so much to her life.

Although Mary stopped making films after her third marriage, she continued to be active in the industry, especially through her partnership in United Artists. The public caught their last glimpse of their "Sweetheart" in 1976, when she was presented with an award from the Academy of Motion Picture Arts and Sciences. Although she was 83, Mary Pickford still impressed all those who watched her being escorted, in her wheel-chair, to the spot she once held nightly – centre stage.

If the public had known that this appearance interfered with what had effectively become complete seclusion, they may have been even more impressed, for early on in the decade Mary had retired to her bed. She rarely left it after that. She was also rarely sober.

Her lawyer, Cap O'Brien, remembered, "If you had seen Mary Pickford before noon in those days you would have thought her still beautiful, intelligent, clear-minded woman she had been for so many years."[30] He left what you'd find after noon open to speculation.

No mention was ever made in the press about Mary's drunkenness and it was tolerated lovingly by Buddy Rogers. He once commented, with obvious affection in his voice, "That little devil, she gets to drinking and she just can't stop."[31]

Mary Pickford died in 1979.

In 1986 the once grand Pickfair mansion was sold – to Pia Zadora. A by-law in Beverly Hills states that the old buildings are not to be demol-ished. Sadly, the intent of that ruling is negated by the addendum that preserving a substantial portion of one original wall (even if every other square inch of the building is flattened by a bulldozer) then the changes to the structure will be classified not as demolition, but as renovation, and therefore be allowed. Presumably Pia Zadora abided by that stipu-lation, but there is nothing recognizable left of the former hunting lodge and famous Pickfair.

The land on which the palatial home stood has also been ravaged by time. The huge property has been sub-divided time and time again. Many substantial-sized homes sit on land that once belonged to the couple that the world loved to love.

If this love story cannot have a happy ending, at least it should have a bittersweet one. At this writing Buddy Rogers, loyal and loving toward Mary to the end, still lives in what was once an outbuilding at Pickfair.

"It's a long way from where Pickfair stood, but it's still an original building and it's in its original location," explained a representative of the Hollywood Heritage Society during a telephone interview.

And so perhaps a part of Mary Pickford, at least, is still where the world always wanted her to be – with a man she loved at Pickfair.[32]

## Endnotes

She may have been born April 8, 1892, according to Robert Windeler's book, *Sweetheart, The Story of Mary Pickford,* Praeger Publishers, New York, 1974, page 10.

[2]*The United Artists Story*, Ronald Bergan, Crown Publishers Inc., New York, 1986, page 8 says that Jack was 2, Lottie 3 and Gladys 5.

[3]*Sunshine and Shadow*, Mary Pickford, Doubleday and Company, Garden City, 1955, page 23.

[4]*Mary Pickford and Douglas Fairbanks, The Most Popular Couple the World Has Known*, Booton Herndon, W.W. Norton and Company, New York, 1977, page 26, and *Sunshine and Shadow*, page 26, and *Sweetheart, The Story of Mary Pickford*, page 16.

[5]*Sunshine and Shadow*, page 16.

[6]Ibid., page 15.

[7]*Mary Pickford and Douglas Fairbanks*, page 83.

[8]*Sunshine and Shadow*, page 119.

[9]Ibid., page 119.

[10]Ibid.

[11]Ibid.

[12]*Mary Pickford and Douglas Fairbanks*, page 172.

[13]Ibid., page 175.

[14]Ibid.

[15]Ibid., page 176.

[16]Ibid., page 168.

[17]Ibid., page 181.

[18]Ibid., page 158.

[19]Ibid., page 189.

[20]Ibid.

[21]*Sweetheart, The Story of Mary Pickford*

[22]Ibid., page 148.

[23]Ibid., page 146.

[24]Ibid., page 153.

[25]Ibid., page 163.

[26]A popular reference of the era and also the subtitle of Booton Herndon's book, *Mary Pickford and Douglas Fairbanks, The Most Popular Couple the World Has Known*.

[27]Ibid., page 292.

[28]Ibid., page 260.

[29]*Sweetheart, The Story of Mary Pickford*, page 181.

[30]*Mary Pickford and Douglas Fairbanks, The Most Popular Couple the World Has Known*, page 276.

[31]Ibid., page 300.

[32]Author's telephone conversation with the Hollywood Heritage Society.

# Evangeline
## & Gabriel

One of Canada's best known love stories may never have occurred at all. The epic poem which immortalized the chronicle of Evangeline and Gabriel may have been entirely a work of fiction. Whether it was based on fact and then embellished or whether it was purely a work of fiction, this poignant Canadian love story was written by an American – Henry Wadsworth Longfellow.

It is a tragic commentary on the prevailing attitude to our country's history that without this work of Longfellow's, much of the information about the tragedy of the expulsion of the Acadians in 1755 would be all but unknown. Likely only a few scholars with a special interest in that particular time and place would be aware of this deplorable event in Canadian history.

Throughout the years Longfellow spent writing the poem (1845 to 1847), little was known of the expulsion. The English, being responsible for the mortal upheaval, were not much inclined to record their considerably less than noble deed and the Acadians, the only other group of people directly involved with the expulsion, were too busy trying to piece their lives back together and find new homes in which to live out the balance of those all-but-destroyed existences. Those seeking barest survival are equally as unlikely as those ashamed of their actions to record events. And so, when Longfellow was crafting the poem, nearly 100 years after the event had occurred, there were only a few obscure written references to the event.

The background against which this legend of love is played out is one Canadians throughout the country's history and geography know well – tensions between the English and the French. The setting for this edition of the ongoing misunderstandings was an area of eastern Canada, then known as Acadia.[1] The era was the mid-1700s.

When the French "discovered" the abundance of untapped natural resources on and around the shores of the New World, they had no intention of trying to create permanent settlements in so inhospitable an environment. They merely wanted to exploit the area's lush reserves.

Those early French explorers were probably unaware that they were not the first Europeans to happen upon the area of the North American continent that would eventually become Canada's east coast. Although the Vikings may have been the first non-natives to "discover" the Canadian Maritimes, a large stone was found in 1912 which provided definitive proof that there had been other visitors before the French. A large, flat-faced boulder was found in Yarmouth harbor. It had an intriguing inscription etched into it. Although the symbols cannot be interpreted word for word, the characters are believed to be part of an ancient Basque system of written communication and the message has been translated to read, "Basque people have subdued this land." Experts estimate this arrogant and presumptuous declaration was carved some time between 500 BC and 150 BC.

Whether or not the translation is absolutely accurate, the message's very existence, to say nothing of its exact meaning, still invite speculation. Does the use of the word "subdued" indicate those early Spaniards battled the North American natives victoriously? If so, did the tribes somehow re-generate or did neighboring tribes migrate to occupy the newly-vacated land? Perhaps the most interesting hypothesis is the possibility that those ancient Basque people might be some of the ancestors of today's Micmac Indians.

By now the debate cannot be resolved, but no matter which European culture, in what century, first influenced what is now Maritime Canada, it is clear that initially no one was interested in establishing communities here. Those early adventurers were only concerned with the profit they could make by returning to their homelands with shiploads of fish, fur and timber for sale. It wasn't until the early 1600s that any thought of establishing colonies in this harsh new land was put into action. At best those first immigrants were deemed to be wildly eccentric, foolhardy folk – at worst suicidal. Those with an interest in preserving the New World's status as merely a supply depot from which to seize valuable natural resources were determined to discourage these would-be settlers in any way possible.

Of course, the existence of Canada as we know it today is proof that in spite of all the adversities, both natural and man-made, those with a bent toward settlement persevered and eventually triumphed. Some of the earliest communities were established by the French in an area identified at the time as Acadia.

Because colonizing this harsh, untamed land was so difficult, population growth was painfully slow. Immigration accounted for little in the way of increased numbers and, as a result, by the mid-1700s most of the people residing in Acadia were direct descendants of the original 40 or so families that had arrived from France 100 years before. This demographic meant, among other things, that the Acadians were an extraordinarily close-knit group. Considering the way the tiny colony was ignored by the inhabitants' homeland, it's just as well the Acadians enjoyed this attitude of self-sufficiency.

While those first settlers were quietly and successfully establishing family farms in what was to become Maritime Canada, England and France continued their disagreements. Throughout the years, only the size and intensity of these altercations ever varied. Which side was victorious, and for how long, often determined whether Acadia was a French or an English territorial holding. Between 1603 and 1760, Acadia's ownership was passed back and forth between the adversaries a total of eight times.

To add to the turmoil, England and France disagreed on the geographic definition of their pawn. The French viewed Acadia as consisting only of the area we know as mainland Nova Scotia. The English, however, also incorporated New Brunswick, part of the province of Quebec and even land in what is now the state of Maine into their definition of Acadia.

Interestingly, these political upheavals had very little effect on the lives of the Acadians themselves. The settlers had already grown away from identifying with their former homeland and had forged a distinctive and independent culture. They asked little of anyone outside their immediate community, wanting only to be left unhindered in their pursuit of happy, peaceful lives.

One of the few times the Acadians were forced to become aware of external political influences was during one of the periods of English rule. Because the settlers were descended from the French, the British were concerned about where the people's loyalties might lie when the next inevitable war between the nations broke out. The English tried to force the Acadians to sign an oath of allegiance to the British. As the ultimate "owner" of their new homeland was of little significance to the average Acadian farmer, they were willing to sign such a document as long as it did not include an order which would force them to take up arms against Britain's enemies. Not only were the Acadian people pacifists, but they were well aware that France would be the first country implied by the phrase "Britain's enemies" and, although the French had done little over the years to assist the Acadians, these people had no reason to want to bear arms either against France or on behalf of England.

As the interminable feuding had been going on so long and with so little effect on the neutral Acadians, they paid scant attention when the British issued an ultimatum – swear unconditional allegiance to England, including bearing arms against that country's enemies, or be deported.

Acadia's population by that time had grown to over 10 000. The settlers had established a flourishing community. Few Acadians were even interested in listening to political rumblings, let alone in getting involved in such affairs. Those who did give the matter any thought found it inconceivable that such an unwieldy plan as a mass deportation would be carried out. And so, to a very large degree, despite having been given clear warnings, the Acadians were naively taken by surprise when in August of 1755 they were ordered to assemble to hear a proclamation

– a proclamation that effectively destroyed their peaceful and prosperous lives.

That proclamation also became the catalyst that, nearly 100 years after the fact, led American poet Henry Wadsworth Longfellow to create one of the world's best known and most treasured love stories.

It is not known exactly how or why Longfellow became interested in such a political event as the expulsion of the Acadians. It is likely he was both drawn to, and appalled by, the happiness and lives of so many being interrupted by government dictate. His lifelong friend and fellow writer Nathaniel Hawthorne may have heard and then passed along a story that became the nucleus for the poem. It is known that Longfellow relied on information in Thomas Chandler's *The History of Nova Scotia* as a historic reference and that Chandler, in turn, had been influenced by a previous work. Because both these sources were decidedly French in their leanings, Longfellow's sympathies were very much with the Acadians.

Prior to his beginning the poem in the late fall of 1845, Longfellow studied notes his sister had made in her journal while travelling down the Ohio and Mississippi Rivers, in addition to relying on travel books of the day. The poet was a bitter-sweet romantic himself. Having been left a widower twice, he could easily empathize with the sorrow that his heroine Evangeline no doubt felt at being separated from her beloved Gabriel.

Whether or not Evangeline, the tragic heroine, was an entirely fictitious character cannot, by now, be accurately determined. During the 1840s when Longfellow was writing the poem, little of the plight of the Acadians had been recorded. What had been noted certainly didn't include any references to a young couple forced apart by the expulsion. Some historians, however, maintain that references to such a couple did exist and have even traced a possible route for the information to have travelled from its origin to Henry Wadsworth Longfellow and his muse. It is interesting to note that the legend has been captured in English – the language of the perpetrators of the expulsion – and stranger still that we Canadians owe much of our delightfully romanticized image of Acadian life to an American poet.

Here, reflecting the timelessness of the theme, is a legendary Canadian love story, re-told this time as a modern tale from the point of view of its heroine, Evangeline.

## April 15, 1755

Dear Diary

Spring is nearly here and I'm so grateful. It isn't that the winter was overly harsh, certainly not like some I remember when I was a young girl. Or maybe it was harsh and I just didn't notice the cold so much this year. After all, Father repaired the thatching on the roof last summer, so there were no draughts to chill the house and for my part I was so busy and happy that the days just seemed to fly comfortably by.

What a relief it's been that those silly neighborhood boys have finally seemed to accept that at 17 I'm far too mature to be interested in any one of them. Even better, Gabriel Lajeunesse has taken to dropping by when his father, Basil the blacksmith, comes to visit my father. Gabriel and I played together often when we were just children. He's grown and changed. Now he's so handsome, all the girls in the village know that, but I know more than that. I know that he has the sweetest nature in the world and I even think I know that Gabriel's the man I want to marry.

He's paying more and more attention to me every time he visits and so I think he may feel the same way about me as I do about him. Pretty soon I'm going to have to say something to Papa, although judging by the extra twinkle, not only in my father's eyes but in Gabriel's father's eyes as well, I suspect that they may have an idea. That's all right, though, because at least it means they won't be objecting to our seeing one another.

Now I should get back to my loom and then out to the fields to tend the heifers. They seem even happier than I am that spring is here. They must be so glad to be free of the confines of the barns where they were stabled throughout the winter.

I shall write again soon, dear diary.

## April 30, 1755

Dear Diary

Basil and Gabriel were over for a visit again this evening, but it wasn't the happy time that the other visits have been. Even though Gabriel and I kept ourselves over in the corner and could not make out exactly what our fathers were saying, we couldn't help but be affected by the mood of their discussion. They were so somber. It was really quite frightening. Perhaps it is as well that I don't know what is going on, but because I don't, it seems that not knowing is the worst.

As best I can figure from gossip around the town, those back in England and France are feuding again. If that's all it is then I'm not going to worry too much. It seems on and off, throughout my whole life, those two countries have stubbornly declined any opportunity they've ever had to make peace between themselves and frankly, it's never made much of a difference to anyone's life here in Grand Pre.[2] There's always been talk of changes, but nothing of any consequence has happened so far and I just can't see why this time should be any different.

Personally, I think the older people in this community, Papa included, take all of this far too seriously. Why pay attention to something that is only ever talked about and never acted on? Adults can be very silly sometimes. I hope I'm not like that when I'm older – no, I know I won't be, because my Gabriel will be with me and that will always remind me of all that is good in my life.

*June 1, 1755*

My dear diary

I have been neglecting you, I know. Believe me it is not from lack of material to note on your pages. The parish priest, the same one who taught both Gabriel and I to read and write, came by this evening. I wonder if he will agree to marry Gabriel and me – if, that is, the young Mr. Lajeunesse ever decides to ask my father for my hand in marriage.

This evening, however, the men's conversation stayed on matters well beyond marriage vows. Why, the talk even stayed well beyond our own village and centered around the ships hovering just away from our coastline. I have never seen everyone so distressed as they are this time.

I know this sounds selfish, but I resent that all of this is taking away from my joy of anticipation. Now please don't misunderstand, my friend, if I were at all convinced that anything untoward was about to happen, I too would be concerned. It's just that I've heard all this talk many times before and know that nothing ever comes of it. That's why I don't think my complaints are selfish – if all this talk of threats will end up amounting to nothing, as I know it will, then all it's done is to dampen everyone's joy at the birth of a new spring.

*June 15, 1755*

Dear Diary

Just as I suspected, the ships are still in the harbor, their guns still aimed at our shores and nothing has happened yet. Well, nothing to do with ships, or war, or England, or France, that is. Something quite exciting has happened where Gabriel and I are concerned. We are to be married, dear diary, on August 7. Yes, just weeks from now. Isn't that exciting? And it's wonderful too, because after that no one can bother us. Gabriel and I will have all that we need – each other.

*June 30, 1755*

Dear Diary

Our rooms are finished. We'll be living with my father, but in new quarters added on to his house. They're going to be just perfect for Gabriel and I even after we start our family. What's funny is that some of the boys who competed with Gabriel for my hand in marriage are the very ones who have helped build the addition to my father's house. And some of the girls, my friends for years, some who hoped Gabriel would look their way, helped to stock the larder. Life is funny, isn't it? Perhaps we shall have the chance to return their courtesies sometime soon. I hope so because I want everyone to be as happy as I am right now.

Oh, and those ships? They're still there, just floating about the harbor. I wonder if it's crossed anyone's mind that they may not be here to wage war against us. They may not mean us any harm at all.

*July 15, 1755*

A very frightening circumstance is at hand, dear diary, and I wish it would all hurry up and finish. My wedding day is less than a month away now and I don't want anything to spoil it for dear Gabriel, or me, or anyone else who is looking forward to the special day.

I refer to those ships, of course, dear diary. All but one of them has remained where they've been for the past weeks, but that lone boat sailed into our harbor and is anchored there. The sailors who had been aboard made their way into the village. They called at each home and left carrying everything that every family owned in the way of muskets and rifles.

Thank goodness I have you, dear diary, because just as soon as I wrote those words I realized the actions of the English sailors are not important at all. Whatever do we in the village of Grand Pre need with weapons, anyway? A firearm cannot help us tend our herds or grow our crops. Let the English have our weapons. We don't need them or want them. All we want is to be left in peace.

*August 1, 1755*

Monsieur Leblanc, the notary, was here this evening, my dear diary. The plans for the wedding are set and it's a good thing too. It's becoming more and more difficult seeing my dear sweet Gabriel so often and yet still maintaining the courteous distance between us. I know he's feeling the strain as well. Soon it will all be over and we'll be united forever. And that is why Leblanc the notary came to call tonight. He made out all the papers necessary for the marriage.

As happy as I am right now, I still have room in my heart to resent what is going on around me and putting a pall on the enthusiasm others are showing for my upcoming wedding day. As soon as the notary arrived here at my father's house, even before the papers for the marriage could be attended to, the threatening presence of the ships in the harbor was discussed by all, at length.

I outsmarted them by the end, though. I got down the draughts' board and set it up for play. I knew the men could not keep their minds on such a depressing subject when there was a chance for a good game of draughts at hand. My plan worked wonderfully well. Not only did it cheer up the company by distracting them, but it gave Gabriel and I a chance for a quiet and almost private conversation.

I can hardly wait to marry this man, dear diary. May the date of August 7 sprout wings and fly to my side!

*August 6, 1755*

Dear Diary

It's all become too confusing for me. All the men in the village, Father, Basil, Leblanc the notary, even men as young as Gabriel, have been called to the church tomorrow – my wedding day. I cannot imagine what this might mean. Please Lord, make whatever is going to happen, happen quickly and then be over with because nothing must interfere with our wedding plans.

*August 7, 1755*

Dear Diary

I can barely believe it. Today is the day that was to be the happiest of my life and it's turned into the saddest. Not only for me but for all the village. I have never seen such sorrow, diary. There is no way to describe it except to say tumultuous anguish has spread throughout the community.

I was wrong to presume nothing would happen. This time the English did have a plan of action – one so cruel that every family in Grand Pre has been struck insensible by shock and mourning.

We must leave. All of us. They have ordered us off our land. Where they will take us I cannot imagine. Perhaps it was just knowing that I may never see a sunset here again that I was struck by the beauty of this evening's twilight over our little community. At least, thank God, no matter where they take us, Gabriel and I will still be united for life. Our happiness together has only been postponed by this idiocy . . . for if we love one another, [n]othing, in truth, can harm us, whatever mischances may happen![3]

I shall keep you with me always, dear diary, but I cannot fathom leaving Grand Pre.

*August 8, 1755*

He's gone, dear diary. Not only have the English separated the two of us, but they have even separated Gabriel from his beloved father, Basil. Our village is in ashes. Those of us who remain on the shore are huddled in pathetic groupings awaiting our fates. The sailors from each ship are herding as many as they can aboard without paying any heed to disuniting families. Generation after generation these people have looked after one another, depended on one another and now we can do nothing but wait in dread.

Father is not taking this well at all. He won't eat or even speak. I fear for him, my dear paper companion.

Oh, my Gabriel, how can this have happened?

*Undated entry*

Father has died.

*July, 1756*

My dear diary

I thought I would never have the strength to open you again. After watching my beloved Gabriel leave on one ship, his father on another, I then had to leave my own father's lifeless body behind, buried near the ruins of the burned-out town on the shores of Grand Pre.

The English have scattered our people as strong winds scatter flower petals. Judging by the calendar, it has not even been a year since that dreadful, fateful morning that was to be my wedding day. My countenance, however, makes the calendar a liar. By now I can barely recall the bloom that was my youth. My eyes are sunken in their sockets now. The glow that once flattered my face was been extinguished. Even my posture is shrunken – deformed by grief.

Every morning when I waken I wonder why I have, and then, slowly, I remember. I face each day with only one goal in mind – to search for my beloved Gabriel Lajeunesse. Each day that I journey I lose more and more hope. How can I not? We have stayed together – the ragged little group that was rudely herded aboard the English ship and then, just as roughly, made to leave at a strange port. Father Felician from our home village is with us and sadly it is a good thing he is, for so often we must pause in our trek to bury one or another of those expelled along with us – those who gave up hope and gave themselves over to eternal sleep. I cannot allow myself such an indulgence, however, for I have a mission. I must find my dear Gabriel.

November 10, 1756

By nightfall last evening I knew the end was near. I had no energy to go on, no desire to keep living. It took until last evening, but finally I understood those who had once been my neighbors and then my ship-mates, those who had simply dropped down at the side of the trail and peacefully breathed their last.

But then as I sat with the others around a campfire, strangers joined us from a nearby town. You'll never guess, my dear diary, they say they've seen him, my beloved Gabriel. They say he is further south, in Louisiana, with others from his deportation vessel. Somehow he found his father and they are together once again. The news renews my vigor. I shall search for him forever.

1756

More news, dear diary, more hope. This evening when our rag-tag group of wanderers stopped to rest for the night, there were other homeless Acadians nearby. We're all so far from our homes and some-how that unites us. Isn't it strange? At home they may only have lived in the next village, but we never spoke with one another. Now I seek them out and make a point to ask them if they think they may have seen my lost love. Tonight I was told once again that someone had seen him. They say he is with his father, Basil. If they have found one another then it must be possible for he and I to reunite, especially as it must be God's will.

November 30, 1756

Oh, my dear diary

He must be close at hand. We have made our way south – into the Louisiana area and the reports of Gabriel are becoming more and more exact. Many say they know of two Lajeunesse men, father and son, who have worked as *coureurs de bois*.

This explains why I have not yet found him. He was not settled in a village as we were at home in Grand Pre. Perhaps neither he nor Basil were able to find enough work blacksmithing in any of the towns they have so far passed through. Once I find him we will find such a village or, if it is God's will, we shall go back home.

December 30, 1756

Diary

I can barely tolerate these people, especially the women. The men at least don't give me their opinions but, oh, these women. Can they not understand the depth of my love for Gabriel? They must have no idea, no understanding. How else could their advice be explained. Forget Gabriel, they say. Look, they say, here is Baptiste Leblanc, the notary's son. Can you not see what a fine young man he is and how he pines for you? Well, dear diary, they might be right on both counts, but I do not care. No one else could ever mean a whit to me.

*June 30, 1757*

Dear Diary

My entries stopped, dear diary, while I recovered from the disappointment of not finding Gabriel. I am sure we were so close to one another. So many people spoke to me of seeing him.

Sadly, the size of our group has diminished even further. By now we all fit in a small boat and we make our way down the river. How I wish I could appreciate the waterway's majesty and grandeur, but my heart will not let me pause, not even in my thoughts. Once again the travellers with whom we stop to speak tell me of having seen Gabriel. Many say they have seen him on a boat floating atop these very waters not many days before. A sad, but perhaps inevitable note that one man added today – he said my Gabriel has lost his youth by now, that he has aged terribly. Alas, how I hate to think of that handsome face having been diminished by strife. I cannot fret too much, however, because I feel only relief at not being able to gaze at my own much-changed reflection. When our reunion with one another reunites us with happiness, surely the strife will leave our faces.

*July 15, 1757*

Dear Diary

We travelled beside villages today, villages built on the sides of this mighty river much as Grand Pre was built at the edge of the water. These villages are so different though, as are the people. Like we once were, they seem happy enough and wave to us as we pass by. I pray those good souls will never suffer as we have.

Tonight as we rest we prepare to turn away from the river and on to the smaller streams. We shall see where this new route will bring us. My only concern is that it bring me closer to Gabriel. My search has taken nearly two years by now. Some days it is so difficult not to give up hope.

*August 8, 1757*

My dear diary

What a strange land this is. I feel most uncomfortable here in this gloom. It is dark as night even through mid-day. The enormous trees and the growths laced through and around them block out the sunlight. Its been more than a fortnight since we've seen the sun. It feels as though evil itself lurks at every turn. I cannot abide this new land and know the others feel the same. We are all so quiet and somber.

Yesterday should have marked the second anniversary of my wedding day. Instead today marks the beginning of the third year of my search for the man who should have been my husband.

*September 6, 1757*

Dear Diary

Today for the first time, I can say that I'm relieved my dear father died on his home shores. He so loved to look out onto the sea and if he saw these waters he would not even call them waters, I know. This water which we make our way through shares no similarities with the water of the sea. It is thick and brown and murky. This water moves so slowly that it is almost as though it doesn't move at all. As our oarsman poles us through the thick, foul-smelling substance, I cannot help but imagine how distressed Father would have been to seen such strangeness.

Equally as strange is the vegetation that grows beside and even above this watery pathway. An arch of moss with eery tendrils hangs suspended, so thick and tangled that they cannot be called boughs or branches. Does it close out the world or seal in our own pathetic world? Such matting could hide all that is good or all that is evil. As long as it doesn't hide my own beloved Gabriel, then I shall have the strength to carry on.

*September 19, 1757*

Diary, can you feel it too? He is here, here somewhere. It is all I can do to sit calmly in this boat and allow myself to be carried so very slowly along the murky water. If only I could jump up and spread aside the tangled dark curtain, it feels that I would see him, my fair Gabriel. What a strange feeling this is.

Father Felician tells me that my feelings are not mistaken because we're finally so close to the town where people have said Gabriel lives. The Father may be right, of course, but it feels as though Gabriel is closer still than even that. I must sit on my hands to keep them from reaching up and out to brush aside the gnarled clusters that hang thickly down around us and prevent me from seeing. My heart tells me that if I could just do that, I could see Gabriel. My head tells me to be patient and listen to Father. He has the greater chance of being right.

*November 30, 1757*

My dear steadfast diary

Is there any point in continuing?

*December 1757*

## Dear Diary

We shall soon leave this strange place. Already the density is lifting and with it my melancholy sense that Gabriel is nearby – closer than nearby – just out of sight. I pray the heaviness in my heart will lighten as the tangle of vines lessens and we make our way back to the river. Gabriel could not be here. One half of my heart, in defiance of the other half, knows that he could not be here, for my beloved could not stay among such tangled overgrowth anymore than I could.

It was with such great gratitude that I noted the oarsmen were turning our small craft around and heading, once again, for the open waters.

*February 1, 1758*

Land, my dear diary, once again proper land, long stretches of land extending back as far as the eye can see. No longer are we surrounded by tangles of tropical vines nor are we floating upon murk. There is land beside us, sky above us and clear water below us. We have emerged safely and I give thanks. Now I know I shall find my beloved Gabriel.

*April 9, 1758*

## Oh, my aged diary

This morning I caught a glimpse of my reflection in the clear water. I left my Grand Pre as a young woman. Now I am far older than my mother ever was.

*June 10, 1758*

## Rejoice diary

This morning, off in the distance, we saw a herdsman tending his stock. The scene was so like and yet so unlike those wonderful farms in Acadia. There was much that was different about the man's countenance, but my eyes feasted only upon the similarities.

*April 15, 1758*

## In joy, diary

It is no wonder that I saw similarities between the herdsman on the shore and those I remember from our homeland, Grand Pre. The oarsman put our small vessel ashore and Father and I began to walk toward this man, who was by then astride his horse. Wonder of wonders – it was none other than Basil, beloved Gabriel's own dear father.

He took us to his home. We wept and laughed and laughed and wept. At first and for a long time no words were spoken of Gabriel. Then after a time of silence, when the pain of not knowing finally exceeded the pain

of possibly knowing the worst, I asked where my dear beloved could be
Basil seemed so surprised at my question. After listening to Father
Felician describe the route we had just followed, Basil assumed we would
already have made contact with Gabriel. He wondered how we might
have floated along through the murky overgrown water paths without
having seen Gabriel, for that is where he is to be found.

Now at last, dear diary, I understand my intense feelings about
Gabriel's proximity, for, in fact, he was close. So close and yet so well
hidden from my view.

At that point, dear diary, I must admit to having collapsed completely
I wept until my weeping was exhausted and then fell into the arms of
Morpheus. I awoke in a panic with the realization that Basil had said
Gabriel was gone once again. Had I come this far, this close, only to have
lost him again? Worse yet was the thought that my beloved might
actually be dead and his father either confused in his grief or wanting to
protect me from the truth had not said so.

No, Basil assured me, this is not so. Gabriel only became restless. His
troubled spirit simply could not have endured even another day of
idleness in this foreign place.

"He told me he could never settle here," the old man told me. "Perhaps,
as it is with you, it is merely the separation from his beloved that causes
this restlessness, but he found no value in this new land. His thoughts
were always of finding you, his dear Evangeline and returning with you
to Grand Pre."

My heart both sang and sorrowed in the same instance. I know now
that we have been so close to finding one another for many weeks and
that Gabriel too, is searching for me. Tomorrow at sunrise we shall set
out on his path. Surely by nightfall we will be reunited.

For today we must visit those from our village who are now, once
again, close at hand.

*April 19, 1758*

Diary

What a strange evening I have had. Because of it sleep will not come.
That and knowing that tomorrow at first light I shall set out on the final
segment of my search for the comfort of Gabriel's warm embrace. Instead
of sleeping, I shall pen a few words on your pages, my friend.

Many who are here now, living near Basil, seem so happy to be here.
They do not speak of finding their way back home to Acadia again, but
rather of how content they are in their new surroundings and how they
enjoy this wonderfully temperate climate.

They speak of freedom from tyranny and an abundance of land to be
had. One soul who hailed from a village neighboring Grand Pre actually

told me he felt nothing by gratitude toward those responsible for the expulsion.

I cannot comprehend their sentiments. I feel only nostalgia for Grand Pre and that I am a stranger in this strange land. Perhaps if Gabriel also felt this way, I would make an effort to understand. As it is, it will be with a smile that I leave this place.

*April 23, 1758*

Oh, diary

Will my life never be anything but frustration? Father Felician and I travelled as planned. We have just arrived in this town – Adayes by name. As soon as we spoke Gabriel's name we were told that he had been here – just yesterday. This is anguish. Tomorrow we shall leave as early as we are able. Surely, by evening.

*April 25, 1758*

Diary

We had to make camp last night out here on the prairies. Is it a mirage or has the anguish I've felt in my heart for months become an image before my eyes? In the distance we can see smoke from a fire lit beside another traveller's camp. My heart tells me it is Gabriel's campfire.

How much longer must I endure this agony?

*May 4, 1758*

Dear Diary

Although we still have not found Gabriel, something occurred at last to bring a measure of relief to my heart. God sent me another woman for companionship. The respite was brief but refreshing nonetheless, especially as we were able to share one another's pain. She was making her way back to her people, the Shawnees. Her husband had been a *coureur de bois*, just as my own dear Gabriel. The Shawnee woman had adored her husband. He is dead now, killed by the Comanches. Young and all as she is, the poor girl feels her life is over. She wants only to find her people once again and live out her last few days surrounded by what comfort their familiarity could bring.

In turn, I told her of my endless search for Gabriel. She spoke of legends told by her people, stories of separated lovers who die apart and broken hearted. Her tales have renewed my vigor and sense of urgency. I must find my own dear Gabriel.

I bid the young widow farewell, while thanking God for having brought her to me.

*May 5, 1758*

Diary

The Shawnee woman spoke of a Christian mission not far from here. We shall make our way there in hopes that this might be the place Gabriel chose to rest.

*May 30, 1758*

Diary

As difficult as it is to comprehend, dear diary, I have to tell you that there is some feeling of pleasure rearing through this pain that wracks my body. The pleasure comes from knowing that I sit, now, exactly where my beloved sat only days ago. The pain, of course comes from the frustration of being so close not yet finding him and more so from the realization that the distance between us has actually increased. Instead of our little party being just one day behind him, my Gabriel is now fully six days in advance of us.

Those here at the mission say that he speaks of little else but finding me and so, oddly, it is his desperation to reunite with me that causes us to be farther apart from one another with each day of fruitless searching.

*June 1, 1758*

Dear Diary

I have decided to rest here at the mission where Gabriel was last seen. I am too weak to go on and the priest who runs the small settlement has told me that my beloved has promised to return and spend next winter here. Father Felician has chosen to return to the company of his old friend Basil and will try to settle there. I will no longer have his companionship to ease the agony of my waiting.

Perhaps those here at the mission can, in some way, utilize my skills toward their Christian purposes.

*September 26, 1758*

Dear Diary

My soul is still weary, but by now my body is rested and able to help tend the crops that feed our little mission. The days drag on. Were they really this same length when I was a girl in Grand Pre?

*April 19, 1759*

Diary

I have shared little with you these last few months, for my news can bring no one joy. Winter has come and gone without sight of Gabriel. There seems little point by now.

*June 27, 1759*

Diary, we must leave at once. Guides who have visited the mission say hey have seen my beloved. They say that he settled in a camp for the winter and so far this season has remained there. I shall set out at once. My heart should be soaring but in all truth, I know I shall pine for this mission that has become home to me and for the others who, over the months, have become as family to me. Only you, dear diary, have been with me through it all and will be with me when my hunt is over.

*Undated*

Again and again and again. All these years, so many times I have come so close to finding Gabriel, and yet still our eyes have not rested upon each other. We have come to the lodge in which he rested and found it abandoned.

*Winter, 1765*

Diary

I wander. Those who see me come and go must think my wandering purposeless and yet the purpose that has driven me all these years remains unchanged. I seek only to find my Gabriel. Through cities and towns and everywhere in between I trudge asking my years and years old question. "Has my beloved been here before me?"

*Undated*

My dear steadfast diary

I am old. Old in body and in spirit. When I was a girl there were old people in Grand Pre, many of them, but their aging was never so grotesque as mine. Perhaps it is because I have aged from the inside out. My soul has decayed through these senseless years. The only beauty that remains in me is the image of dear Gabriel. Even the years of relentless anguish have been unable to tarnish that lovely portrait. It has remained in my heart, unaffected by the years of torment.

*March 26 (no year given)*

Diary, there is nothing left for me. I shall search for Gabriel no more but seek now only to do God's work, tending to the destitute, the sick and the poor of this city until death can ease their suffering forever.

*This entry was also undated. We know only that the events Evangeline recorded here took place on a Sunday in 1793.*

I have found him, dear diary. In death I have found the one I searched for in life. He discerned my image as I came to him on his death bed. I held him and kissed him and laid his cheek upon my breast. And so it was that Gabriel's last breath rattled my chest as it did his. I thanked God for granting us that much at least. Now I welcome the Angel of Death to heal my wounds as well.

Evangeline's death wish was apparently granted and so the once-young-lovers, she, "fairest of all the maids" and he the "noblest of all the youths"[4] were united in death as they had wanted to be in life.

Without this poignant and possibly fictitious poem of lovers separated by the "Grand Derangement," a tragic and important event in Canadian history might have been all but lost.

The story of the love between Evangeline and Gabriel may have been imaginary, but his settings were as geographically accurate as the description of the expulsion was historically accurate. Even Gabriel's death can be tied to historical records, as Longfellow had him dying of a virus (yellow fever) which ran a fatal course through Philadelphia in 1793.

Because so much of our popular knowledge of the event comes from Longfellow's epic poem, we are inclined to think of the expulsion as having taken place in Grand Pre, Nova Scotia. In fact deportations occurred throughout the Maritimes, wherever there were settlers of French descent who refused to agree to take up arms against Britain's enemies.

A few of those about to be exiled escaped and eventually made their way into what is now the province of Quebec. The rest were herded onto English vessels which then sailed south along the eastern seaboard of the United States. The ships deposited their human cargo at various English settlements along the coast in the hopes that the French-leaning Acadians would be assimilated into the English-dominated societies. Some were even taken as far as the Caribbean Islands.

Those who found themselves exiled in the Spanish-held territory of Louisiana became a significant part of the area's evolving culture. (The moniker "Cajun" is a further corruption of the original term "Arcadie.") Others made their way back to Acadia and, although they found the English had already begun to build villages in the areas the Acadians once called home, the returnees quietly and successfully re-established themselves on their beloved land. Today many Acadian settlements dot Canada's east coast. The northwest stretch of the island is known as the Evangeline Trail. Acadia University in Wolfville serves a wide student body, while the Université Sainte-Anne, located in Church Point, is a French-language university and a centre for the preservation and celebration of Acadian culture. Each summer a play commemorating Evangeline's poetic plight is produced at the university for the enjoyment of both residents and tourists.

Many homes and businesses along the Evangeline Trail proudly fly the Acadian flag (the Stella Maris) alongside the Canadian flag. At the Grand Pre National Historic Site, visitors are encouraged to explore both the area's history and geography. A statue honors Evangeline as a symbol of the Acadian suffering and eventual victory of sorts over seemingly insurmountable adversity.

Pockets of Acadians also populate New Brunswick. While descendants of the original settlers live their lives in the villages that dot the Acadian Peninsula, each year the area also attracts tourists by the thousands. In addition to the exquisitely scenic Maritime geography, the visitors come to enjoy the

*The statue of Evangeline.*

Acadian way of life as it actually is today, as well as a look at the past courtesy of the Acadian Historical Village.

The province of Prince Edward Island also honors its ancient roots. In addition to the Acadian Pioneer Village, there is a museum devoted solely to telling the story of this unique culture from the days of their emigration from France in the early 1700s to today. The descendants of the exiled Acadians who did not return to the Canadian Maritimes now make their homes virtually all over the world. Despite this geographic scattering and the passage of years, those expatriates have created something of a cultural anomaly. The majority of these people still strongly identify with their Acadian origins, speak a modified version of archaic French and proudly protect and practice the Acadian culture.

In August, 1994, 239 years after the dispersal, the World Acadian Conference was held in Moncton, New Brunswick. The turnout for the reunion exceeded even the organizers' expectations. An incredible quarter of a million people from all over the world converged on the city to share, celebrate and explore their common heritage.

And so, whether or not Evangeline and Gabriel's love story is fact or fiction, it represents a depth of attachment that has endured through hundreds of years.

## *Endnotes*

[1]The word "Acadia" evolved from the area's earliest recorded European name, "Arcadie." It was likely chosen to both reflect and indicate the extraordinary physical beauty of the area.

[2]Grand Pre (which means Great Meadow) is located on the southwest shore of the Minas Basin in the province of Nova Scotia.

[3]*Evangeline*, Henry Wadsworth Longfellow, Nimbus Publishing Limited, Halifax, 1951, page 67.

[4]Ibid., page 59.

# William Lyon Mackenzie King
# & His Mother

## With Cameo Appearances by a Selection of "Other Women"

William Lyon Mackenzie King served as Canada's Prime Minister three times, during very different periods of our history. His record for length of term in office – more than 21 years – will likely stand unthreatened forever. If, just for a moment, we were able to view the world through the enduring leader's eyes, we could appreciate the enormous satisfaction he would have derived from that single statistic.

Despite the confidence Canadian voters demonstrated in the man, even while he was in office Mackenzie King was viewed as an enigma. Some held that he was a nondescript, do-nothing sort who accomplished almost nothing during his terms in office. Others said he guided the country gently, patiently and skillfully through some of its most trying and dangerous times.

Clearly, Mackenzie King's style did not promote consensus then, and today, nearly 50 years after his death, historians have still not reached any sort of accord about the man's political accomplishments, or lack of them.

On other issues concerning William Lyon Mackenzie King, however, there is agreement. For instance, few would argue against the premise that he was a pompous, self-centered egoist. Fewer still would dispute the existence of his Oedipus complex. The man was consumed, from his youth to his death, by devotion to his mother.

Despite the strength and longevity of this unhealthy obsession, there were other women in the man's life – many of them – and the term "other women" is not used by happenstance. The women with whom Mackenzie King had the most significant relationships (including his mother, of course) were married – and certainly not to him. (An extensive, although possibly incomplete, list at the end of this chapter enumerates the women with whom Mackenzie King contemplated marriage.)

*William Lyon Mackenzie King. (photo courtesy of the Liberal Party of Canada)*

William Lyon Mackenzie King was born on December 17, 1874, to John and Isabel King, in what was then the small, southern Ontario town of Berlin (now the city of Kitchener). John King was a lawyer who lacked the competitive nature that his stronger, more ambitious wife would have appreciated. Although she viewed him as one who never made much of a success of his life either personally or professionally, an objective look at John King's record of achievements tells quite a different story. He was an involved father, active in both community and church affairs as well as being a respected member of his profession – not the curriculum vitae of a ne'er do well. John King was simply not aggressive enough in the pursuit of either financial well-being or social status to suit his wife and this apparently overshadowed, in Isabel King's mind, his many admirable qualities.

The fact that Isabel King was the 13th child of the failed rebel leader William Lyon Mackenzie, no doubt influenced her mindset considerably

WILLIAM_LYON_MACKENZIE_KING

Oddly, she assessed her father by a yardstick quite opposite that with which she measured her husband. Although she disliked her father's rebellious nature, she was inordinately proud of the man's accomplishments and was very willing to overlook his evident failures.[1]

Isabel King was a woman of great determination, a characteristic bred, no doubt, by the abject and exiled poverty in which her defeated father was forced to raise his family. This background may also have provided the impetus from which her highly developed manipulative qualities grew; for throughout her adult life at least, Isabel King made sure that she got her own way most of the time.

Like many mothers, Mrs. King was determined that her children would do better than the generation that had gone before them and she had special hopes for her elder son, on whom she bestowed her father's name. It is possible that so naming him created specific sorts of responsibilities and rewards for the boy. It is also possible that Willie, as his parents most often called him, was just a very different sort of child right from the start. A third possible explanation for William Lyon Mackenzie King's seemingly unique, and definitely bizarre, personality is the hypothesis that all four of John and Isabel's children were equally affected by their upbringing, but because Willie became a national leader (and kept extensive diaries) we know more of the intimate details of his life than we do about his siblings' lives.

There may have been a point when, had parental intervention not occurred, William Lyon Mackenzie King *might* have developed a normal attachment to a woman and so been able to avoid much of the mental and physical anguish he spent the balance of his lifetime enduring. The incident revolved around a woman named Mathilde Grossert. By the time this "[d]ear little soul"[2] makes her debut on the stage upon which King's youth was played out, he was in his early 20s and had already established at least two significant and enduring behavior patterns – diary keeping and prostitute visiting. His strong sense of superiority had already become evident in the not-very-subtle speech habit of appending the adjective "little" to virtually every reference he makes to a female.

Miss Grossert, as he frequently referred to her, was one of the nurses who attended King when he was hospitalized in March of 1897 at the age of 23.[3] Having graduated the year before from the University of Toronto, he was continuing his studies in Chicago when he became ill. Comments King recorded in his diary indicate that although he might have been sick, he was well enough to have thoroughly enjoyed all the attention he received from the nurses, especially Mathilde Grossert.

Whether she simply fit into his idealized (and oedipal?) image of what a woman should be or whether she was the catalyst which created that image cannot, by now, be known. There is considerable proof, however, that for the balance of his life, William Lyon Mackenzie King was consistently attracted to older women (Grossert was 12 years older than King) whom he saw as serving the Lord (either directly or, as in the case of nursing, indirectly through service to people in need). He also showed a strong preference for those same women to dress in white, as nurses traditionally did in that era.

After recovering from his illness, thanks in part to Mathilde Grossert's ministrations, King left Chicago to study at Harvard. While in Boston he kept in touch with Nurse Grossert, who had remained at her job in St Luke's Hospital in Chicago. Letters back and forth between King and the American nurse initially demonstrated that the nurse and her former patient were equally interested in one another. Within a year, however, two events coincided to terminate the long distance relationship. First, King's lusty libido began to infiltrate his letters to the woman, frightening her badly and secondly, he informed his family that he intended to marry the fair Mathilde.

Had either Isabel King or Mathilde Grossert been aware that the other was most effectively accomplishing what they both wanted, one of them could have saved her breath. Be that as it may, the combined actions of the women terminated the love affair. This had the additional benefit of clearly establishing a directive which, up until then, had likely been nothing more than an unwritten and unspoken family rule – William Lyon Mackenzie King was responsible first to his mother, then to the rest of his family. Anything or anyone else stood a distant and unalterable third or lower.

With these ground rules established, Mathilde Grossert disappeared from the roster as a potential Mrs. King. She married not long after the relationship with King had ended, but amazingly, the two former love birds remained in casual contact with one another until King's death.

The termination of the romance with Nurse Grossert was difficult for the young man. Although it is likely the relationship was never physically consummated, its very existence had succeeded in temporarily putting an end to an activity King practiced but abhorred. Willie King was still in his teens when he discovered the joys and sorrows associated with visiting the ladies of the night.

Being very much a product of his Victorian era, Mackenzie King viewed his own, and everyone else's, sex drive as an evil affliction, something one should strive to overcome. Of course, he was no more successful at suppressing his naturally occurring urge than any other human animal would have been, but in King's case he paid a high mental and emotional price for his failure. Scattered throughout his diary are references to "strolling." The fact that he found it necessary, even within the covers of his personal diary, to describe the activity euphemistically, is a strong indication of his attitude toward his own immoral behavior.

If these paid-for trysts bothered the young man so much, one might wonder why he would commit them to record at all. Surely a protective attitude of denial would have been possible if only the events had not been so methodically noted in his diary each time they occurred. Unfortunately for King's peace of mind, it had been a brutally honest attempt to identify and then overcome his weaknesses that had prompted him to begin his journal keeping in the first place.

The mental, emotional and spiritual turmoil caused by his strolls are pathetically evident in King's diary entries. "Tonight was practically wasted" he noted on September 7, 1893. October 9 of the same year was "[w]orse than wasted." On other nights he "committed a sin," was "ashamed" or "cried after coming home."[4] The man was clearly tormented, wracked with guilt. It is a given that anyone partaking in the illicit sex trade is endangering his physical health and that in itself could provoke strong feelings of remorse, but in Mackenzie King's case his mental stability was also severely threatened, for when he was not availing himself of the women's services, he was attempting to reform them.

On one occasion at least he tried to combine the two counter-productive activities of reformation and utilization. After the incident, King assessed, with his usual pomposity, that the prostitute felt as distraught about the outcome as he did. Of course, it is possible the man's assessment of the situation was correct – she may well have felt ashamed of herself. Perhaps, though, it is more reasonable to assume that the woman viewed that business transaction exactly as she had the dozens that had gone before and the dozens yet to come. After all, she was a prostitute – exchanging sexual favors for money was simply her job.

Despite his best efforts to the contrary, William Lyon Mackenzie King continued on a decreasingly regular basis throughout the years to pay for sex. It was one of the unhappy aspects of his life that he hoped marrying would eradicate. As he never did marry, no one shall ever know whether or not that might have been so. What can be surmised is that, having abided by his mother's wishes regarding that very first, potentially serious relationship with a woman, King settled into a pattern in which Isabel King would always be not only the dominant female, but the dominant person.

In spite of this, or perhaps because of it, there were a tremendous number of women in and out of King's entire life (see listing at the end of the chapter) and getting married was an ever-present, never-to-be-resolved issue. By the turn of the century, however, 26-year-old King's life's work in public service was as established as his Oedipus complex. His career path had taken him, by then, to Ottawa. His parents were living in Toronto. This distance may have helped to make his mother less attainable and therefore even more desirable.

❦ ❦ ❦

As peculiar a combination as King's desire to both access and reform prostitutes was, his next significant relationship with a woman was stranger still. Always a deeply religious man – a Christian with decidedly limited tolerance for any derivation from that perspective – he began in the autumn of 1900 to attend St. Andrew's Presbyterian Church in Ottawa. The minister was the highly regarded Dr. William Thomas Herridge, whose wife possibly became William Lyon Mackenzie King's lover.

"You must come away with us for awhile this summer, Rex," Marjorie Herridge implored, using King's recently adopted nickname – Latin for his surname.

"Oh, but I couldn't – not and leave mother to swelter in the Toronto humidity for weeks at a time," King countered.

"Well, then bring her, for goodness sake. The Reverend will be in England and I'd love to have the lot of you there for company," the preacher's wife protested and apparently convincingly, because King, his mother and his close friend Bert Harper spent the summer of 1901 with Marjorie Herridge and her children at Kingsmere, Quebec. The area was to have deep significance for the balance of Mackenzie King's life.

(A short aside here – Kingsmere has, by now, almost become synonymous with William Lyon Mackenzie King. The fact that "Kingsmere" translates to "King's mother" is merely an interesting coincidence. The area was named in honor of an early Quebec pioneer – long before the subject of this narrative was born. Perhaps that "King" also suffered an Oedipus complex.)

Obviously Mrs. King did not carry the same objections to her son's relationship with Marjorie Herridge as she had to Nurse Grossert, because Mrs. King and Mrs. Herridge spent an enjoyable summer together. Despite this contrast, Mathilde Grossert and Marjorie Herridge did have at least one characteristic in common – they were both very much older than King, Herridge by 16 years and Grossert by 12. King's attraction to older women had become evident.

Most of King's activities were dutifully recorded in his diary and his encounters with Marjorie Herridge were no exception. His references to her, however, are decidedly odd, even considering the relationship they reflect. King rarely referred to Marjorie Herridge by her first name. When he was feeling fondly toward her, King used the condescending moniker "child." Most other references to her are formal – he calls her "Mrs. Herridge."

Just which term, if either, reflected the evolving relationship between King and Herridge is open for speculation. Leaning only on currently available evidence, it would be folly to conclude whether or not the two had become lovers over that summer. About all that can be attested to with surety is that by the time the happy little group of summer campers returned to Ottawa in the fall of 1901, the city's gossip mongers were in high gear. After all, both Marjorie Herridge and William Lyon Mackenzie King were reasonably high profile members of the community. It is also clear that Marjorie's husband, the Reverend Dr. Herridge, was not at all pleased with the situation he found upon his return from England.

"You must not continue to see my wife the way you have been, King. Can you not imagine the talk that has been going about? I shall not put up with it. I forbid you to see Marjorie ever again," Herridge implored before qualifying his sweeping directive, "unless there is a third party present."

It is likely that at that time the initial intensity of the relationship between Marjorie Herridge and Mackenzie King had weakened to the point that the possibly-cuckolded husband's directive was not terribly difficult to follow – at least while the main characters in the drama were all back in Ottawa. With the arrival of the summer of 1902, however, the setting shifted back to Kingsmere.

King once again joined Marjorie Herridge and her children for their summer holiday and once again Dr. Herridge was obvious only by his absence. During the early part of the year, he had suffered a bout of what would today be termed "depression." Whether to recuperate or perhaps to fulfill duties for the church, Dr. Herridge spent that summer in the Canadian Maritimes.

For reasons we can only guess at, the pages of King's diary are uncharacteristically blank throughout that summer's stay at Kingsmere. Entries do not begin again until late September, but once they do they are very revealing.

> The story of my life for the present is the story of its relation to the Child. Our summer has been lived together, lived to ourselves . . . What is to be the outcome of this love, the love which binds her to me and me to her . . . She loves me more deeply than ever before if that is possible . . . I tremble at moments when I think of what our lives are to each other.[5]

If King's mother accompanied them during that second summer in Kingsmere, she must have turned a blind eye to a great deal. When they returned to Ottawa in the fall, Mackenzie King and Marjorie Herridge continued to see each other frequently, although usually in the company of Dr. Herridge as well. By the following summer, King had purchased property adjoining the Herridge's at Kingsmere Lake. This move had a dual and seemingly contradictory effect on the liaison. On the one hand it seemed to guarantee a continuity of the relationship, but on the other hand, as King was living in his own cottage, it also succeeded in separating the pair from one another.

The change in summer living arrangements may or may not have had any influence on the relationship. It is not known *what*, eventually, tore the strange union asunder. Approximately *when* the interdependence ended, however, is considerably easier to spot, for by the autumn of 1911 King couches all references to a friendship with the Herridges in the past tense.[6]

This particular segment of the William Lyon Mackenzie King narrative has a sad ending. Marjorie Herridge died early in 1924 at the age of 66. She had been in failing mental health for at least a year prior to her death, while King had been the Canadian Prime Minister for the three previous years. In reviewing his more than 20 year long relationship with the older, married woman, King hardheartedly assessed that, in the end, both the relationship itself and his life had been badly affected by the woman's "selfishness."[7] This conclusion is especially distasteful considering that he continued to see other women, (one of whom was also married) throughout his association with Marjorie Herridge, even during those first, intense years together.[8]

Mackenzie King spent much of the next few years working (and womanizing) in the United States. By 1918 he had returned to Ottawa, written and published a book (*Industry and Humanity*) and become involved (unsuccessfully to that point) in federal politics. He rented a residential suite in the prestigious Roxborough Block. The apartment next door to King's was occupied by a bank manager and his family — hence Joan Patteson became William Lyon Mackenzie King's version of the "girl next door."

At first blush the similarities between Joan Patteson and Marjorie Herridge are striking. Both women were married to well-established men, had children and were older than King. The more subtle differences in the two, however, are pivotally important. Joan Patteson was only five years King's senior, not 16 years as was Herridge. Patteson's husband was apparently most accepting of his wife's relationship with the bachelor Prime Minister. Further, Joan's agenda was uniquely unselfish. Being there whenever King wanted her to be was all the satisfaction Joan Patteson required. The man had found nirvana – devoted, loving and totally undemanding companionship.

King frequently recorded his interactions with Joan in his diary. As were the notations about Marjorie Herridge, the references to Joan Patteson were also often formal. He uses "Mrs. Patteson" occasionally, even "Mrs. Pattison" [sic], rather than the woman's given name, which surely would have been a more accurate reflection of their relationship. Perhaps in that era the use of title and surname, rather than given name, might not have seemed as odd or as great a contradiction as it does now. Today, however, especially considering the nature of their bond to one another, it certainly adds a perverse quality to the reporting.

Despite those overtones of propriety, the enduring relationship between Joan Patteson and the Prime Minister of Canada was quickly and firmly established. King became a regular fixture in the Patteson household, dropping in whenever he could fit a visit into his schedule. Regard for the family's routines never seems to have been an issue, in King's mind anyway. He would knock on their apartment door early in the morning, at meal times, or at 10:00 at night after a session in Parliament. No matter when he showed up it is clear from his diary notations that he always expected to be cordially admitted – and was.

This sort of open hospitality would be amazing even if it were Godfroy Patteson that King was interested in visiting, but it was most assuredly was not Godfroy's companionship King was seeking. It was Joan's. In his diary, the man's initial reference might obliquely suggest he visited with "the Pattesons." Reading not much beyond that, however, it is obvious that Godfroy Patteson was often not included in the meetings and even when he was present he was of little significance, neither contributing to nor detracting from Joan and Rex's liaison.

As it developed, from 1918 on, Joan Patteson effectively fulfilled most of the functions King had always anticipated that his elusive "wife" should have. She helped him dress for state dinners, was the first woman to offer congratulations on special accomplishments, prepared meals for him and offered unconditional love and acceptance to him.

Altering a previously established pattern only slightly, King invited the Pattesons to join him at his home in Kingsmere for the summer of 1920. And it was then that, once again, the vacation spot brought a relationship of King's with an older, married woman to an increased level of intensity. To give him credit, however, this time around King saw the situation unfolding and recognized the significance of those changes. Whether or not he acted on those changes and if he did, what form his actions took, must forever remain a mystery, for King committed an extremely uncharacteristic act by ripping the pertinent pages from his diary.

Despite the lack of existing evidence about what might have occurred within the love triangle, it remains reasonable to deduce at least two convincing scenarios from that summer's fallout. Mackenzie King and Godfroy Patteson may have had a direct confrontation – or King and Joan Patteson may have become lovers. Even if the truth lies somewhere between or beyond those two premises, we do know from implications in the remaining diary entries that something very provocative occurred. Surprisingly, this upheaval did not terminate the bizarre relationship. Within weeks the intensified emotions had calmed down and the association continued very much unaffected until Mackenzie King's death some 30 years later.

During that same summer of 1920, King's political ambitions became considerably more successful. He had been elected to the House of Commons and had also won the leadership of the Liberal party. Joan was the "first lady to congratulate" him on his victory.[9]

As his political successes and responsibilities increased, the intensity of the possibly adulterous neighborly situation seems to have leveled out.

Perhaps some of the emotional energy King had once devoted to Joan was now required at and applied to work. Joan Patteson may have been relieved to have a little less attention paid to her day-to-day activities, as King was often highly critical and unreasonably demanding of the woman.

"I'm so very glad to see you both," King gushed when he dropped in to the Patteson's apartment during a break from the campaign trail of 1921.

"Let me fix you something to eat, Rex," Joan fussed while the "other man" in her life took his usual spot on her living room sofa. "You look so worn out but I think once you've eaten and heard my news you'll be somewhat renewed."

"News? What news?" the man inquired as he settled himself into the familiar corner cushions.

"I've been so bothered, Rex, by your concerns about my playing cards with friends but your being away has actually helped me put it all in perspective and I've decided these hands have played their last game of bridge. You were quite right. There are far more important matters that I could be attending to," she announced, alluding to an angry discussion the two had had before King's temporary departure from Ottawa.

The woman's obedience to his request was rewarded just days later with an expensive, engraved bracelet. This seems a highly personal and therefore inappropriate gift to present to a married woman, especially considering the inscription he chose read, " A strength was in us from the vision." The dedication was completed with a reference classically typical of the self-involved King – "The campaign of 1921."[10]

Shortly after presenting the gift, King realized his long-standing goal of becoming the Prime Minister of Canada. It is both revealing and symbolic that he celebrated this enormous victory by having dinner with the Patteson's in their apartment. From that point on it seemed that this was to be Joan Patteson's role in Mackenzie King's life – to make herself and her resources available to him whenever he required either. In other words, Joan Patteson was to fulfill all the obligations of a wife, while imposing none of the responsibilities upon him. As he had previously worried that he could not attain political office without a wife, it is hoped that he fully appreciated Joan's role in his victory. (Some may see Joan's role as more closely approximating that of a mother than a wife.)

As mentioned earlier, Marjorie Herridge died in 1924. The surviving Herridges were not interested in preserving the vacation home at Kingsmere that she had loved and so the property came available for sale. At King's urging, Joan and Godfroy Patteson purchased the Herridge's estate, thereby extending the strange chain-like entanglement by a crucial link.

By now King and the Pattesons were only immediate neighbors during summers at Kingsmere. King had inherited Sir Wilfrid and Lady Laurier's enormous home in Ottawa. Once he was settled into the impressive residence, King began to entertain extensively. Joan Patteson was often present during these festivities, occasionally acting as hostess. Whether from lack of interest or lack of invitation, Godfroy rarely attended. If Joan and Rex spent a social evening apart, they would drop into the other's home for an intimate, if brief, encounter before returning to their own.

Despite the intensity and longevity of his friendship with Joan Patteson, King continued to look for a wife. Showing incredible insensitivity, he even recruited Joan's cooperation in his search and, demonstrating that her role was well understood, she acquiesced. Just as he had during the years with Marjorie Herridge, Mackenzie King managed to find another married woman to become involved with while maintaining the status quo with the long-suffering Joan Patteson.

In the earliest years of their union, Joan Patteson probably gained little beyond the extra work inherent in tending to the needs of another person who had virtually become another member of the household. She must have loved the man deeply in order to have given so much for so long with so little forthcoming from her investment of time and effort. By the time King had become Prime Minister, there was certainly some additional status to be gained from her unusual position and, unlike Marjorie Herridge who had some social status through her husband, Joan Patteson had none apart from that derived by her special role in King's life.

As the years passed, Joan Patteson and Mackenzie King's relationship deepened even further. The most significant single cause for this change was the discovery of their shared interest in spiritualism. There would not have been many with whom either one could have confidently satisfied such a quirky curiosity and so through this mutual intrigue, they each gained a great deal.

As with most new interests, it took awhile for a pattern to become established. King's attraction to contacting the spirits' of the dead likely developed immediately after the deaths of his sister Bell, his father and then his mother all in the months between April 1915 and December 1917. His bereavement left the man vulnerable and eager to embrace that which he had once denounced. It is not known whether Joan Patteson had harbored a latent interest in the metaphysical or whether, as with so many aspects of her life, she merely reflected Mackenzie King's desires. Wherever Patteson's impetus may have come from, she quickly became a passionate participant in the sessions with the "little table."[11] (Given King's propensity for the adjective "little," one wonders what the actual measurements of the paranormal communications device might have been.)

This new and extremely time-consuming activity did not develop until King was in his mid-50s and Joan her early 60s. This was a period when King was out of office and so had minimal demands on his schedule. Although Godfroy apparently joined them for a few sessions, he remained very much a background figure. For the most part the psychic encounters consisted of the Prime Minister and his neighbor huddled intimately around the "little table."

Their method of communicating with those "who are beyond"[12] through the tapping table followed a numerical pattern with a pre-determined number of taps meaning "yes" or "no" and enhanced by the occasional drawn out spelling session where one tap symbolized the letter "a," two, the letter "b." If that were the case, one hopes, for expediency's sake, the spirits chose to avoid words spelled with letters such as "w" or "y" or "z." It would be interesting to know whether or not the "little table" made as many spelling mistakes as William Lyon Mackenzie King did.

One of their first encounters together around the table was in conjunction with birthday celebrations for Joan in November 1933. Judging from the numbers of spirits who reportedly "came through" that evening, it was a highly successful initiation to the new hobby. "They came trooping in with their birthday greetings. Joan's family & mine, many friends, members of prlt. & others."[13]

Even in this activity King was incapable of fidelity. He shared his spiritual table with at least one other woman in whom he had some romantic interest – Julia Grant, the granddaughter (or daughter) of the United States President Ulysses S. Grant, who later married a Russian Prince and became the Princess Cantacuzene.[14] Perhaps Joan's occasional derision of the extent to which King carried his belief in paranormal communications encouraged him to seek feminine corroboration from an alternative source.

Joan and King's increasingly frequent use of the tapping table as a communications device eventually forced them to weave elaborate explanations for occasions when the "little table" dispensed inaccurate information. It must have been disconcerting to the pair when those "from a higher realm,"[15] who were supposed to be in an all-knowing and all-seeing position, came up with incorrect predictions. After one such incident, Joan was conveniently contacted by the spirit of Sir Wilfrid Laurier who, by way of an explanation for the troubling inconsistencies, advised her that the perfidious messages had been supplied by an "evil spirit."[16]

King accepted that explanation as gospel, but then that really shouldn't be too surprising – it had been told to him by his beloved table partner. He and Joan were deep confederates and King believed to the core of his being that they had a divinely assigned pipeline to the privileged knowledge available from the souls of the dead.

"We might have to restrict ourselves to seances with mediums, rather than directly communicating ourselves through the table," Joan suggested. "The mediums minds will be empty of the conflicts our intelligence might create. Perhaps it is the knowledge already in our minds that occasionally creates inaccurate messages."[17]

Both Joan, and the spiritual encounters he practiced with her, were, by then, equally important in Mackenzie King's life. Even when explanations such as the one from Laurier were required, King was not able to bring himself to forego the intimate sessions.

"Perhaps in part you are right, Joan. Perhaps we should rely on an objective medium where prophesies are concerned, but surely we can continue to call on mother and the others to come through and visit us in the intimate fashion they always have," King responded.

The birthday sessions with the table developed into something of a tradition with a most remarkable sitting occurring on King's 60th birthday. He and Joan were huddled together over the table once again and King noted the spirits "trooped" in, although this time, in typical King-fashion, he spelled the word incorrectly and so actually had the spiritual visitors "trouping."[18] On other occasions the couple was suddenly joined by a whole host of entities – some whose stay on earth dated back to Biblical times.

This commitment to spiritualism developed while the Liberals were out of office and Mackenzie King therefore was only the leader of the opposition. For such a politically ambitious man as King, this was not a situation he was happy with, even if it did allow him the luxury of free time to dabble in the paranormal. The spirits were apparently as anxious to get King back into office as he was. They even offered specific, if rather ordinary, advice on how he might best prepare himself for that eventuality. King was directed to take care of his health – physical as well as spiritual, and his re-election as Prime Minister would be granted to him. Unfortunately, in the interest of completeness it must be added that the reinstatement to office occurred fully 13 months after it was prophesied to occur, and in all probability more correctly reflected the nation's dissatisfaction with Prime Minister Bennett's leadership than with directives from other-worldly political movers and shakers.

Predictably, with the reinstatement, King's leisure time was cut substantially. He did, however, still manage to fit in the odd psychic session – usually with Joan Patteson but occasionally by himself. After one seance conducted by a medium, which Patteson didn't sit in on, King made his way to another woman's (Beatrix Robb) apartment for dinner and something of a spiritual debriefing. It is not known whether Joan was ever aware of this odd form of infidelity and if she was, what her reaction might have been.

What would no doubt have become a concern to the majority of Canadians had it been widely known, was King's reliance on messages from beyond regarding matters of international politics. As the world stumbled toward the outbreak of the Second World War, King's continued involvement in the spirit world was, in retrospect, a fairly serious matter. The year before the war broke out, he met with Adolph Hitler and came away with a most positive impression of the mass slaughterer. Of course, Hitler's Oedipus complex was easy for King to identify with. The Prime Minister also admired what he felt was Hitler's spiritualist side. Like himself, King felt Hitler had been divinely appointed to lead his people.

Despite this major mis-calculation of character assessment and intent, King continued in his role as Canadian Prime Minister through the Second World War and even into the first prosperous years of peace. By the time he retired in 1948 at the age of 74, William Lyon Mackenzie King had led the country longer than anyone else. This in dramatic contradiction to his own prediction that he could not successfully hold political office as a bachelor. Had many Canadians known that a married woman was fulfilling an interesting number of the functions usually performed by a wife, King's political career might have been dramatically altered.[19] (Canadians realizing the depth to which their country's leader was mystically inspired might have had a similar effect.)

By the time he finally retired, King's health was a very real concern. He had celebrated his 74th birthday and the years had definitely taken their toll on his mental and physical health. He had never been an innately confident man, but now required almost constant reassurance of both his accomplishments and his current worth. This must have been an extremely difficult period for Joan. She was nearly 80 and so could not possibly have been as energetic and robust as she once was. In addition, Godfroy's health had declined and so his needs became more time-consuming than ever before. Having to care for two men under those circumstances must have been extremely trying.

We know at least some of King's thoughts about the love triangle, but what about Godfroy Patteson's? What could he have been thinking during all those years that his wife was involved in an intense and intimate (although not necessarily physically intimate) relationship with another man? Today we can only speculate, for history has not left us much in the way of information about what kind of a man Mr. Patteson was. Was he endlessly patient, trusting and understanding or was he a disinterested man with a broad lazy streak running throughout his being? If the latter were the case, then his wife's close and enduring relationship with Prime Minister King must have relieved him of many of the normal obligations of a husband and thereby accomplished as much for him as it did for Joan and King, the other two players in the tawdry little drama.

In later years King records in his diary that he thinks Godfroy is warming to him. As that is King's report, however, it certainly isn't a necessarily reliable indication of anything Mr. Patteson might have felt. On balance, because so much must be left to assumption, any ruminations on Godfroy Patteson's involvement in this love story have a distinctly inadequate feel to them.

Despite, or perhaps because of, Joan Patteson's unfailing love and loyalty throughout the years, Mackenzie King often treated her disrespectfully – even to asking her to help him choose a wife.[20] Later, in 1939, at the age of 65 and after enjoying all the advantages that Joan's great fondness for him provided, he invited the Princess Cantacuzene back into his life, this time having her join him at Kingsmere. He cruelly had Joan Patteson act as hostess during this visit.

King cannot be excused for his hardheartedness on the grounds that he was unaware of Joan's deep love for him. Right from the earliest days of their friendship and frequently throughout the years he acknowledges her evident fondness for him and even expresses concern about the possible nature and outcome of their feelings for one another.[21] He writes of his love for her and his assuredness that he would have been happy married to her[22] as well as noting, rather pompously, her occasional displays of jealousy in reaction to some of his associations with other women.

More than once King even acknowledged that Joan Patteson was, to him, the ultimate consolation prize – "She has filled the place of my mother in my heart over the years."[23] For it was King's utter devotion to his mother – initially as a person and later as a memory, that represents the ultimately bizarre Mackenzie King love story.

No matter where he lived, Mackenzie King decorated his bedroom with photographs of Isabel King. In social settings he would wax eloquent about his mother's exquisite beauty and then, to the great embarrassment of all those around him, he would support his claims by producing at least one of the pictures of his mother which he carried with him at all times.

In retrospect, King had little chance to have become a well-adjusted man. His mother, Isabel King, had been the pivot around which her husband and children operated. Only matters which were personally important to the self-centered Isabel had become family issues: and, as previously noted, the one thing that mattered to Isabel King, above all others, was financial security. Her father had not provided it for her and much to her disappointment, her husband was apparently incapable of providing it in amounts adequate to meet her needs. In her mind then, the responsibility, therefore, to provide Isabel King with financial security fell to her older son, William.[24]

"You must think of home, Willie," she implored when she heard about the youthful William's proposal of marriage to Nurse Grossert. "You have responsibilities here. How can you think of marriage and shirk your duty to your family?"

The fact that Willie might have wanted to start a family of his own apparently had not occurred to the woman – or perhaps it had and the fear of such an event and its ramifications was precisely what motivated her to manipulate her son's plans so determinedly. Whichever the case, that altercation proved to be the catalyst that ensured the depth and breadth of Mackenzie King's devotion to his mother – a devotion that lasted long after the woman had died.

King's decidedly mundane physical appearance invites speculation that his was a face only a mother could love. If this was so, then King managed to balance the equation by loving his mother more deeply than any other woman in his life, but even she, King managed to love utterly selfishly. His mother was only significant to his life in so far as she was able to contribute directly and positively to his well-being. This self-serving attitude extended beyond the mother/son connection to their shared heritage, for it was Isabel King who directly linked him to one of his heroes – William Lyon Mackenzie.

"It is wonderous to me that the man who was my grandfather should have endured and survived all that he did. The fact that under the most difficult of circumstances he then produced a thirteenth child – the one who was to become my mother – this to me is nothing short of miraculous. This evolution speaks a clear and profound message to me. My life has a purpose. I have been born for a reason. I must and I will make something of my life," King mused vainly when he was in his mid-20s.

Shortly afterward Mackenzie King confided, in his mother of course, the goal that would focus those free-floating delusions of grandeur.

"I whispered to mother that I believed, that if opportunity came in the future I might become the Premier [sic] of this country." This was more than just a young man's ambitious goal – God had engineered the man's heritage such that William Lyon Mackenzie King was predestined for greatness.[25]

This hyperbole is undeniably difficult for anyone, except possibly King and his mother, to stomach. It was most effectively backed up, however, by King's quite extraordinary combination of intelligence and energy. The man was able to finish four university degrees while still in his early 20s in addition to participating, with great enthusiasm but lesser amounts of skill, in a full schedule of extra-curricular activities. Through all this his sense of divinely assigned mission became something of a self-fulfilling prophesy.

It was as King's career progressed that he concluded remaining single would be a real detriment. "To go into politics without marrying would be folly,"[26] he stated on one occasion and on another, "I feel I should seek to become married. It is a mistake not to, and if my life is to be what I wish it to be I believe a home is all important."[27] Those assertions left no doubt as to *why* Mackenzie King wished to be married, but he also had an extraordinarily clear image of *what* his future bride should be like. "If

I can only win such a wife as I have such a mother, how infinitely happy!" To this requirement he added "wealth in association with marriage."[28] He and his mentor, Sir Wilfrid Laurier, began a campaign together – not a political campaign, but a crusade to seek out a suitable candidate for the role of Mrs. King Jr.

A look back indicates that not only were the matchmaking efforts unsuccessful, but also apparently unnecessary. In part thanks to the selfless devotion of Joan Patteson, King remained a bachelor all of his life while also becoming Canada's longest serving Prime Minister. Proof that marriage was not a prerequisite to achievement of his political goals. And that is most fortunate, for any woman married to a man with as enormous an Oedipus complex as King displayed would have been doomed to a most unhappy life – to say nothing of mother-in-law problems (even posthumously) of colossal proportions.

Few women would want to compete for the affections of a man who at the age of 24 wrote, he wouldn't feel "a longing for the love of another if she [mother] were always with me."[29]

Worse, King's affections were evidently returned – in kind – by "dear little mother."[30]

Because Isabel King made no secret of her disappointment in her husband's accomplishments, her feelings toward the man spread to their children and created a generalized attitude of toleration tinged by condescension toward John King. William grew up secure in the demented conviction that his mother loved him far more deeply than she loved his father and in time the young man reciprocated by adopting his mother as the benchmark beside whom all women were judged.[31]

Of course, it goes without saying that in order for King to have made that judgment, he would first have to develop relationships with women – and develop he did! (There have been occasional allegations made over the years that King was homosexual. Such a theory is simply inaccurate.) Isabel King's interference at the time of her son's infatuation with Nurse Grossert certainly marks a determining point in the ongoing importance of mother and son to one another. It was not entirely Mrs. King who spawned the change. John King too was also vocal in his disapproval of the potential marriage and a quick review of almost anyone's life will turn up at least one instance where parents have attempted to exert some control over their youngsters' love lives. Rather it is young King's reaction to their meddling that forms the basis for the change. He is overwrought with guilt and completely convinced that he was wrong to consider a relationship outside his immediate family.

"Why was I not always with mother. I should have shown more love to her. If God Spares her and me may he give me strength to prove my love. I must work now for all at home, keep them before me, deny self, work for my mother, father, sisters and brother first."[32]

As a result of the family crisis brought on by Mathilde Grossert's presence in her son's life, Isabel became acutely aware of her position of power where young Willie was concerned. In response she sought to tighten the knot on the apron strings.

After the crisis with Mathilde Grossert was resolved and just as the young man was settling into his studies at Harvard, he received a letter from his mother. In it she virtually propositioned her son by indicating that if he would have her, she would go immediately to Boston and live with him.

"If you and I were together we could take long walks and talk over things in general." She explains before adding the dramatically indicative closing sentence – "Now remember . . . Barkis is willing."[33] This phrase is from a Dickens novel with which, presumably, Willie and his mother would both have been familiar. In the original, it is a reference to a marriage proposal.

In the end, however, Mrs. King stays home with her husband and Willie finishes his degree at Harvard. It was, perhaps, the last time King denied his mother anything and really he only succeeded in delaying her living with him, not negating it completely.

In the years in between, William Lyon Mackenzie King found many ways of operating his life around his Oedipus complex. Sometimes he would censor information about his love life from his mother. Other relationships he handled differently. As we have already noted when Marjorie Herridge was King's love interest, he merely took his mother along for the affair and trusted that she would note only as much as her blinded mother-eyes would let in. The fact that his methods were effective is simply a reflection of her utter devotion to King. Where her older son was concerned, Isabel King had an apparently endless ability to overlook the obvious in order to see only what she wanted to see.

In 1916 John King died, thereby removing the "other man" from the incestuous love triangle. Mackenzie King arranged to have his mother come to live with him in Ottawa. She was in poor health and King hired caregivers to attend to her around the clock. Despite this, the old woman's 74th birthday the following February was treated, at Laurier House anyway, as though it were a historic event. Tributes poured in and were duly noted – as were those that were not received. Mackenzie King terminated the services of one of his mother's physicians because (among other things) neither the man nor his wife had acknowledged Isabel King's birthday. Such an oversight was clearly an unforgivable omission in her son's eyes.

Predictably, Willie pulled out all the stops and truly outdid himself on what would prove to be his mother's last birthday. (Judging by the glowing write-up in his diary, it's clear that King was delighted with himself and his performance on this most auspicious occasion.) He waited until 4:00 o'clock in the afternoon to begin the real celebrations of the day, because he had discovered that was the time at which his mother had been born. He later recorded in his diary that at that moment, "I began to give her a kiss for the years that had gone by since then, and so I kissed her 74 times. . . . I gave her a few more kisses for the years to come."[34]

Oddly, once the excitement of the birthday party settled down, Mackenzie King found himself beginning another of his periods on the street, cavorting with the ladies of the night. His behavior this time distressed him as much as ever, but one instance vexed him even more than usual. While King was supporting the underground sex trade, his mother took a turn for the worse. His feelings of remorse, which were always high after his visits to prostitutes, were virtually beyond his ability to manage when he came home and discovered the doctor tending to the emergency. Had his beloved mother died when he was being unfaithful to her by indulging in an act he found abhorrent, it is doubtful that Mackenzie King's tenuous hold on sanity could have survived.

By the end of that year (1916), King was back out on the campaign trail, leaving his "dear little mother" to the care of trained nurses. He was doing the best he could for the two most important aspects of his life. Sadly, neither arrangement was successful. On December 17, 1917, King's 43rd birthday, he lost his election bid for his grandfather's old riding of North York and the following day, before he could get back to Ottawa, his mother died. King retired to seclusion for months.

When he emerged, his hold on sanity had not improved. He had become obsessed; with numbers especially as denoted by the hands of the clock. It also marked the beginning of William Lyon Mackenzie King's slow, steady movement toward spiritualism – the realm which brought his dearly beloved mother back to him. He began to sense his mother's presence frequently and felt that she was near him, guiding him through his career path. She appeared to him in dreams, with messages. Once again King felt divinely connected and empowered.

Soon he sought out the services of fortune tellers in order to have closer contact with his dear departed mother. Initially his attitude to availing himself of that type of service was much like his attitude toward availing himself of paid sexual services – he was remorseful and angry. There did eventually prove to be a difference in the two endeavors, however, as he came to accept and even embrace the spirit world. There was never any level of acceptance for King where pay-for-play sex was concerned.

King's journey into the paranormal proceeded gradually until October 1929, when the crash of the New York stock market heralded the beginning of the Great Depression. Just months later King was voted out of office as Canadian Prime Minister. This left him not only terribly humiliated and in need of comfort, but with a considerable amount of spare time. Joan Patteson, who must have had at least some curiosity about communications with the dead, was very much a fixture in the man's life by this point and so all the variables were in place.

If Isabel King thought that she would be spending eternity resting in peace, she was sadly mistaken, for as soon as King and Joan found they were able to reach/or connect with the "other side," the deceased woman was called on more consistently than she ever had been during her life. Joan and King adopted a method incorporating "the little table" through which the spirits could communicate their messages. They spent countless happy hours huddled together in paranormal intimacy around the table while the spirits, one by one or in a group, visited.

But, as mentioned previously, Joan was not King's only choice of partner for these bizarre sessions. One seance partner, Senator Fulford's widow, received the ultimate compliment from King after a spiritual session. "I know no one who is more like mother . . ."[35] Nor did he restrict his method of contacting the departed to the table. Even then, more than 10 years after her death, King was desperate to receive affirmation of his worth from Isabel King. He "spoke" to her through Ouija boards, mediums and people who would today be called 'channels.'

Not surprisingly, mother came through frequently and with messages of great praise, encouragement and consolation. To be fair, many other spirits also came through, but none as consistently as mother's. What had been a lifelong Oedipus complex now extended past life on earth and into death. This version of the mother/son relationship was interrupted somewhat in 1935 by King's re-appointment as Prime Minister, thereby severely restricting his time available to indulge in such pursuits as seances. Despite this, William Lyon Mackenzie King managed to lead Canada through the final years of the Depression, through the Second World War and on into the first years of peace and recovery, while communicating with dead politicians, dead dogs, dead Biblical characters and dead relatives – most notably his beloved "little mother."

Throughout the years after his mother's death, King rather optimistically assumed that his psychic relationship with her was a secret. Apparently his confidence was somewhat misplaced.

"He was awfully naive in some ways . . . He thought an awful lot of things were secret that in fact weren't," according to Jack Pickersgill, who had been an aide to King.[36] Fortunately for King and his career, the press in that day and age weren't quite as fond of stirring up scandals as they later became.

When King retired in 1948 he was 74 years old and had been the Prime Minster of Canada longer than anyone else. Joan Patteson had also served her country during most of those years by serving its leader. She continued to serve her dear "Rex" until the end. Joan was with him at death, but it's possible that by that time her loyalty would have meant nothing to King if he was finally reuniting with the true love of his life – his mother.

Death came to William Lyon Mackenzie King on July 22, 1950, at Kingsmere during a highly localized, severe summer storm. "It was a lovely evening but just at the moment he died thunder and lightning and torrents of rain came without any warning . . . the rain only fell at Kingsmere."[37]

Perhaps one of the claps of thunder that was heard there that day was the sound of William Lyon Mackenzie King and his mother lovingly re-uniting beyond the veil.

A short afterword is most fitting for the King love story, because it somehow seems very unfair to be criticizing the man for what he revealed in the contents of his diaries. After all, he ordered his diaries to be destroyed at his death and so, by rights, we should have none of the information we do. King's literary executors, however, decided that his directions were unclear and therefore should be ignored. Had the man's instructions not been overruled we would not have been privy to any of the details about King's peculiar love stories.

J.E. Handy, who had been King's personal secretary for many years, told author Arthur Myers, "I sometimes feel those diaries should have been destroyed."[38]

King imposed himself upon the Pattesons' hospitality for many years – impositions that often implicated extra expenses. Nowhere is there any note of his having repaid them for any of their out-of-pocket expenses. During his lifetime, there was a general presumption that Mackenzie King did not have a lot of money. When he died, however, it was revealed that in fact he had been a very rich man. In fairness, it must be noted that Mackenzie King did leave a joint annuity to Joan and Godfroy.

There is a second, totally unrelated postscript – one that King himself would have enjoyed immensely. In 1955 two magazine articles were published[39] that indicated that Percy J. Philip, a well-respected journalist, had conversed with the ghost of William Lyon Mackenzie King. The meeting apparently took place in the summer of 1954 at the former Prime Minister's summer home at Kingsmere. If King updated the esteemed (and no doubt surprised) reporter regarding his heavenly love life, such information was, sadly, not recorded.

❦   ❦   ❦

The following list has been compiled from a survey of the literature by and/or about William Lyon Mackenzie King. The names on this list are all women in whom King had varying degrees of romantic interest at one point or another in his life. Some he has merely noted as having been attracted to. Others he had pursued, having declared he was "falling insensibly in love"[40] with them. The question of which ones fit into which categories matters little at this point. It is the sheer volume of women to whom he found himself attracted that makes the accounting significant.

Isabel King, Mathilde Grossert, Marjorie Herridge and Joan Patteson have been omitted only because their stories have already been told. The only other woman purposely excluded from the list is Mackenzie King's long-time friend Violet Markham. She and King were good friends through most of their adult lifetimes, but there was never any romantic intention by either.

This enumeration doesn't pretend to be all-inclusive. As a matter of fact, despite its impressive length, it may be woefully inadequate. William Lyon Mackenzie King certainly adored women – and lots of them. The ladies are listed in approximate chronological order and first names are given whenever they've been available.

Miss Cascadden, Miss Hunter, Florence Lynch, Miss Mab Moss, Miss Sheridan, Lelia Lash, Miss Street, Miss Edith Jones, Miss Robertson, Miss Worth, Miss Marwood, Miss Dowd, Miss McQuestion, Miss White, Miss Lamports, Miss Mackenzie, Miss Kerr, Miss Worthy, Miss Lamports, Edith and Florence Macdonald, Kitty Riordan, Nurse Cooper, Nurse Scott, Nurse Rogers, Nurse Harding, Miss Stairs (also a nurse), Mina Cameron (a prostitute whom King attempted to "reform" – for unexplained reasons C.P. Stacey refers to her by the pseudonym "Millie Gordon"), Miss Rohrer (a nurse), Miss Hall (another mysterious use of a pseudonym), Mrs. Lily Hendrie (married to William Hendrie), Miss Catherine Keith, Mrs. Cheney ("a wealthy widow"),[41] Lady Ruby Elliot, Beatrice Burbidge, Irene Herridge (Marjorie's daughter – King never demonstrated an interest in the young woman until she "married well" – he then reacted angrily as though her marriage to another man had somehow taken something away from him.), Miss Fowler, Miss Frances Howard, Miss McCook, Miss Dorothy Stirling, Miss Carnegie, Miss Jean Greer, Miss Larkin, Beatrix Henderson Robb and Julia Grant aka Princess Cantacuzene (another married woman).

## Endnotes

[1]*Knights of the Holy Spirit, A Study of William Lyon Mackenzie King,* Joy E. Esberey, University of Toronto Press, Toronto, pages 11-12.

[2]*A Very Double Life, The Private World of Mackenzie King,* C.P. Stacey, Macmillan of Canada, Toronto, 1976, page 53.

[3]Ibid., page 47.

[4]Ibid., page 42.

[5]Ibid., page 93.

[6]Ibid., page 101.

[7]Ibid., page 104.

[8]Ibid., page 94.

[9]Ibid., page 120.

[10]Ibid., page 123.

[11]Ibid., page 171.

[12]Ibid., page 165.

[13]Ibid., page 172.

[14]Ibid., pages 75-6. (*More Than A Rose, Prime Ministers Wives and Other Women*, Heather Robertson, Seal Books, Toronto, 1992, page 194, indicates Julia Grant was the former President's daughter.)

[15]Ibid., page 177.

[16]Ibid., page 179.

[17]Ibid., page 180.

[18]Ibid., page 181.

[19]*Knights of the Holy Spirit*, page 100.

[20]*A Very Double Life*, page 133.

[21]Ibid., page 120.

[22]Ibid., page 137.

[23]Ibid., page 138.

[24]*Knights of the Holy Spirit*, page 14.

[25]*A Very Double Life*, page 68.

[26]Ibid., page 118.

[27]Ibid., page 109.

[28]Ibid., page 112.

[29]Ibid., page 69.

[30]Ibid., page 70.

[31]*Ghosts of the Rich and Famous*, Arthur Myers, Contemporary Books, Chicago, 1988, page 146,

[32]*A Very Double Life*, page 69.

[33]*Knights of the Holy Spirit*, page 40.

[34]*A Very Double Life*, page 151.

[35]Ibid., page 167.

[36]*Ghosts of the Rich and Famous*, page 154.

[37]*A Very Double Life*, page 222.

[38]*Ghosts of the Rich and Famous*, page 158.

[39]Ibid., page 158.

[40]*A Very Double Life*, page 37.

[41]Ibid., page 97.

# Francis
# & Alma Rattenbury

Every seat in Toronto's venerable Massey Hall was occupied. A rush of excited, last minute conversation echoed through the auditorium. The Concert Master, who had been chatting with the violinist on his left, now stood and faced the orchestra. With a flourish, he raised his bow to signal an oboe player in the back row, who sounded an extended tone, the note from which the others would tune their instruments. Ear-scratching cacophony answered. Seconds later the discordant sounds streamed themselves into a single, uniform cadence and the Toronto Symphony Orchestra was ready to perform. The Concert Master took his seat once again, the orchestra and the audience fell into an anticipatory silence.

The Conductor stood in the wing, just off stage. He breathed deeply, absorbing the energy the crowded hall exuded. This was the moment he loved best, this millisecond of absolute silence. He took two more deep breaths and at the very moment he knew he could not endure another moment's latent stimulation, he strode on stage. The Concert Master rose from his seat again, this time to greet the Conductor with a handshake. Members of the string section tapped their bows on the metal music stands in front of them. Musicians playing woodwind, brass or percussion instruments tapped their feet on the floor or against their music stands but, after the perfunctory handshake, the Conductor noticed nothing "his" orchestra did or didn't do. He was turned away from the musicians, toward his adoring and paying audience. Earnestly, and with as much humility as he could muster, the man accepted their ovation.

Of course every performance was special, but tonight was even more special than most. After a short opening number, the Polonaise in D Sharp Minor by Chopin, he would leave the stage for a moment and return with an exquisitely beautiful young woman on his arm. Alma Victoria Clarke was the guest soloist this evening. Rehearsals had gone wonderfully well and he thought she may have been the most talented youngster to ever grace this stage. The Heintzman grand piano Alma had chosen stood just to the right of his dais. She would carry her Stradivarius to the stage herself.

This would be a wonderful evening, he was sure. He had thought fleetingly this afternoon that Alma had actually been flirting with him!

Despite his advanced years and usual dignity, a small smile etched itself into the corners of the Conductor's mouth.

Perhaps in an unknowing response to their leader's recently stimulated feelings of masculinity, the Toronto Symphony Orchestra performed the Polonaise as they never had before. It wasn't a complex work, but tonight there seemed to be increased vigor infused into the piece. It came off beautifully. After receiving the audience's expressions of appreciation, the Conductor should have left the podium to escort his soloist to her piano. Instead he took a moment and turned to the orchestra once again. He spread his arms and bowed deeply to his fellow musicians to show them that he, too, had appreciated their fine presentation. The night was off to a splendid start!

"May I?" he asked rhetorically as he offered his arm to the beautiful young virtuoso waiting just behind the red velvet curtain.

She nodded demurely, placed her hand lightly on his outstretched arm and accompanied the man to centre stage.

Alma Clarke was never surprised by the warm greetings audiences extended to her. She was already an accomplished veteran of the stage, having grown up performing. Everywhere she went Alma had always been surrounded by praise verging on adoration. The experiences had nurtured her until she had become completely comfortable and confident before an audience.

Comely and vivacious, Alma charmed all she met, but it was when she sat down at a piano keyboard or placed her violin bow against the strings of her treasured Stradivarius that she left those same people speechless. It was said that her talents and abilities as a musician were so great that she could make even an average composition sound wonderful.[1]

Tonight she would outdo even herself. On this night, in Massey Hall accompanied by the Toronto Symphony Orchestra, Alma Clarke gave the performance of her young life. Her piano concerto was indeed remarkable but, oddly, it was the concerto for violin that nearly brought down the house. The usually restrained crowd jumped to its collective feet amid calls of "Brava, Brava."

Years later, a much-changed Alma continued to delight in re-living and re-telling the victory that was hers that evening in Toronto.

That same year, renowned architect Francis Mawson Rattenbury incorrectly believed his life was at its lowest ebb. The adulations heaped on him during the five years it took to construct British Columbia's Parliament Building were all forgotten. Worse, the fault-finders had come out of the woodwork by now. The project had gone well over budget, they complained. Undeniably, this was true, but it was not something Rattenbury felt responsible for.

Next the press got on the bandwagon. The reporters squawked that the building's Press Gallery was sadly inadequate, and now, fully 15 years after the Government had gratefully accepted his plan for the spectacular building, there were complaints about the design of the Lieutenant-Governor's suite. Discouraged and frustrated, Rattenbury wondered what else could possibly go wrong.

*The B.C. Parliament buildings – Rattenbury's prize-winning design.*

He had arrived in Canada in 1892, a brash 24-year-old architect with a strong entrepreneurial bent. He brought with him a great deal more energy than humility and leaving his native England meant he could embellish his credentials with little fear of being found out. And embellish he did. Rattenbury credited himself with designing buildings with which he hadn't been remotely connected and even one which had been completed when he was a very young child.

*Francis Mawson Rattenbury. (photo #b-09502, B.C. Archives and Records Service)*

The self-aggrandizement may have been dishonest, but it did produce the desired results, for less than a year later Francis Rattenbury was an integral member of Victoria's elite society. He was invited to every occasion that mattered. William Oliver, a respected Victoria lawyer and close friend of Rattenbury, described the aftermath of an exclusive New Year's Eve gala he had hosted this way, ". . . Rattenbury's dress coat, which was bought for the occasion was hanging in rags as he left. It was a successful celebration."[2]

Apparently Rattenbury clearly understood which occasions allowed him to abandon his inhibitions and which ones required more decorum. He was an important addition to the guest list of any social gathering and played game after impressive game of tennis at the city's most exclusive clubs. After a match he could usually be called upon to entertain the other guests by playing the piano. Society's matrons adored the handsome, successful young man. Mothers with marriageable daughters were especially anxious to include Rattenbury in their plans.

Oddly, Rattenbury never showed much interest in the eligible young women paraded before him. Then on June 19, 1898, the man shocked everyone who knew him by marrying Florence Eleanor Nunn, a woman no one of any importance had ever heard of.[3] The marriage dashed the hopes of many of Victoria's eligible young ladies and Rattenbury paid for his seemingly strange choice by becoming the subject of citywide gossip.

"Why ever would he marry her?" the wags wondered. Florrie was certainly not a pretty or vivacious woman and her humble background could not bring Rattenbury any additional standing in the community. Perhaps the gossip-mongers' excited discussions kept them from recognizing the most obvious possibility. Seven months after the wedding, Florrie gave birth to a child – a son. What should have been a joyful occasion was not. Francis Burgoyne Rattenbury, or Frank as he was called, was born with hideously deformed clubfeet. Doctors predicted the child might never walk.[4]

Young Frank adored his father. Rattenbury, perhaps disappointed or repulsed by the child's disability, paid little attention to the lad. Florrie, however, lavished every available moment on the child.

Rattenbury threw himself into his career with even greater fervor and determination. Multi-millionaire cattle baron Pat Burns offered the Victoria architect a series of contracts. These were not artistically exciting, they included warehouses and other industrial buildings, but they were profitable. And when Burns decided to move his place of residence from British Columbia to Alberta, he called upon Rattenbury to design and oversee the construction of the residence. Burns's love of the ostentatious and Rattenbury's flamboyant style combined well. A 10-bedroom mansion resulted.

The profit from these commissions would easily have supported the three Rattenburys for several years, but his growing reputation meant he was much in demand. Rattenbury-designed banks, office buildings and grand residences sprang up throughout Western Canada.

Rattenbury's success would probably have bought his wife entrance nto the social milieu that once rejected her presence. Florrie, however, showed absolutely no interest in joining their elite ranks. She had never been particularly outgoing and since Frank's birth, she had withdrawn even further. By the turn of the century her whole life consisted of her home and her young, crippled son. Even Rattenbury was somewhat of an outsider in his own home.

The gregarious man merely accepted the odd set of circumstances and continued to enjoy all the social functions to which he'd always been invited. Hostesses gave up including Florrie in their plans, because she never attended. Who needed her, anyway, they rationalized. She'd likely only sit sulking in a corner and undermine all the other guests' high spirits.

Despite this apparent duality, there must have been something more left of the marriage than was obvious to outsiders, because on May 11, 1904, a second child was born. Rattenbury took one look at his daughter, a tiny pink and white bundle and, for the first, but not last, time in his life fell head over heels in love. He named her Mary, after his mother, and proceeded to dote on her as his wife doted on Frank. The combination, of course, was lethal to the already suffering marriage and soon all pretenses of domestic bliss were dropped. Rattenbury and Florrie took separate bedrooms in the home which, in more optimistic times, they'd named *Iechineel*, a Gaelic word meaning "a place where a good thing happened."

It is prophetic that the phrase is in the past tense, because very little that was "good" would ever happen in that home again. Husband and wife even stopped speaking to one another. When both children were away at boarding schools, the family members existed as four entirely separate lives.

For the next 20 years Rattenbury's career experienced both substantial gains and losses. He rode out the peaks and valleys as well as he was able, but it was clear to all who knew him that this was not the fun-loving, aggressive man who had taken Victoria by storm some 30 years before. The unhappy home life took its toll on all the family members. Perhaps young Frank was the least affected, but his chances for a normal life had already been badly damaged, not only by his deformity, but by each of his parents' reactions to it. In turn, Florrie became a full-blown recluse, Mary developed a speech impediment and Rattenbury, with increasing frequency, sought solace in the bottle.

This unhappy situation continued until the last few days of 1923. Rattenbury's career, which had recently been plagued by both criticism and a slumping economy, suddenly took off again. The city fathers had agreed to build a spectacular amusement centre. Soon Victoria would be graced by yet another of the architect's magnificent buildings, The Crystal Garden. On December 29, 1923, celebrations were held to acknowledge this plan. Rattenbury was once again where he loved to be – at the very centre of attention.

He left the reception basking in the once-familiar glow of triumph. In the lounge of the Empress Hotel, which he had designed some 25 years before, Francis Mawson Rattenbury was introduced to Alma Victoria Clarke Dolling Pakenham.

She was no longer the demure, naive and innocent Alma Victoria Clarke, the teenager who had performed so stunningly on the concert stage in Toronto. Alma was now in her late 20s. She had been married briefly to a man she adored. When he was killed in the war, she sought active duty herself and served as an ambulance driver until the armistice. Shortly after returning to Canada, Alma remarried. Very quickly she became a mother and then, almost as quickly, a divorcee.

The day Alma and Rattenbury, met she was a 28-year-old divorced mother with a two-year-old son. He was a lonely, successful, married man who drank far too much. He was also twice her age.

Despite the age difference, or possibly because of it, Rattenbury was totally smitten the moment he laid eyes on the sensuous young woman. Their whirlwind courtship began immediately, without regard for Rattenbury's marital status.

Initially, the two made an effort to keep their romance a secret. Inevitably, word leaked out and soon Victoria's society matrons were once more wagging their tongues over Rattenbury's tastes in women. At first "Ratz," as Alma had affectionately dubbed him, didn't care a whit. His unhappiness and celibacy were finally over. Thanks to the sexually aggressive Alma, he was having the time of his life.

He was puzzled and offended by his friends' reactions to his newly found happiness. He'd expected they'd not only be delighted for him, but anxious to include Alma at their numerous social occasions. After all, she was a beautiful young woman who had gained quite a reputation first as a musician and more recently as the composer of popular songs.

William Oliver, who had so enjoyed Rattenbury's antics at his New Year's Eve party some years before, agreed with the others in Victoria's elite. Francis Rattenbury was suddenly a very changed man. Conjecture raged. Could the young woman's charms alone have caused the man's indiscreet behavior? Perhaps it was something more. Perhaps it was drugs. Cocaine, among others, was rumored to be behind the man's personality shift.[5]

Rattenbury was hurt to be ostracized this way, but the feeling did little to impinge on his newfound bliss. Fear, however, did – the fear that he would lose his beautiful Alma to another, probably younger, man. The very thought was more than he could bear. He had to marry her to make her his for all the world to see. And he had to do it soon.

Marriage, he predicted, would not only secure his place in Alma's life, but it would also facilitate acceptance back into the social life he'd so enjoyed. Of course, first he needed a divorce. Toward this end, Rattenbury spoke to Florrie for the first time in years.

"Please, Florrie, I will give you anything you ask. Just give me a divorce."

"No." The monosyllabic reply was followed by complete silence – for months.

Desperate, Ratz set about changing the woman's mind anyway he could. He moved out of the house and took most of the furniture with him. When this did not have the desired effect, he arranged to have first the heat and then the power turned off. Considering his beloved daughter, Mary, also lived in the house, these ploys explicitly reveal the extent to which Ratz had fallen under Alma's spell.

Much to Ratz's surprise, Florrie fought back. By court order, she won the right to live in the house. The injunction, however, apparently did not ban Rattenbury from *Iechineel*, nor did it prevent him from entertaining there.

He began to bring Alma to the house, where she would sit for hours at the piano playing loudly and disturbing the ailing Florrie. Eventually the poor beleaguered woman gave in and consented to a divorce, naming Alma Victoria Clarke Dolling Pakenham as the co-respondent.

Rattenbury had won, but he had also lost. Part of the divorce agreement stated that he should buy a new house for Florrie. She insisted the house be designed by Rattenbury's former partner and situated overlooking *Iechineel* where Ratz and Alma lived with her son, Christopher.

It isn't known where or when the lovers became husband and wife, but becoming Mr. & Mrs. Rattenbury did not buy them the social acceptability they'd hoped it would. None of his former friends or business acquaintances would associate with him. Both Alma and Ratz were highly social people who thrived on recognition and appreciation from those around them. Ratz was especially devastated.

The very members of his social circle who had gossiped so viciously when he married Florrie continued to display their disapproval with his choice of women. Once again *Iechineel* became a retreat. Alma and Ratz became as reclusive as the home's former tenant, Florrie.

Being ostracized did not dampen the ardor between the apparently mismatched couple. In December, 1928, the Rattenburys welcomed an addition to their home. John, a second son for each of them, was born.

Alma, especially, was delighted. She loved children and loved being a mother. She proudly took her two boys out for regular afternoon walks, John contentedly propped in his pram and young Christopher running here and there around his mother and younger brother. Anxious to engage in the traditional exchange of oohs and aahs with other young mothers, she waved expectantly to all she passed. No one returned her overture or even acknowledged her presence. To a young woman used to praise and acceptance, this condemnation was intolerable.

By now, Ratz realized that he would never work in Victoria, and possibly in all of British Columbia, again. Terribly insulted and discouraged, he took Alma and their sons and sailed back to England. Fleeing the detritus of his personal life was Rattenbury's only hope of salvaging anything of his once-flourishing career.

Ratz knew just how far he'd fallen from the days when crowds would offer him ovations of recognition. His departure from Canada was as lonely as his arrival had been. Only Frank, his son from his previous marriage, was at the dock to wave good-bye to his snubbed father.

Fortunately, much of the capital he had amassed during his boom years remained intact and Ratz was able to support his young family while they settled into their new life. Alma was delighted with her new surroundings and quickly made friends. Ratz, however, found the orientation process considerably more difficult. His work was not known in England and he had no grapevine to help him become known. Besides, his drinking had not diminished and the toll it was taking on the aging man was becoming evident to even the most casual observers. His frustrations were mounting. The imposed idleness and isolation were interfering with his mental and emotional stability.

"I must work, Alma. I am wasting away here," he told her repeatedly. And to give the man his proper due, he did have a specific project in mind. No one, however, was willing to back his plan financially.

Alma had not been used to a lot in the way of material goods. Her father had been a journalist and her mother a music teacher. While this meant the girl's music lessons hadn't been expensive, it also meant the family lived at a modest level. To her, Rattenbury's wealth seemed astronomical, a veritable bottomless pit. She couldn't understand his preoccupation about money. There always seemed to be enough as far as she could see and besides, Alma was as happy as she had ever been.

Ironically, the city of Bournemouth, where the couple had taken up residency, was almost the English equivalent of Victoria. Both cities were on the southern tip of islands, enjoyed pleasant climates and were known as retirement communities for the upper-middle class. In his book, *Murder at the Villa Madeira*, Sir David Napley tells of a cleverly vandalized road sign near Bournemouth. Evidently the marker is located at a cross roads leading to either Devon or Bournemouth, depending on which way you turn. At the top it reads, "Devon for the continent." Under that, the road to Bournemouth is indicated with the rider, "for the incontinent."

Despite the apparent lack of young people in the community, Alma truly enjoyed living there, just as she had enjoyed Victoria until the wrath of society fell on them.

In September, 1930, the Rattenburys rented a house, pretentiously called "Villa Madeira." Christopher, Alma's son by her second marriage, spent most of his time away at boarding school, but there was a bedroom for him in the Villa and he was home every weekend. John, the younger lad, stayed at home with his parents and shared his mother's bedroom.

Ratz and Alma had apparently ceased having any sort of a sex life. As he had in his first marriage, Ratz moved out of his wife's bedroom. He took a small room off the parlor as his bedroom. This move likely wasn't motivated by any lack of affection. He remained genuinely fond of Alma. The move was probably to avoid embarrassment. Rattenbury was in his 50s by now and his advancing years coupled with too great a love of liquor had, it would seem, rendered him impotent.

Conversely, Alma had always had a healthier than average libido and continued to do so. Three books written about the Rattenburys maintain that Alma contracted tuberculosis and that this disease is known to dramatically increase feelings of lust.[6] Alma's methods of sublimation remain open to conjecture.

Despite Ratz's concerns about money, the Rattenburys did employ at least two full-time employees at the Villa Madeira. One was Irene Riggs, Alma's paid companion and helper. She "lived in," having been assigned the bedroom next to Alma's on the second storey of the home.

The two women quickly became friends. Within weeks they were absolutely inseparable. Everywhere Alma went, Irene went too. The relationship was far deeper than that of mere employer/employee. If Alma had tickets to the theatre, Miss Riggs knew she'd be invited along. The family never went on a picnic without Irene. She was there for any events that might have been held at either of the boys' schools. In return, Irene was everything Alma could have wanted in a domestic. She was hardworking, loyal and unabashedly fond of her employer.

For those wondering if this friendship could have provided the sexual outlet for Alma's reportedly intense passions, F. Tennyson Jesse, editor of *Trial of Rattenbury and Stoner*, is careful to point out that Alma Rattenbury, "had no unnatural tendencies."[7] How Jesse would have known this is, disappointingly, not documented. Although Irene's duties may or may not have included sexual services, they certainly did go well beyond the duties normally expected of live-in domestic help.

The wags who'd driven Alma and Rattenbury out of Victoria often speculated on the possibility of Alma having become addicted to cocaine and/or morphine during her war service. The gossip may or may not have been based in fact. There is no doubt that by 1930, as she and Ratz settled into life at the Villa Madeira, Alma was drinking far too heavily. In addition she was reportedly given to "fits" or "attacks" of frenetic activity. Often these episodes, which may have been drug induced, lasted all night. Irene patiently stayed with her employer during each and every one of these bouts. When the manic condition had run its course, Irene would see her mistress safely into bed before getting any rest herself.

Cocaine use could certainly have prompted such behavior, however, it is also possible that sheer frustration from the unsatisfying life she was leading could have been responsible for Alma's occasionally bizarre behavior.

The other employee in the Rattenbury household was a hired man named Gregory. He was not nearly as devoted to the mistress of Villa Madeira as Irene was. As a matter of fact, he left his employer without notice in September, 1934. Gregory never did explain himself to either Ratz or Alma, but apparently confided in Irene, whom he no doubt viewed as a peer.

"It's the Misses, Miss Riggs. She keeps making up to me. I think I'd be better off out of the way."[8]

Despite Ratz's obsession about their financial problems, he clearly didn't expect his wife to run the household without adequate help. And so, on Sunday, September 23, 1934, the following advertisement ran in the *Bournemouth Daily Echo*, "Daily willing lad, 14-18, for housework. Scout-trained preferred. Apply between 11-12, 8-9, 5 Manor Road, Bournemouth."[9]

It is known that at least one young man applied for the position, was accepted by Alma, but turned the job down. He explained that his sister told him the job sounded too good to be true. A second lad did not have the advantage of a concerned sister. He also didn't have much in the way of what we'd now call "street smarts." George Percy Stoner was, in fact, terribly naive.

Stoner had been raised by his grandparents. They loved the lad dearly, but were candid enough to admit that he had always been quite slow witted. He hadn't learned how to walk until after his third birthday and his learning process hadn't improved much by the time he reached the age to begin school, so that he only completed three years of formal education. He spent most of his time happily tinkering with various pieces of equipment found around his grandparents' property. All who knew him considered the young man to be completely inept socially and totally inexperienced sexually. Thus equipped, Stoner, then just short of his 18th birthday, answered the Rattenburys' newspaper advertisement. Alma hired him on the spot.

Much to his grandmother's surprise, Stoner's first job seemed to be working out incredibly well. At first Stoner continued to live at home and report to the Villa Madeira each morning. Within a month, however, the young Stoner had moved in with the Rattenburys. He was assigned an empty bedroom on the second storey of the house. It was right beside Irene Riggs' room which, in turn, was right beside Alma's.

Just about this time Alma succeeded in selling some songs she'd composed. The tunes were to be recorded by England's heartthrob tenor of the era, Frank Titterton. The music publisher would begin forwarding royalty cheques to Mrs. Rattenbury in the very near future. Alma was ecstatic. It was wonderful to be involved with the world of music again and she knew Ratz would be delighted that she'd have a bit of an income.

When she approached her husband with the good news, Ratz had good news of his own. An old friend, a man named Jenks, in nearby Bridport, had expressed interest in providing financing for the housing project Ratz was so determined to build. The two men would need to meet soon for discussions.

"We'll have to make a trip to Bridport the week after next, Alma. Let Stoner know so he can get the car ready for the trip. He'll have to drive us, of course," Ratz explained with more emotion than Alma remembered him showing since they'd left Canada.

Alma was truly delighted for her husband. She congratulated him warmly and the two celebrated by polishing off a bottle of whisky. That was one tradition that had become firmly entrenched in the Rattenbury's household – they would drink either in celebration or depression. It didn't really matter, the constant in the equation had become alcohol.

In her Introduction to the book *Trial of Rattenbury and Stoner*, editor F. Tennyson Jesse offers these interesting and contradictory statements within a dozen words of each other – "Every night Mr. Rattenbury drank the best part of a bottle of whisky . . . he was not a drunkard."[10]

Stoner, however didn't share the enthusiasm his employers felt. He had been thoroughly enjoying the unique conditions of his employment. Filtered through his severely limited intellect, the recent developments between he and Alma indicated they had a long and exclusive future together. Upon hearing about the planned trip to Bridport, Stoner became outraged with jealousy. Nothing Alma could say would convince the young man that the time away would not include having sex with old Ratz.

Finally Alma thought of a way to appease her "hired man."

"We're not going to Bridport until the week after next. Let's you and me go away together next week. Just the two of us. I'll get some money from Ratz and we'll have some fun together, just the two of us," Alma offered.

Stoner, who'd never travelled away from Bournemouth and who, his grandparents later maintained, had been virgin until he met Alma, was as excited as a child with tickets to the circus.

One obstacle, however, lay in the path of the lovers' fling. Money. None of Alma's royalty cheques were in yet and although Rattenbury gave her a regular housekeeping allowance, there weren't any surplus funds. Certainly not enough to finance the proposed trip. Fortunately,

Alma knew how to correct the situation. She'd done it before and it had worked.

"Ratz, Dr. O'Donnell was here yesterday and he said I needed another operation to help cure my tuberculosis. It will cost 250 pounds but he can arrange to have it done in London next week," Alma lied.

Well, actually, only part of the story was a lie. Dr. O'Donnell, the family's doctor, had indeed dropped in the day before. But then that wasn't unusual. In her book, *Rattenbury*, Terry Reksten states, "Dr O'Donnell, Alma's physician['s], . . . calls to the house were too frequent to be entirely professional."[11] Reksten does not speculate on what the exact nature of those visits might have been.

Despite the fictitious component to the request, Rattenbury immediately issued Alma a cheque for 250 pounds.

"Stoner will be driving you, then will he?" Ratz enquired.

"I presume so, dear, and Irene will be here to look after you. I'm sure I'll be back home by Friday evening," Alma predicted, tucking the cheque into the pocket of her dressing gown.

Although it was early afternoon, Alma wore pajamas and a dressing gown. By now even her manner of dress had become a reflection of the strange life she was leading. Visitors rarely came to the Villa Madeira, other than Dr. O'Donnell, and except to attend the occasional events at either Christopher's or John's school, the Rattenburys rarely left their home. The planned excursions, first to London and then to Bridport, were exceedingly unusual events in their increasingly reclusive lives.

The following Wednesday morning, Alma and Stoner pulled away from the house before dawn. Ratz was not even aware they had left. He slept on, undisturbed, in his first floor bedroom. Irene, however, was awake and watched with a heavy heart as the distinctly odd but happy couple pulled away from the house.

Once in London, Stoner and Alma booked into the Royal Palace Hotel. They took rooms across the hall from one another and claimed to be brother and sister. That was one of the few ruses the pair could have offered. After all they could hardly pass themselves off as husband and wife – Alma was old enough to be Stoner's mother.

Moments after checking into the luxurious rooms, they set off to scour some of London's finest shops. The two days were a veritable frenzy of spending. Alma bought Stoner an array of expensive clothes, including crepe de Chine pajamas, but perhaps the most outlandish purchase made that weekend was a diamond ring which Stoner bought for Alma with funds she gave him.[12]

When Friday evening, came Alma suggested that they pack their bags and head back to Bournemouth. She had had fun but was now anxious to get back to the Villa. She wanted to see young John, check on her husband and titter with Irene about the adventures she'd had while they were away.

Stoner, however, was appalled at the thought of returning to routine. He'd thoroughly enjoyed illegitimately rising above his station in life. He had no desire to leave this fantasy behind and return to reality. Even he, however, realized that with their finances exhausted there was no way to avoid returning to the Villa. Still, he complained about what he viewed as the great injustice of it all during the entire drive home.

Stoner's life was the only one to have been changed by the weekend. When Alma opened the front door of the house she stepped back into the circumstances she'd left two days before. John was sleeping soundly in his bed in the corner of her room. Ratz had passed out in his chair in the parlor and Irene sat in the kitchen having a cup of tea before bed.

The next day Alma was truly disappointed that Irene didn't seem much interested in a full report on her employer's escapade. Conversely, she was relieved that Ratz appeared to have forgotten about the surgical procedure she was supposed to have undergone in London.

That trip over, it was time to prepare for the second one – the one Rattenbury hoped would set his life back on a positive, prosperous course. Lately, in his alcohol-induced daydreams, Ratz had been fondly recalling his glory days years before in Victoria. He looked forward to reveling in public adulation once again.

His delusions, of course, were precisely that. The fact that humans are rarely able to see themselves objectively can be a great gift – a gift of protection against a reality too difficult to accept. Although Alma was still genuinely fond of her husband, even she must have known in her heart that Francis Mawson Rattenbury was, by now, merely a drunk and a has-been.

In retrospect, no one but the most cold-hearted soul would have denied Rattenbury his self-deceptions. They were almost all he had left. Increasingly, his drinking was bringing on bouts of depression and even the occasional talk of suicide. Alma always kindly and patiently diverted his attentions during these periods. On the Sunday afternoon after Alma and Stoner's trip to London, Ratz fell into another of his melancholy moods.

"I've been reading this novel," he explained waving about a book entitled *Stay of Execution*. "It has made me realize that I'm old and not truly a husband to you. I know now that you must be satisfying your desires with someone else. I cannot live with that, Alma. I am going to kill myself."

Alma was aghast at the proclamation. She'd assumed her affair with Stoner was safe. Ratz appeared either not to know about it or not to care about it. Apparently her presumptions had been incorrect. Quickly, she set about righting the potentially lethal situation.

Stoner, who was still not delighted at his return to hired-man status eavesdropped as husband and wife made love with the lust they'd enjoyed in the earlier days of their relationship.

"And don't forget, dear," Alma said as she left the room later. "We're going to Bridport tomorrow. By the end of the week you'll be working again. Why in just a few days everyone will once again know that the name Rattenbury is synonymous with exquisite architecture."

Relieved that she'd been able to avert a most serious crisis, Alma closed her husband's bedroom door. She turned to go into the kitchen. She needed a drink badly. Instead she bumped headlong into Stoner. He was in a rage, sure Rattenbury had discovered their ruse and that Alma had slept with her husband in order to appease him.

Now, instead of relaxing with a much needed drink of whiskey in her hand, Alma had to calm the other man in her life. Fortunately, handling men had become a finely-honed skill of Alma's and soon Stoner seemed considerably less agitated.

"Besides, Stoner, this is your afternoon off. Even Irene's away visiting with her parents. Why don't you take the motorcar and go off for a nice visit with your grandparents. I'm fine here, really I am," she told Stoner.

Stoner's second favorite part of his job at the Rattenbury's was driving Ratz's car. The young man smiled contentedly at her suggestion and moments later drove down the street pretending that the car and Alma were both his.

Alma was right. She was fine alone. Certainly she was more composed than she had been an hour before when Ratz was still conscious and Stoner was still in the house. Little John was playing happily in the yard and Alma took a strong drink of whisky, drew herself a hot bath and proceeded to soak and drink away the frustrations of the day.

By evening Ratz seemed to have forgotten the upsetting episode earlier in the day. Little John remained innocent of the problems around him and was happily tucked into bed by 7:30 that evening. Ratz and Alma played a few hands of cards together before turning in about 9:30 that evening.

"Don't forget, Ratz, we want to be well rested for our trip tomorrow. If you get lots of sleep tonight you'll be at your best in the morning. Jenks will be positively dazzled by your scheme. I know he will," Alma offered as she kissed her inebriated husband good night.

Just as she usually did, Alma left the semi-conscious man sitting in the parlor in his favorite chair. She made sure the doors were locked before going upstairs to bed.

Irene came in before 10:30, but as her dear friend and confidante, Alma, had obviously retired early, Irene decided to do the same. A few minutes later, however, the woman realized that despite the delicious dinner she'd eaten only hours before at her parents home, she was hungry. Irene went back downstairs and into the kitchen to fix herself a snack.

As soon as she got downstairs, Irene could hear the sounds of labored breathing coming from another room. Frightened that Mr. Rattenbury might be ill, Irene cautiously peered around his bedroom door and into the room. The bed was empty and showed no signs of having been slept in.

"That's a relief," she said to herself, for she knew that Alma often left Rattenbury to fall asleep sitting up in his chair.

"He's probably just slumped over with his head at an angle and snoring," she assessed without checking further.

The little adrenaline rush that the strange sounds had given her succeeded in doing away with her appetite and Irene Riggs proceeded back up the stairs for the second time in less than half an hour. This time she saw Stoner standing in the upstairs hall, peering down into the darkened stairway.

"What are you doing?" she asked sharply.

"Just wanted to make sure all the lights were out," Stoner replied before returning to his bedroom, next to Irene's.

As the woman was finally settling into bed for the night, Alma popped her head in the door.

"Irene?" she called. "You're not asleep yet, are you?"

Riggs gave a small laugh. She was always glad to see Alma.

"I may never get to sleep tonight at the rate I'm going," the woman told her employer, who by now was seated cross-legged at the end of Irene's bed.

The two exchanged reports on how their days had gone, Alma describing in some detail the difficult time she'd had with both Ratz and Stoner. After their brief chat, Alma retired to her own room where, moments later, she was joined by Stoner.

The two were making passionate and noisy love when Alma heard a groan from the floor below. It was a horrible sound, one that sent Alma running from her lover to her husband's side. There, as oddly slumped as Irene had assumed he must have been, sat Francis Mawson Rattenbury. He was struggling to get air. Alma came around to the front of the chair and moaned herself.

"Oh, poor Ratz, poor Ratz," she screamed, bringing the other two hurrying to her side.[13]

She stared in horror at the large purple mark on the side of her husband's face and seemed oblivious to the fact she was standing, barefoot in a pool of her husband's blood.

"He's trying to talk," Alma announced to no one in particular. "But he can't because something's knocked his teeth out. Look, here they are on the floor."

Alma tried in vain to put the dentures back in her dying husband's mouth. She gave up and instead put the false teeth on the table near Ratz's chair. There they lay, reposing in a macabre smile beside Ratz's half-full glass of whisky. Alma apparently noticed the drink for the first time. She picked up the tumbler, held it to her mouth and drained it in single swallow.

Stoner and Irene stood paralyzed by all that was going on around them.

"Don't just stand there, you two," she screamed. "Irene call the doctor. Stoner, help me move him onto his bed. My poor dear Ratz must be so uncomfortable."

By the time the beleaguered Dr. O'Donnell arrived at the Villa Madeira less than 15 minutes later, Irene had regained some of her composure. Both Stoner and Alma, however, had become even more distraught.

In an effort to calm her nerves, Alma had taken a straight shot of whisky. The drink did not produce the desired results, for by the time the doctor arrived she was verging on hysteria.

O'Donnell realized there was little he could do for Ratz. He called a local surgeon who arrived at the house within the hour. By this time, Alma had sneaked at least a second straight pull from the whisky bottle. She ran about the house incoherently attempting to explain the situation to the others in the house.

Fortunately, Christopher, her elder son, was back at school, no doubt fast asleep in his dormitory. John, however, was at home, but his ability to sleep through noise and chaos had been well-documented during Alma's nocturnal "fits." Blissfully, he stayed asleep through this pandemonium as well.

Rooke, the surgeon O'Donnell called for, was barely in the door before Alma came flying at him. She was, by now, quite drunk.

"Look at him, my poor Ratz. Someone has finished him. Someone has done him in," she explained incoherently and most unnecessarily.

"If you want to finish him off, then you're going about it the right way," he informed the nearly hysterical Alma. "Now get out of my way and let me get near enough to the patient to at least get a good look at him."

Pouting at having been spoken to so gruffly, Alma slunk back to the corner of the room. When she was within reach of the cabinet which held the liquor, she reached for the bottle. She emptied it in two large swallows.

"This man's been hit," the second doctor determined. "There's nothing I can do for him here. We'll have to get him to a medical centre right away. I'll need to operate."

The room fell silent.

"I'll call the police," O'Donnell announced.

Stoner helped the surgeon move Ratz into the car and then drove them to the closest medical centre with the equipment Rooke would need. As the odd trio arrived at the hospital, a police officer, an Inspector Mills, made his way to the Villa Madeira. Here both Dr. O'Donnell and Irene were doing their best to calm the seemingly inconsolable Alma.

Mills inspected the crime scene with a practiced eye. He noted the blood covered carpenter's mallet lying just under the chair and the blood splattered about the room. He also noted the parlor's French doors which led out to the backyard.

"Were these open when you first came down and found your husband?" he asked Alma.

Her brain, well sodden with alcohol by now, was not working well.

"No, of course not. It's night time. They were closed and locked," she replied before realizing that she'd just closed and locked out the possibility of the crime having been committed by an intruder.

Hearing this, Mills called back to his office.

"I'll need someone else to come 'round here for a bit. I want to check on the victim. He's been taken for surgery."

Constable Bagwell replied to his superior officer's request and arrived at the house minutes later. Mills met him at the door and quietly explained what the younger man's duties would be.

"Dr. O'Donnell and I are going to see what they've found out about Mr. Rattenbury's injuries. The wife and a hired girl are here. Keep an eye on things for me, Bagwell. Make sure those two don't get into anything. I don't want anything re-arranged or cleaned up."

Bagwell indicated he understood what should have been straightforward instructions. The man was totally unprepared for the grotesque melodrama he was stepping into. Alma, having realized she had given away a good opportunity to diffuse the investigation from either herself or Stoner, tried to pull herself together.

"Hello!" she greeted the uniformed man as he walked down the hall toward her. "Thanks for coming round so quickly. We've had a problem here tonight."

Bagwell nodded, trying to absorb his strange surroundings.

"I know who done it," Alma said simply.[14]

Bagwell quickly pulled his notebook from his tunic pocket.

Seeing that her words would be noted, Alma changed her mind about confessing. She offered the officer ten pounds, apparently to encourage him not to record her confession and then quickly withdrew her offer.

"No, my lover did it."

Alluding to Stoner may have made Alma feel romantic because she put a record on and suddenly the house was filled with the romantic strains of ballads. No doubt this reminded the woman that there was a more efficient way of bringing the policeman over to her side. Historically, Alma Victoria Clarke Dolling Pakenham Rattenbury had been able to get her way with men by letting them have their way with her.

Unfortunately, this time the man was acting strangely. She was having to chase him all around the house in order just to get near enough to start kissing him.

"What peculiar beasts men are," she thought as she pursued her mission.

All this running around was making Alma feel quite dizzy and ill. She decided to revert to her earlier tack.

"I know who did it – his son," she said, cruelly and stupidly implicating Rattenbury's older son, Frank, who, of course, was thousands of miles away in Victoria, British Columbia.

Much to Bagwell's relief, his superior officer and Dr. O'Donnell returned just then. As they got into the police car outside the clinic, they noted Stoner, fast asleep, behind the wheel of Ratz's car, waiting to drive the surgeon home when he was done.

As Mills and O'Donnell entered the Villa Madeira, both men were taken aback. Almost every light in the house was on and music was blaring from the gramophone. Irene had wisely sought refuge in her bedroom upstairs. Both Alma and Bagwell, however, remained on the first floor and looked considerably the worse for what they'd been through together since Mills and the doctor had been gone.

O'Donnell went directly to Alma. He opened his black bag, spoke quietly to the woman who responded by suddenly sitting on the nearby chesterfield. There, with wildly dilated pupils, she watched in detached awe as the man introduced a half grain of morphine into her body by inoculation. Seconds later, Mills and O'Donnell carried the semi-conscious woman upstairs to bed. They were surprised to find little John still fast asleep in his bed in the corner of Alma's bedroom.

"Mine never slept like that!" Mills commented before leaving the doctor with Alma.

Dr. O'Donnell nodded.

"I should check on Bagwell. He didn't look to be in a very good way himself," the Inspector continued.

O'Donnell looked up from his patient and shot Mills a knowing smile.

"No, he certainly didn't," the doctor agreed.

Mills' concerns were considerate but unnecessary. Bagwell's training and experience as a policeman had begun to surface again as he watched Alma being carried from the room. By the time his superior officer came back downstairs he had fully recovered from his encounter with Alma's drunken nymphomania.

Ratz had not regained consciousness yet but he was, at least, still alive. The surgeon, Rooke, had done all he could for the man, for the time being. Stoner drove the doctor home and then drove back to the Villa Madeira. There was little else he could do, considering it was still the middle of the night. He could hardly go to his grandparents' home. He'd waken them for sure and then there would be questions. Lots of them.

A couple of hours later, just before daybreak on Monday, March 24, 1935, a third policeman arrived at the Rattenbury's house. Detective Inspector Carter first questioned Stoner, who testified that he had not overheard a quarrel of any sort earlier in the evening and that he had never seen the mallet before.

Next, Carter was interested in Alma's version of the evening's events. He went up to her bedroom where the very drunk and drugged woman was attempting to regain consciousness. He called for a police matron to make coffee for Alma and help her wash and dress.

Amazingly, she appeared quite rational when Carter interrogated her.

"He dared me to kill him," she explained quietly. "He wanted to die. I picked up the mallet. He said, 'You have not guts enough to do it.' I then hit him with the mallet. I hid the mallet. I would have shot him if I'd had a gun."

Before she knew what was happening to her Detective Inspector Carter was whisking Alma off to the Bournemouth police station. She was charged with wounding her husband.

In response to the charges, a very subdued Alma replied, "That is right. I did it deliberately and would do it again."

Alma was then escorted to a cell where she was allowed to sleep off the depressants remaining in her system.

At the Villa, Stoner and Irene proceeded with their individual tasks as best they were able. It was Monday, so Irene got John ready for school and he had left the house without being aware that anything out of the ordinary had happened to his parents while he slept.

All morning the two did their best to ignore one another. Irene was dreadfully confused about how best to help her beloved Alma. She was sick with worry, of course, the poor dear woman was being treated like a common criminal when she'd done nothing wrong, but at least her affair with Stoner hadn't been uncovered yet.

Later in the day, partially confirming the reasons for his lack o. academic success as a child, Stoner commented to Irene that he'd bor- rowed the mallet from his grandparents'.

"Your finger prints will be on it, then," she pointed out to him.

"No they won't. I wore gloves," the slow-witted lad bragged.

The already fragile state of Alma's mental stability had been pushed over the edge by her confinement in jail. She began writing unintelligible and self-condemning letters to Stoner. In these she pledged her love for the boy, called him by terms of endearment and then signed them "Lozanne," a stage name she'd used years ago. Her postscript succeeded in adding an even more ghoulish quality to the notes. Here, as though an afterthought, she inquired as to the state of her husband's health and requested that Irene bring her some hairpins.

Alma did get the report she requested about Ratz, for he died the next day.

Upon hearing the news, Irene knew that Alma would now be charged with murder. She couldn't keep Stoner's confession to herself any longer. She called the police station and Detective Inspector Carter, now in charge of the case, came out to take her statement.

Stoner's self-protective qualities may have faltered under the stress of the last three days. Or he may simply have agreed with Irene that Alma could not be charged with a murder she did not commit. Either way, he did not protest when the authorities arrested him.

The police were in an unusual situation. Commonly, they would have been looking for the murder suspect. But in this case, two people were claiming to have swung the fatal blows. Technically, however, Alma had only pleaded guilty to wounding while Stoner's plea was registered after Rattenbury's death and so he was charged with murder.

The case was scheduled to be heard in London's Old Bailey courthouse on Monday, May 27, exactly two months after Rattenbury had died. Both Alma and Stoner were held in jail until the trial began.

Alma apparently spent much of her time writing letters to her friend and employee, Irene Riggs. In these long, rambling epistles, Alma fre- quently requested particular cosmetic supplies and as the trial date drew closer she enumerated what clothes and toiletries she'd need for her appearance before the judge. She signed all her letters, "Lozanne." The name may have served to remind her of happier times.

Word of the sensational case had shocked and titillated the entire south of England. Back in Canada, most particularly Victoria, Rattenbury's former colleagues reeled at the news. The gossip began immediately. Showing amazingly consistent predictive powers, everyone had "seen it coming." This didn't, however, dampen their interest in following the case. Ever sensitive to their readers' whims, the papers back in Victoria, British Columbia, covered the story in great detail.

All the rituals associated with British law were carefully adhered to as the case came to court. The most respected criminal magistrate of the time, Mr. Justice Richard Sommers Travers Christmas Humphreys, presided over the proceedings. In keeping with tradition, he entered the court room carrying a posy of flowers, a custom dating back years to the days when stench and fever permeated the courtrooms.

A Mr. T.J. O'Connor, K.C., had been appointed as Alma's lawyer and Mr. R.P.Croom-Johnson, K.C., served as Crown prosecutor. Stoner, however, had to select his counselor from those available through the Poor Prisoners' Defence Fund. The job fell to a man named Mr. J.D. Casswell, chosen from a pool of lawyers available to those with limited financial means, was not nearly as experienced or adept as his better-paid counterparts. Even after the sensational Rattenbury case, Casswell returned to his distinctly mediocre law career and in his years of retirement recorded his memoirs a book he called *A Lance For Liberty*. The titles he chose for the chapters in the book acknowledge his less than spectacular career.[15]

Stoner and Alma gave very different impressions during their turns in the witness box. Stoner, now exactly half way between his 18th and 19th birthdays, was uneducated and certainly not quick witted. He made a very nervous and uncomfortable witness. Irene Riggs' sworn statement of his admission of guilt served to stack the deck heavily against the lad.

Alma's presence on the witness stand, however, was completely different. She had spent many hours reclining in her cell mulling over her extensive and attractive wardrobe. After mentally rejecting several possible outfits, she asked the ever-faithful Irene to make sure certain dresses and suits were in good repair and then bring them to her. As a result, Alma, looked her best. She even sounded her best. Recalling her days on the stage, Alma kept her voice low and mellifluous.

The viewing areas in the courtroom were packed to capacity for the opening of the trial. As allusions to drug addiction, alcoholism and marital affairs spewed forth day after day, from witness after witness, the crowds increased until a standing-room-only situation had been reached. The press was having a field day. Canadian representatives had even been sent abroad to cover the trial.

Five days later on Friday, May 31, 1935, the jury retired from the courtroom at 2:48 p.m. to consider the evidence they'd heard throughout the week. At 3:35 p.m. they returned to their seats at right angles to Mr. Justice Humphreys. The foreman of the jury rose, holding a slip of paper in his hand.

Presently, the Clerk of the Court asked, "Are you agreed upon your verdict?"

"Yes, sir," was the reply.

"Do you find the prisoner, Alma Victoria Rattenbury, guilty or not guilty of murder?"

"Not guilty," the foreman replied.

"Do you find the prisoner, George Percy Stoner, guilty or not guilty of murder?"

Here the foreman paused for a moment. He was not used to the glare of publicity's spotlight being shone upon him and he was not enjoying it one bit.

"Guilty, but we should like to add a rider to that; we recommend him to mercy."

"Then you find Alma Victoria Rattenbury not guilty and you find George Percy Stoner guilty of murder, and that is the verdict of you all?" the clerk confirmed.

"Yes," the foreman assented and gratefully sat down.

Turning to a pale and shaking Stoner, the Clerk of the Court informed him, somewhat redundantly, he stood convicted of murder.

"Have you anything to say why the Court should not give you judgment of death, according to law?"

Stoner replied in a barely audible voice, "Nothing at all."

The trial of Rattenbury and Stoner was over and in all likelihood justice had been served. Alma was a free woman as she probably should have been. It is unlikely that Alma was capable either physically or mentally of issuing the blows that killed her husband. She simply wasn't strong enough to muster the power that had been behind the lethal swings. But perhaps more importantly, she was still genuinely fond of old Ratz.

In addition, Alma had been around long enough to realize that the arrangement, as it had stood before Ratz's death, was the most advantageous one for her. She was over 40 years of age and had two sons she was responsible for. As flighty as Alma could occasionally be, even she couldn't have deluded herself into thinking that running off and marrying an illiterate teenage hired hand would provide her with any sort of a life.

Stoner apparently didn't agree. He was jealous of any little kindness Alma showed to her husband and thought that if the older man were out of the way, he'd have no competition for Alma's time and affections.

Despite her love for Ratz, Alma was also deeply attached to Stoner and she nearly fainted in the courtroom when she heard the jury's verdict. She had to be helped out of the courtroom and the next day arrangements were made for Alma to be admitted to a nursing home while she recovered from her recent ordeal. Many feared that if she were allowed to return to the Villa Madeira she would become overwhelmed and attempt to kill herself. In the medical facility, she would not only be relieved of the responsibility of caring for herself, but she could be watched by medical personnel.

Alma's reaction to Stoner's conviction was interesting. All through the trial she had been content to let a poorly paid, court-hired solicitor defend her lover. Now that she had been cleared of any wrongdoing, Alma would see no expense spared that might save Stoner.

It is well that she felt this way, for the first trial had effectively used up the portion of the Poor Prisoners' Defence fund to which Stoner was entitled. Although an uncle of Stoner's offered to subsidize his nephew's legal fees, without a contribution from Alma it would have been difficult for him to have financed an appeal hearing.

On Tuesday, June 4, before any financial arrangements had been made for Stoner's new lawyer, Alma borrowed two pounds from an employee at the nursing home and walked out the front door. She was not seen again until 8:30 that evening, when William Mitchell,[16] a farmer from near Christchurch, spotted a woman sitting and smoking on the bank of the River Avon.

Mitchell paid close attention to Alma's every move, convinced that something very out of the ordinary was unfolding before his eyes. It was hard for him to imagine why a woman would be wandering there, alone, especially wearing a fur coat on a June evening.

As he watched, Mitchell's interest turned to horror. Alma calmly extinguished the cigarette she'd been smoking, and walked toward the river. She paused for a moment and withdrew a shiny, pointed metal object from her clothing. Mitchell, paralyzed by panic, watched as Alma plunged a knife into her left breast, over and over again.

As she collapsed into the fast running river, Mitchell ran to the spot where he'd last seen her. He picked up Alma's discarded fur coat and threw an end of it out to within her reach. A nonswimmer, there was little else the man could do. She held his gaze for a moment but made no move to grasp the hastily devised lifeline. Soon the dying woman was floating downstream surrounded by an orb of bloody water. Mitchell ran for help and Alma's lifeless body was pulled from the river minutes later.

And so, Alma Rattenbury died as dramatically as she had lived. An inquest confirmed that she had managed to inflict a total of six knife wounds into her own chest. Three of those had pierced her heart. Understandably, this medical fact renewed rumors of Alma's cocaine addiction.

Her funeral would have pleased the woman no end. Thousands attended, drawn, no doubt, by morbid fascination. Both Stoner and Irene Riggs were inconsolable. On a particularly macabre note, a man circulated among the mourners, gathering signatures for a petition to reprieve Stoner.

Once he'd recuperated from the shock of his lover's death, Stoner developed a very different story of the events at the Villa Madeira that fateful night of March 24, 1935. He claimed that he had brought the murder weapon from his grandparents' house for innocent reasons and that Alma had found it outside and had used it to kill her husband.

His re-trial began on June 18, 1935. A week later, George Percy Stoner was sentenced to prison for seven years for his part in the murder of his lover's husband, Francis Mawson Rattenbury.

And so the love story that began in 1923 at Victoria, British Columbia, ended 12 years later at Bournemouth, England, as a double tragedy.

## Endnotes

[1] *Rattenbury*, Terry Reksten, Sono Nis Press, Victoria, British Columbia, 1978, page 144.

[2] *Rattenbury*, page 90

[3] *Rattenbury*, page 46

[4] *Rattenbury*, page 119

[5] No proof was ever found, however, rumors of Alma's drug addiction persisted throughout her life and, indeed, the possibility does exist. Many First World War veterans returned home with cocaine addictions. In that era the addictive properties of the drug were not understood, but it was known to increase alertness and enhance the ability to work the long hours that were required under those circumstances.

[6] *Murder at the Villa Madeira*, Sir David Napley, Weidenfeld and Nicolson, London, England, 1988, page 16, and *The Trial of Alma Victoria Rattenbury and George Percy Stoner*, F. Tennyson Jesse, Editor, William Hodge and Company, London, England, page 5, and *Rattenbury*, page 145.

[7] *The Trial of Alma Victoria Rattenbury and George Percy Stoner*, page 5.

[8] *Murder at the Villa Madeira*, page 27.

[9] Ibid., page 35.

[10] *The Trial of Alma Victoria Rattenbury and George Percy Stoner*, page 11.

[11] *Rattenbury*, page 142.

[12] Ibid., page 149.

[13] *The Trial of Alma Victoria Rattenbury and George Percy Stoner*, page 22.

[14] *Rattenbury*, page 155 – the quotation is given here as, "I know who done it." In *The Trial of Alma Victoria Rattenbury and George Percy Stoner*, page 52 – the quotation is given as "I know who did it."

[15] *Murder at the Villa Madeira*, page 87.

[16] Ibid., page 209.

# John
## & Mildred Ware

"John Ware the Negro Cowboy." That's how history has recorded one of its most colorful characters. While the designation sounds offensive and racist today, it is undoubtedly easier on present-day ears than the moniker the man lived with – "Nigger John."

Of course, like any story, this one must be viewed in context and at the turn of the century in the Canadian west, nothing derogatory was intended by the use of those appellations. As a matter of fact, if anyone ever made a disparaging remark about John Ware, it has not been noted. To have known the man, it seems, was to admire him.

Over the years, John Ware has become a legend of the Canadian west. And like all legends, it's difficult, by now, to separate facts from embellishment.

In their December 23, 1903, issue, *The Farmers Advocate* carried an amazingly detailed account of John Ware's life. Whether or not it is accurate is anyone's guess. That writer would, at least theoretically, have had the advantage of interviewing Ware. And he may have. The information given may be correct. If it is, then it is strange that no wordsmith who came after the nameless *Advocate* writer ever chose to repeat the facts in their own work.[1]

Even the most basic statistics about John Ware are unknown. Where was he from? Georgetown, South Carolina and Fort Worth, Texas, have both been put forward as Ware's possible birth place. That article in *The Farmers Advocate* has him born in Alabama.[2] It is also, of course, possible that none of the above is correct.

Was he born into slavery? He may have been, but because his birth date and place aren't known we can't be sure. Abraham Lincoln abolished slavery in 1865, so Ware would probably have been in his late teens or early 20s at that time, but depending on where he was, the man may or may not have been a slave. If he was from Texas, then it's unlikely he was ever a slave, because slavery was not widely practised in that state. If, in fact, Alabama was his American home, then he most surely was a white man's possession for his childhood and youth. As Ware's birth, like thousands of other African-Americans born in the 1800s, was not deemed to be of enough importance to have been recorded, we'll never know.[3]

And what of Mildred Ware, John's adored wife? We know a little more about her, but still there are uncertainties. All historians appear to agree that she came with her parents from Ontario. Her father, Daniel Lewis, was a carpenter who moved his family to Calgary about 1890. His eldest child, daughter Mildred, was in her teens at the time.

But from where in Southern Ontario did the Lewises hail? Some say Toronto and some say Whitby. Still other sources specify Chatham, which was a northern terminus for the underground railway and there-fore, indeed, a possibility.[4] It is also possible that that assumption was covertly racist. Because the Lewis family was black and from Ontario, it might have been presumed that Chatham was the only place they could have been from.

Fortunately, what is unknown is of little importance to the essence of this story. History may not have been scrupulous in its record keeping, but it has left us a wonderful love story.

Whatever John Ware's background, he'd evidently spent a great deal of time around horses. It was natural, then, that as a young man striking out, he gravitated to the career of "cowboy." Whether or not Ware was an oddity as a black cowboy is another matter left fuzzy by the passage of years. Some say most cow hands were black, hence the origin of the somewhat disparaging term "cow*boy*." Others maintain that a black man riding with a herd was most unusual. Either way, around 1865, when he was about 20 years of age, John Ware joined a cattle drive north to Montana.

His employer must have thought he'd found the perfect cow hand. Ware was a big man, standing 6'3" and weighing over 200 pounds. He was as strong as an ox, well used to hard work and reportedly afraid of nothing except snakes and lightning. He was a quiet man who may have spoken with a speech impediment. John Ware could neither read nor write.

In accounts of his life, historians, with annoying frequency, have Ware "drifting" from place to place. Did the man really arrive at any given place more by accident than choice?[5] It's possible, of course, but it is also very likely that any young black man would have moved as far away from the southern States with as much purpose and speed as he could muster.

Whether he "drifted" or purposefully fled, by 1882 John Ware had seen the foothills of the Canadian Rockies.[6] The splendor of the geography and the opportunities to ranch convinced him his travels were over. He'd fallen in love with the enormous, rugged landscape.

"This is where I want to spend the rest of my days," he decided with deep contentment.

Ware immediately made himself part of the community around High River, Alberta (40 miles southwest of Calgary). His skills as a cowhand were soon recognized and admired by those who knew how to judge such qualities.

The *Calgary Tribune* carried the following report about a roping contest in the area. "John Weir [sic] . . . was fortunate . . . in catching his animal . . . the time was so short that the spectators were hardly aware it had been done."[7]

In the spring of 1890, as tiny crocuses poked their mauve heads out from the newly thawed prairie soil, John Ware made an important decision.

"I'm going to buy me a place of my own," he announced to his employer, a ranch owner named Duncan McPherson.

"John, you can't do that," the shocked man replied. "I'll never manage without you."

John laughed quietly and assured the man, "I won't be ready to stock a ranch of my own for another season at least, boss. You'll have lots of time to pick another foreman from the boys you got here. Besides, we'll still be neighbors. The place I have my eye on is just over there by Sheep Creek."

That news was a great relief to McPherson. He'd come to value the huge, hardworking young man as a friend as well as an employee.

"Next thing I know you'll be telling me you're going to get hitched, John!" The older man teased good-naturedly.

"I doubt that, sir. There's no one around here for me. I needs to find a colored girl if I'm gonna get married. And there just ain't no other coloreds around these parts."

There was no denying the truth of what John Ware told his employer that day. Black settlers in central Alberta were a rarity. Further north there were black settlements. Pine Creek (re-named Amber Valley in the 1940s, now a ghost town) had been flourishing for years and even the black community at Wildwood was prospering by now.

But John's life did not include trips away from the foothills area around Calgary and he may not even have been aware that a cache of eligible black girls existed only a few hundred miles away. Besides, John already had more in his life than he'd ever expected to and he was more than satisfied with his lot.

His friends, however, did not share their friend's contentment. They liked and admired Ware and felt he deserved to have a home life, too. They agreed, however, that he must marry within his race and no one's intentions could simply make a marriageable, young black woman suddenly appear in the area. Still, all who knew Mr. John Ware kept their eyes open for a suitable Mrs. John Ware.

About this time, Daniel and Charlotte Lewis, accompanied by their children, began their trek from Ontario to the west. They settled at Shepard, on the outskirts of Calgary, where Dan Lewis took up his trade as a finishing carpenter. He specialized in building ornate staircases. These had recently become a fashion focal point and an important status symbol in the homes of many wealthy ranchers.

Charlotte Lewis kept the family home and tended to an ever-increasing number of little ones. Her elder daughter, Mildred, a girl of 19, helped out where she could.

On Saturdays, the family made its way into town to shop for the provisions which they weren't able to grow or make themselves. Here Dan Lewis occasionally met some of the men he'd seen around the palatial homes where he worked through the week. Before long the men's tongues were wagging and plans were afoot to have John Ware and Mildred Lewis meet.

The eventual plot was long on good intentions but decidedly short on camouflage. A man named J.J. Barter, owner of Calgary's splendid new Alberta Hotel, and one of the many who were in on the scheme to introduce the two young people, called out to John one day when he saw the big man in town.

Barter was familiar with the Lewis family's Saturday routine by now. He knew that by early afternoon, they would be stopping at the shops along Stephen Avenue.

"John," Barter hailed. "Will you be back in town next weekend?"

"I figure so," the new ranch owner replied. "Seems I need supplies almost every week these days. I'm building myself a bit of a cabin out there on my land."

Barter and McPherson and the others involved in the plan to get "Nigger John" married off must have chuckled at the timing of the Lewises' arrival in the area and John's home construction. Both occurred in the early summer of 1890. Now, all that was left to them was to assure that the two young people actually met. Fate had taken care of the rest.

"Good, John, I'm glad to hear that. Drop in and see me at the hotel when you're here. I want to wander over to the store with you."

"Shore, J.J.," Ware confirmed before making his way back to his tethered horse a few blocks up the dusty street.

The following week all went as well as the cowboy-cupids had planned. In the dimly lit I.C. Baker store, John Ware first cast his eyes on his future wife. Never a great man with words, Ware was reportedly struck dumb at the sight of this teenage beauty. She was as shy as he and neither spoke a word. Fortunately, Charlotte Lewis, Mildred's mother, knew what needed to be said and she wasted no time saying it.

"Hello, Mr. Ware," she responded formally to their introduction. "We're indeed happy to meet you."

John merely nodded.

"Would you care to join our family for a meal sometime? Perhaps a week next Sunday?"

Still awestruck by the beautiful young woman standing at her mother's side, just inches beyond his reach, John Ware was again only able to nod. Mrs. Lewis, however, took this gesture as an acceptance of her offer of hospitality.

"Good. We'll look for you that afternoon, then," she confirmed. "And now I must bid you goodbye. We need to be finished here and back out in Shepard in time to tend to the chickens."

John Ware remained silent. It took all the self-discipline he could muster to manage to nod at the kindly woman for a third time. Watching John staring at Mildred as she and her mother left the store, the matchmakers knew they'd done their job.

John thought of little else for the next 10 days. Then, when the date for his dinner invitation drew nearer, he began to wonder whether the whole thing wasn't just a dream. Perhaps he just imagined it. What if he got all the way to the Lewises' homestead at Shepard and found they weren't expecting him. When he thought back to his glimpses of Mildred's exquisite face and lovely dark eyes, he wondered if the meeting had been real or if his mind was merely playing tricks on him. He'd just stay home on Sunday. It was better than risking making a fool of himself.

Content with his decision, John set about his Friday night routine, in preparation for another trip into town the next morning. He needed more spikes by now. Construction on his simple cabin was nearly complete and to John Ware's eyes the rough dwelling was a truly magnificent sight.

Picking the needed hardware out of a barrel, Ware found himself standing next to Dan Lewis.

"Greetings, my friend," the older man said, offering his large, rough hand for John to shake. "It's because of you, my boy, that it's just the young lad, Spencer, here, and me in town today. The women are back at home cooking up a storm. I can guarantee you won't leave our place hungry tomorrow, John!"

A thousand thoughts flooded Ware's mind.

"See you tomorrow, John," Dan Lewis called as he paid for his purchases and left the store.

John had still not moved from in front of the barrel, his hand hovering above the required spikes.

"You nearly through there, young fella?" A voice behind John inquired, breaking his reverie.

"Shore, shore I am," Ware replied, leaving the store and then the town, without accomplishing his original purpose.

John Ware arrived at the Lewises' home nervous and excited. How would he ever be able to eat, he wondered. He was sure he'd be far too anxious, but Mr. & Mrs. Lewis anticipated that reaction and were prepared to put John at his ease. For one thing, they had invited another couple, the Hansons, to join them for dinner and so the already boisterous household was a veritable flurry of activity. John was far from the center of attention that he'd dreaded being and before long everyone in the house was thoroughly enjoying everyone else's company.

After a delicious meal, Dan Lewis suggested that his guests might enjoy a ride in the democrat. Jim Hanson and his wife took the back seat, leaving John to drive with Mildred perched prettily beside him. With warnings not to stay out too long, that the sky looked like rain, the four headed out happily for a late Sunday afternoon drive.

The warm and friendly atmosphere that had pervaded the Lewis' home extended itself to the outing and the foursome laughed and chattered as they bumped along in Dan Lewis's democrat, powered by two of McPherson's horses, which John had borrowed for the day.

The time passed quickly and the miles with it. Before they knew it the Hansons, Mildred Lewis and John Ware were a long way from Daniel Lewis's homestead. The sky had begun to darken ominously.

"We'd better head back quickly," John announced, seeing the threatening clouds rolling across the prairie.

He no sooner got the wagon turned around when the rain started. It pelted down ferociously.

"Wrap yourself in this," John told Mildred as he took off his heavy coat and handed it to her.

The Hansons, meanwhile, had fashioned a tent of sorts from a tarpaulin under their seat.

"I'm going to have to push these horses as hard as I can. We got to out run this storm," John called as loudly over the noise of the rain. Although he had a voice as big as his body, most of the sound, this time, was lost in torrential downpour.

Seconds later a sword of lightning lit up the sky and a clap of thunder shook the wagon. There was little in this life that badly frightened John Ware. Snakes certainly did – snakes and an electrical storms terrified the otherwise courageous man. He couldn't let his fear get the best of him here, though; he'd have to fight his natural inclination because people had put their faith in him. Duncan McPherson had trusted him with his horses, the Hanson's with their safety and comfort and Dan Lewis with his democrat and most importantly his daughter. John had to get the group back to the homestead.

Standing now and driving the horses as hard as he could, John focused everything he had on reaching their destination safely. He was making good progress when a second crack of thunder sounded from the heavens and lightning eerily lit up the entire sky for measurable seconds. The wagon shook as the ground beneath it received the power of the electrical current. Then the wagon lurched and stopped with a tremendous jolt.

Badly frightened, shaken and bruised, the four stared in disbelief at the ground in front of them. The lightning bolt had hit the horses and the poor animals, still tethered to their harnesses, now lay dead.

Later they all agreed it was a miracle that no one was thrown to the ground, but for now they had to find a solution. The bald-headed prairie was a dangerous place to be in any kind of severe weather. There was no shelter for as far as the eye could see, and the storm that killed the horses was worsening.

John jumped down and unhitched the carcasses from the wagon. Using every bit of strength he could summon, he freed the harnesses from the corpses and turned the wagon around. Then, at a trot, he began to pull the democrat. With the three riders huddled together on the floor of the wagon, John hauled his responsibilities away from the danger.

Charlotte Lewis stood at the door of her house scanning the horizon for any signs of her guests and, even more importantly, her beloved daughter, Mildred. Despite her protestations, Dan was saddling up to go looking for the missing group. She feared within minutes she'd have lost all of them to the ferocious prairie storm.

Then something on the horizon caught her eye. She tried to call to her husband, but he didn't hear her over the noise of the storm. What was that, she wondered, straining to identify the approaching figures. Seconds later her husband looked up and must also have seen the outline on the horizon, for he rode directly to it.

Even when Dan Lewis came close enough to clearly make it out, he could scarcely believe his eyes. The form that Charlotte had seen approaching from a distance was, in fact, their family's democrat, but the horses were gone. Only John Ware's enormous strength powered the wagon. He'd pulled the cart, with three people in it, through the storm, across deepening mud and back to safety.

Everyone hurried inside amid confirmations of being either, "all right" or "fine." Once they were bundled in warm blankets and sitting in front of the roaring fire Dan had stoked in the stove, the whole story came out.

Charlotte Lewis listened to the tale of adventure with ever so slightly mixed emotions. She was deeply grateful that these dear people hadn't been hurt, but still, she knew this trip marked, at least partly, the loss of her elder daughter. Mildred's mother watched the young woman's face as she recounted her part of the episode and she watched the girl's eyes as John recounted his. With resignation, Charlotte accepted the inevitable

– she had effectively lost at least a part of her daughter, the girl's heart, to the storm.

The courtship which began in that storm continued for a year and a half. On February 29, 1882, John Ware and Mildred Lewis became man and wife. On Wednesday, March 2, 1892, the joyous occasion was noted in the *Calgary Tribune*.

### Orange Blossoms

Very many of our readers will join with us in wishing Mr. John Ware and bride, who were married Tuesday [probably should read Monday] morning. All happiness and prosperity in their new sphere of life. The ceremony was performed by the Rev. Mr. Cross, pastor of the Baptist Church at the residence of the bride's parents [in] Calgary. The bride is of a happy disposition, well cultured and accomplished, and probably no man in the district has a greater number of warm personal friends than the groom, Mr. John Ware. The *Tribune* extends heartiest congratulations.

With those kind words, the newlyweds set out on their lives together. John's cabin was rough, but adequate. He had hewn a few pieces of furniture in anticipation of Mildred's arrival, but the bulk of his efforts had gone to establishing his ranch as a viable enterprise. His herd of cattle, marked with the distinctive 9999, was increasing and that was vastly more important, in anyone's estimation, than store-bought luxuries for a house.

*John and Mildred Ware and family. (Glenbow Archives, #NA-263-1)*

How John came to use his unique four 9 brand is another matter for speculation. One theory holds that he was nine years old when slavery was abolished, but many years later Bob Ware, John's younger son, explained that he doubted the likelihood of that story. For one thing, Bob wasn't convinced that his father had ever been a slave. Another story suggests that John's first child, a daughter, Janet, was born on March 9 and that's why he adopted the symbol. Although it's undeniably a great story, that version doesn't hold water either, because he used the brand years before Janet was born. The simple truth is that no one knows why the man chose the brand he did.

A matter with no confusion surrounding it was Mildred Ware's attitude to ranch life. She tolerated it only out of love for John. Married to one of the finest horsemen in the country, Mildred would never get on even the tamest foal. She hated cattle too, although, of necessity, she did learn to milk the cows.

Despite these great differences in interests and preferences, John and Mildred's relationship blossomed. Just over a year after they were married, the Wares presented Amanda Janet Ware to the world. "Nettie" as she was soon nicknamed, single-handedly reduced her father, John Ware, the formidable horseman, to emotional jelly.

The family continued to grow and prosper. On September 11, 1898, twins William and Mildred were born, followed by Bob and later Arthur. The last child was named Daniel, after his maternal grandfather. Little Daniel was a sickly child, however, and didn't survive past infancy.

Spring weather in the Canadian west has only one predictable quality to it. You can absolutely count on it being unpredictable. Even the May snowstorms don't always hit and if they do, some years their devastation is worse than others.

In May of 1903, however, few people in cow country had their minds on the weather. Most people's attention was on another force of nature — that which had caused an enormous piece of Turtle Mountain to crack off and thunder lethally down on the sleeping town of Frank, some 400 miles to the south and west of Calgary. By May 16, rescuers had done all they could for the town which lay buried under tons and tons of rock. Salvage and rebuilding operations were underway by those who had survived the devastating Frank Slide, in the Crowsnest Pass. Against this background, it's no wonder that few people, in what would soon become Alberta, took much notice when it began to rain.

John Ware certainly didn't. As all the ranchers did, he had felt shock verging on disbelief when he heard that almost an entire town full of healthy, productive people had been buried. But, for the most part, his mind was on other matters. His dear Mildred wasn't well. Hadn't been since the last baby had been born the year before. To make matters worse, the child himself was a sickly baby. It seemed Daniel was never long without some sort of a sickness or another.

John hated to leave Mildred alone with the children when she was feeling so poorly, so he waited an extra day to see if she would rally at all. She didn't, poor woman. It seemed to him that she was weaker at the end of the day than she'd been in the morning. He felt he had no choice.

He had to get to Calgary and buy the medicine the doctor said Mildred needed.

As he mounted his horse and left their cabin, John knew he'd have to hurry. Mildred wasn't even able to get out of bed by herself and even though Nettie was a responsible little thing and a big help to her mother, she was only five years old. The child would have her hands full just looking after the twins, Bob and Arthur, to say nothing of Mildred and poor ailing Daniel. But John had no choice. He had to get the medicine Mildred needed or she'd be weak and in bed even longer.

John rode through the pelting rain as fast as he dared. There was no point in trying to go too fast. Haste would only lead to an accident. He couldn't risk having his firm-footed animal losing its footing in the deepening muck. And so, trying to be satisfied with the pace he and the horse set, John headed toward the town of Brooks. From there he would leave his horse in the livery stable and take the train to Calgary. If all went well he'd make it home around midnight.

And all had to go well. He couldn't bear to look up at the sky. The clouds were darkening and the prairie air smelled suspiciously of snow. Convinced that he had no choice but to carry on no matter what weather developed, John tried to avoid even a quick, disheartening glance at the threatening horizon.

The clapboard buildings of Brooks were a welcome sight to both rider and horse. The trip had taken considerably longer than it usually did and so John just had time to leave the animal's reins in the liveryman's hands before running for the last train of the day to Calgary.

By the time he'd boarded the train, there was no need to avoid searching the sky for clues to approaching weather. The blizzard had already started to whirl ferociously. For the time being, though, John was as comfortable as he was going to be for the next few hours. The bench seat offered no padding, but at least his long Prince Albert coat provided something of a cushion. The trainman stoked the car's welcoming fire in the wood stove and Ware was, at least temporarily, out of the direct force of the storm.

The wind and snow heightened as the train approached Calgary. John knew that wasn't good news. It meant the weather was moving from the west and by the time he finished his emergency round trip, he'd be in the centre of it.

John was ready to get off the train fully five minutes before it began to slow. He knew he'd have to hurry. The chemist would need time to make up the suspension for Mildred and the last train back to Brooks left the city station just after 10 o'clock each night.

Calgary's streets were nearly deserted when he arrived. Everyone who could had already made it to the safety of their homes. The drugstore's door was locked for the night, but John knew that wasn't a problem. He climbed the stairs at the side of the building and knocked at the druggist's door.

"Lord help us, John!" the man exclaimed. "Whatever brings you such a distance in a storm like this?"

"It's Mildred, sir. She's poorly. The doc says she needs more of that medicine. Can you make me up some? Will it take long?"

The words tumbled out one after another. Had the pharmacist not known John Ware, he might have doubted the man's sobriety. As it was, the drugstore owner understood the big man's near panic.

"Come on downstairs with me, John. You'll be back on the station platform before you know it," he confirmed reassuringly.

Less than 20 minutes later John once again boarded a train. This time it was heading toward home and he had the medicine for Mildred. His journey was half over now, John thought optimistically.

With the brown bottle of vile smelling liquid safely in an inside pocket, John stared fruitlessly out the train window. It was dark outside. Even if it had been broad daylight, though, he could only have seen a reflection - the reflection of a curtain of snow.

Once again John was ready to leave the train long before it pulled into the station. He stood impatiently by the warmth of the stove as the train slowed. He watched and listened as the conductor came through the car with an announcement. Apparently the engineer had decided that he couldn't go any further than the Brooks' station tonight.

"The wind's blowing the snow around so bad he can't even see the tracks in front of him. It's just too dangerous to continue. Even people's cattle's being blown around. There's lots of 'em up against fences near the tracks and he just can't take the chance of going on. There's a stopping house in Brooks that'll put us up for the night and we'll make our way, the rest of the way in the morning when the storm's cleared," the conductor informed his passengers.

To John, of course, the news was neither here nor there. Brooks was as far as he could have gone by train, anyway. From here he'd have to pick up his horse and ride the rest of the way.

John made his way toward the stable from memory. The tiny white granules of snow obliterated everything and stung the man as he strained to search out the stable. Much to his relief he finally spotted a light, just to the left of where he estimated the horse stable was. Dimly at first, and then a little more clearly, John was able to make out a lamp burning at the side of the building. It was the owner's quarters.

Banging on the door and shouting against the force of the wind, John made his presence known. The stable keeper looked incredulous when he opened the door and saw the huge black man, already covered with snow, standing before him.

"Come in, come in," the man shouted and John did as he was instructed. "You'll have to bunk in with me here tonight, I'm afraid, John. There's no way your horse would make it through this blizzard. This must be one of the killer storms you sometimes hear the old-timers talk about. I'll tell you boy, mother nature must sure be mad at us for something. First Turtle Mountain and now this."

John stood as politely as he could and listened to the man.

"I can't stay here tonight, sir, although I do deeply 'preciate the invitation. I gotta get home to my Mildred and the children. They need me and I got Mildred's medicine right here too and she needs that," John explained.

"You're telling me you're going to try to ride through this blizzard? You'll never make it, my boy. You'll be doing Mildred no favor by even trying. What good is a dead husband on a dead horse?"

"We'll get through, me and my horse. We have to," John said simply.

"You've parted company with your senses, young man, but I'll open up the stable for you anyway. I won't lock it up again, though, you'll be back in a few minutes."

John didn't waste any additional energy arguing with the man, he merely followed him to where his horse was, thanked the barn's owner, mounted his horse and turned the animal in the direction of home.

For the first time in his life, John Ware wasn't able to get a horse to do what he wanted it to do. No matter how he prodded and yelled the steed would not take more than a few steps before trying to turn around and head back to the warmth of the stall. The animal had no blinders on and the snow and the wind were stinging its eyes mercilessly. Before long John knew it was hopeless to keep trying. The liveryman was right. No one could expect a horse to get through this storm. The next time the mount tried to turn back, John Ware let him.

The barn door was unlatched as the owner had said it would be. John walked the cold and badly frightened animal back to its stall.

"Glad to see you back," the man called. "I figured even someone as stubborn as you would catch on eventually. There's no way you can ride home through this snow."

"You're right, sir. The horse just wouldn't move. I'll have to come back for him when the wind lets up," John answered before turning his coat collar up to cover his face.

The liveryman didn't understand the implication of Ware's words until he was out of sight. John Ware was setting out in a blizzard the likes of which had rarely been seen – he was going to walk the 14 miles from town to his homestead.

Mildred was frantic. Had she not known her husband so well, she mightn't have been worried at all. She might have presumed that he'd have been sensible and not tried to make his way through the weather – at least not until morning. But Mildred knew, as she lay there in her bed, listening to the wind howling, that John was out there, fighting to find his way home to her and the children.

From inside all that could be heard was the sound of the children's even, regular breathing, deep in innocent and unaware slumber. Mildred tried to concentrate on the rhythm of the children's breath. She tried to hear it so clearly that it would block out the horror of the wind sounds, for Mildred Lewis Ware knew her husband was out there somewhere and there was nothing she could do to help him.

John trudged on, one heavy footstep after another. His face and hands and feet were, thankfully, numb by now. Well beyond hurting. There was no turning back. There never had been. John had to get to Mildred. Her life depended on him. There was no decision to be made. He merely had to do it.

For miles and hours he pushed on blindly. Nothing existed except him and the harshly stinging snow, first assaulting his face and then piling up at his feet. His mind was blissfully blank. If he'd realized the situation he was in, even John Ware might have panicked. One moment's hesitation out there in the middle of nothing but a prairie blizzard would have brought sure death.

The emptiness of the world had become all encompassing, both in time and in space. He would walk forever through this endless snow, he was sure. Then, without warning, his foot hit against something solid. The jolt threw him off balance and he fell forward. Instinctively holding out his frozen hand to cushion his fall, John didn't feel the wire fence rip into his flesh. He only knew his heavy woolen mitt was torn and that he had fallen, but not to the ground.

Groping under the snow to help himself up, John discovered what it was he'd fallen against. It was a cow. Dead, poor thing, blinded by the snow and driven into a fence by the wind. Now it lay, frozen to death in its tracks. The discovery jarred John terribly. By now he had few defenses that the cattle did not. Thankfully, one of those was the ability to reason.

Talking to the huge corpse all the while, John hurriedly wiped snow from its carcass until he could find the brand.

"It's a sign from God," he told himself for he'd recognized the brand. The cow belonged to his neighbor. He wasn't far from home now. If he could just follow the fence line he should be able to see his own place in no time.

Checking to see that no harm had come to Mildred's medicine in his fall, John set out again. Not many minutes later he thought he saw a light off in the distance. It couldn't be, could it? On and on he trudged, by now so worn that he stumbled and fell with almost every step.

In his badly stressed mind, the man could already feel the warmth of his cabin. But that warmth would be nothing compared to the warmth of holding Mildred next to him, once again. He was almost upon it before he could make out the silhouette of the small dwelling. No sooner did the outline become clear but he thought he spotted Mildred at one of the windows. Of course, that must be an illusion, John realized. He knew she was far too sick to have gotten out of bed without assistance.

But he was wrong. As soon as he laid his frozen and badly cut hand on the door knob, it turned, seemingly of its own accord. There on the other side of the door, was the loveliest sight John Ware had ever seen. His Mildred. She and John were reunited, seven hours after he left his horse behind in Brooks.

If the story of John and Mildred Ware had been a work of fiction, it would end here, with everyone's future happiness assured. The children would grow up strong and healthy and John and Mildred would live well into their old age while enjoying legions of grandchildren. Real life, however, rarely works out nearly that well.

Mildred's recovery from her sickness, thanks to the medicine John risked his life to bring her, was probably as close to fiction-perfect as life ever gets. Sadly, from there the storybook quality of this love story ends.

Little Daniel, weak from birth, never did develop enough strength to live. He died in the first weeks of 1905, before his third birthday. Mildred, who had never fully regained her strength after Daniel's birth, became seriously ill again that spring. John called for his mother-in-law to come and stay with the remaining children. He needed to take Mildred to Holy Cross hospital in Calgary. Within weeks, Mildred Ware succumbed to typhoid and pneumonia.

John was devastated. Mildred's parents now lived in Blairmore, in the Crowsnest Pass near Frank, Alberta, and Grandmother Lewis needed to get back there. She still had youngsters of her own. But John could not even begin to think of caring for his children himself. Even under the best of circumstances, that would have been a challenge for the kindly rancher. And these were certainly not the best of times. He was in deep mourning, virtually incapacitated by his grief. He could barely care for himself, his livestock and his land, let alone cope with the responsibility of the five surviving children.

There seemed no alternative. John Ware packed his children off on the train back to Blairmore, with his mother-in-law. Once again, the cabin was as empty as it had been 15 years ago when he first built it.

John struggled on through the balance of the spring, but by summer the loneliness was unbearable. He took the train to Blairmore himself. After visiting with his children and reassuring himself that they were all right, John returned to the cabin near Brooks. But he brought Bob, the youngest boy, with him.

The child's company helped ease John's pain. The little boy went everywhere with his father. On September 11, 1905, Bob happily trailed along on foot as his father rode out to tend to the herd. From a distance, the little boy watched in horror as the horse his father was riding, the gentlest one the Wares owned, one that Bob's sisters used to ride, tripped in a badger hole and fell forward.

As though in suspended animation, Bob watched his father, widely reputed to be able to ride any horse alive, fall from this gentle one. The huge man struck his head on the nag's saddle and died instantly.

As bad news will, word of the tragedy spread quickly. The unthinkable had happened. John Ware was dead, killed by a fall from a horse.

For those who had not heard, by word of mouth, the *Calgary Daily Herald* carried the following report:

**John Ware Killed**

Well Known Colored Rancher Meets Sudden Death

Brooks, N.W.T., Sept. 12 – John Ware, commonly called "Nigger John," an ex-slave from the south and for twenty-five years a rancher and cow hand in the west, owner of a thousand head of finest range cattle on the Red Deer river, was killed today by a horse stumbling and falling upon him, killing him instantly. Deceased was 60 years old and leaves a family.[8]

The funeral service was held at the Baptist Church in Calgary. "It was the biggest [funeral] seen in Calgary up to that time. . . . hours before the service, wagons, buggies, democrats and saddle horses were converging upon the city, bearing men and women in whose hearts pride in knowing John Ware now mingled with sadness."[9]

Daniel and Charlotte Lewis took in the newly orphaned Ware children.

"After the sale [of the Ware's ranch] Grandma took us to live with her at Blairmore. She was the most kind-hearted person in the world. She raised eight children of her own so five orphans must have been an added burden but she and grandpa made us feel welcome and loved," Janet Ware recalled.[10]

❦  ❦  ❦

"Us Wares just aren't the marrying kind, I guess. My one brother, Robert, was married, but he lost his wife and they had no children," Janet Ware explained to a newspaper reporter in the summer of 1967.[11]

When Janet was asked why she'd never married, she bluntly informed the interviewer that she'd never met a man she could respect the way she respected her father, the legendary John Ware.

At the time of his death, records indicate that John Ware was a credibly wealthy man. He owned a large ranch, nearly 1000 head of cattle and 100 horses. Whether or not he was born a slave, Ware did start with nothing but determination and enthusiasm. He succeeded, unquestionably.

It is interesting that at the time of his death, the number of livestock John Ware owned was officially recorded and yet his own birth never was.

All the Ware children are deceased now, leaving no descendants. The name John Ware is still held in high esteem in Canada's ranch country. Ware's grave is highlighted in a booklet about famous people buried in Calgary's Union Cemetery, a building on the Southern Alberta Institute of Technology is named for him, books have been written about his life, the Wares' cabin has been preserved in a provincial park and a movie tentatively named *John Ware the High Rider* was planned in the mid-1980s.

It is only fitting that these tributes be paid to a Canadian pioneer. Sad though, that the strength of the love between these two is an aspect of the legend which is rarely re-told.

## *Endnotes*

[1]*Farmers Advocate*, December 21, 1903.

[2]*Farmers Advocate*, December 21, 1903, *Alberta Report*, January 23, 1984 and the *Calgary Herald*, July 23, 1960.

[3]*John Ware's Cow Country*, Grant MacEwan, Western Producer Prairie Books, 1973, page 2.

[4]Ibid., says Toronto, page 130; unpublished document from the Glenbow Archives, Calgary, written in August, 1956, specifies Whitby, Ontario; *Western Producer Magazine*, April 22, 1954 and *Calgary Herald*, March 9, 1955.

[5]*Calgary Herald*, March 9, 1955, *Farmers Advocate*, December, 21 1903, unpublished, undated, document from the Glenbow Museum and Archives written by Slim Marsden of Vulcan, Alberta.

[6]*John Ware's Cow Country*, page 25.

[7]*Calgary Tribune*, June 28, 1893.

[8]*Calgary Daily Herald*, September 12, 1905.

[9]*John Ware's Cow Country*, page 187.

[10]*Calgary Herald*, July 23, 1960.

[11]*The Albertan*, July 17, 1967.

# Louis
# & Marie Hebert

This Canadian love story begins in Paris sometime during the late 1570s.

Young Louis Hebert's fascination with the New World was well known by all who were acquainted with him. Even as a little boy, Louis would seek out men who had returned from explorations of the exciting far-off land and assault the traveller with question after question about the adventures they encountered. Most of the explorers welcomed the opportunity to share their stories with such an enthusiastic audience of one and would gladly spend a few minutes filling the boy's head and heart with romantic tales of vast expanses of shoreline, forests where enormous strange animals hid and where noble savages threatened at every turn.

Hebert was the son of the most highly esteemed apothecary[1] in all of France – the man charged with guarding the health of those within the royal household. When Queen Catherine de Medici nearly died from overeating, the elder Hebert saved her life and, in so doing, guaranteed himself a lifelong position of favor at court.[2]

When the royal house entertained sailors who had returned from trips to the New World, the apothecary attended the sessions, often taking his son with him. M. Hebert never had any concern that the normally lively child might misbehave in such a formal setting, for the father knew little Louis was so fascinated by the stories of derring-do that he would sit, spellbound, for as long as the travellers took to tell their tales.

Perhaps Louis' father hoped that exposing his son to as many of these stories as possible would serve to satisfy the lad's curiosity about the strange new land the explorers had visited and curb his dreams of travel and adventure. For M. Hebert had dreams of his own and one of those was to have his son serve an apprenticeship in order to follow in his father's footsteps.

And so, when Louis finally asked to spend time in his father's shop, the older man was relieved. His plan had worked – or so he thought. It was not until some time later that the lad announced to his father that he wished to learn the skills of an apothecary, not to become chief defender of the royal health, but to take his expertise with him to the New World.

"Don't talk foolishness, my son," M. Hebert admonished in reply to his son's announcement. "You will be throwing away the opportunity for a fine life right here in Paris. You will be killed by the savages they say roam the woods in the New World. No, Louis, I cannot allow this. You must give up this dream. Paris is where you belong. You will marry a nice girl and take over my business. Let those young men with less to lose seek their fortune across the ocean."

Out of respect for his father and in order to avoid an argument, Louis did not plead his case any further at that time. Nor, however, did he let his father's words change his plans. He knew the man's counsel was motivated by love and besides, one portion of the picture the older man was painting was appealing to young Louis – that of marrying. Louis had always admired his parents' marriage and he very much enjoyed the company of a woman. Although he did want to marry eventually, Hebert had already seen that his two goals of married life and adventures in the wilds might prove to defeat one another.

Despite this dichotomy he certainly wasn't ready to give up either plan. There was no shortage of desirable young women in Paris, especially for someone as eligible as Hebert. As an apothecary and son of the royal apothecary, Hebert enjoyed an elevated standing in the city. He was also a cousin to Sieur de Poutrincourt, the well-educated and famous explorer.

Hebert's cousin must have been considerably older than Hebert, for he had an adult son who had journeyed with him to the New World. Poutrincourt knew of his cousin's burning desire to travel to see the New World. He also knew that the famous explorers, Sieur de Pont-Grave and Sieur de Monts, were organizing another trip to Acadia and that it was de Monts' intention to establish a colony on the new land.

Such a voyage would undeniably be a test of endurance, taking as long as three months for a crossing. Each trip across the ocean was fraught with danger and disease. It was wise, therefore, to have someone with sound medical knowledge along on the trip. Recruiting Hebert for the expedition seemed to Poutrincourt to be an ideal arrangement. A deal was struck in no time and on March 7, 1604, when the next ship sailed away from the French port with Hebert aboard, it was the beginning of a dream come true for the man.

The trip was a comparatively easy one. The ocean's huge swells were a constant danger for such a small vessel, but for this crossing at least they were spared the threat of attacks by pirates. And because they completed the crossing in only two months, the hearty little group was never in danger of running out of water or food. They came ashore in time to enjoy the earliest days of spring in what is now Nova Scotia.

The land was beautiful – more beautiful than Hebert could have imagined. At first, however, there was little time to enjoy the natural splendor, for the industry of settlement began immediately. Land was cleared and buildings, even a saw mill, were erected. As soon as Hebert was able, he was off exploring the strange woods, studying plants, mosses, vines and any other vegetation he could uncover. As an apothecary, he was as well trained as a botanist in the examination and identification of plants. Unlike the botanist, however, Hebert's reasons for interest were solely the medicinal properties of the plants. In these vast tracts of unexplored land he discovered many unfamiliar species. He collected samples and set about testing the potential healing properties of each.

Shortly after the ship's arrival, Samuel de Champlain, the royal geographer and cartographer who had sailed with the de Monts' company, prepared to set out again, this time down the coast of the New World on a map-making expedition. Hebert was delighted to be invited along and to have the opportunity to explore and collect even farther afield in this wonderfully abundant new land.

Just before the winter of 1604 settled in, Sieur de Monts prepared to set sail back to France where he hoped to solicit additional funds for the burgeoning little community. Those who stayed behind, including Hebert, set about preparing for their first winter in the new land. The construction of the buildings was as sound as they were able to make it and the larders equally well stocked. Had the winter not been so dreadfully severe, the colonists would have passed the months in reasonable comfort. As it was, however, the would-be settlers found themselves constantly bombarded by cruel storms and devastatingly low temperatures.

As week after week of severe and unrelenting winter weather assaulted their camp, the group's morale sank lower and lower. No one could sleep for the noise of the biting winds howling around them. Everything they possessed froze solid and became unusable. Proper food and water were little more than memories to the ravaged men.

With his medical knowledge and supplies, Hebert tended the men as best he was able, but as one after another of the men became ill, it became apparent that there was little that could be done to help them. The young man watched in horrified impotency as his fellow colonists writhed in agony – their arms and legs swollen and bruised. It didn't take him long to realize that once the scurvy affected a man's gums, death was close at hand. Through it all the dreadful coughing persisted. In the final stages they coughed so hard their teeth right flew from their swollen, purple gums. There was nothing Hebert could do for those who were sick. None of his training nor carefully collected herbs were effective against this terrible disease and many men died agonizing deaths that first cruel winter.

Spring was late that year, but by the time it arrived those who had survived realized that in order to save themselves, they must abandon any plans of establishing a permanent settlement. They would have to return – a failed expedition – to the safety of France.

As the snow melted and the winter began to subside, the devastated group set about making preparations for their retreat from the hostile area. Hebert dreaded having to return home in defeat. Not only did he feel humiliated by the failure, but he knew he would have to be patient in listening to those who had counseled against the trip in the first place. What's more, he knew he would have to endure the stifling restrictions of the European city. After enjoying the freedom of the Canadian wilderness, this would not be easy.

Just days before their planned departure, one of the group spotted a ship on the horizon. It was a fellow Frenchman, one who had made the original voyage with them, but had chosen to go back to France before the killing winter had set in. Now he was returning with a shipload of new settlers and additional supplies. Hebert was overjoyed by the possibility of a reprieve. Surely this would give the worn-out colonists a chance to re-group and hopefully make a success of their settlement.

A meeting was held and the new arrivals listened in dazed silence as those who had survived the winter described the hardships they'd endured. Lead by Sieur de Monts, the colonists decided that they must relocate to the more protected south shore of the Bay of Fundy.

Hebert was delighted with the change. As soon as they were settled in the new location, the apothecary cleared and planted another garden. Again he used cuttings and seeds from those specimens he had collected on his excursions with Champlain and his less ambitious solo trips into the surrounding forests. Some were plants he believed held medicinal properties and others were vegetables, for Hebert theorized that a better diet through the coming winter could help to prevent a second outbreak of scurvy.

His fellow adventurers admired the special way he seemed to have of coaxing the best crop from the soil. Hebert's garden soon became the pride of the community. Champlain noted in his diary:

> It was surrounded with ditches full of water, in which I placed some fine trout, and into which flowed three brooks of very fine running water, from which the greater part of our settlement was supplied. I made, also, a little sluice-way towards the shore, in order to draw off the water when I wished. . . . I made there also, a little reservoir for holding salt-water fish, which we took out as we wanted them. I took especial pleasure in it, and planted there some seeds which turned out well.[3]

As one of the leaders of the expedition, Champlain's support of Hebert's efforts was extremely important. It demonstrated to one and all that not only did the energetic and idealistic young apothecary think this settlement could be a success, but so did he, Samuel de Champlain, the royal geographer.

Hebert was pleased and relieved when it was announced that they would definitely stay on at least one more winter. The winter of 1605/06 was not nearly as severe as the previous one had been and the colonists survived in relative comfort. Still, by the following summer, when supply ships from France had not arrived, it was determined that they would have to abandon the camp, for they would have been inviting disaster to attempt another winter with provisions so low.

Although Hebert was disappointed, he was also realistic about the potentially lethal severity of winters in the New World. Besides, they were leaving a party of two men behind to guard the fort and Hebert had firmly decided that he would be back – this time for good.

Having come to that decision, Hebert wondered if he had doomed himself to a life of celibacy, for there were still no women in the colonies. What's more, he certainly couldn't imagine finding a woman who would attempt such a foolhardy feat as marrying him, knowing she would live out the rest of her days in the wilderness. This realization disappointed Hebert because, although he had enjoyed the freedom of his new life, he had often been very lonely.

And so, as Hebert and the other colonists prepared once again to return to France, it was not with the same feelings of defeat as they had struggled against the previous year. Once again, however, their plans were cut short. A party of ships was spotted on the horizon. A small vessel reached them first with the advice that Poutrincourt's ship the *Jonas* was following close behind laden with additional workers, tools and all manner of supplies. Perhaps this reprieve was met with slightly mixed feelings, especially by Hebert who might, by now, have looked forward to the opportunity to settle out his affairs in Europe once and for all.

Nevertheless, for the present, a celebration would be enjoyed by newcomers and colonists alike. A scribe aboard the leaky old *Jonas*[4] described the festivities this way, "Monsieur de Poutrincourt ordered a tun [sic] of wine to be set upon end and gave leave to all comers to drink freely as long as it lasted, so that there were some who made gay dogs of themselves."[5] Presumably, after allowing a day or so for the "gay dogs'" headaches to ease, the colonization process began anew.

Champlain continued his trips to explore and record the area around the colony and Hebert continued to occasionally accompany him. When he stayed behind, Hebert tended his own flourishing garden and assisted the others in developing theirs. In return for his guidance and assistance, the colonists made sure Hebert's house was well fortified against the approaching winter and well stocked with fish and game.

Although the previous winter had not been the killer that the first one had, the leaders couldn't help but note that the men's morale dropped considerably during that season. They knew the men, like Hebert, were lonely and would have benefited greatly from the company of women, but they too doubted that any reputable woman would come to this hazardous new land. Of course they knew of men who had gone off with native women, but they had never returned and one could only guess at the terrors that may have befallen those lust-driven comrades.

As women were clearly not a possibility, then some other form of companionship and diversion must be found. And so in the last months of 1606, the colonists' third winter on the shores of the Bay of Fundy, The Order of Good Cheer was born. The colony's lawyer, a man named Marc Lescarbot, left a wonderfully colorful description of the fellowship. He noted,

> To keep our table joyous and well provided, an order was established at the board of . . . M. De Poutrincourt, which was called the Order of Good Cheer, originally proposed by Champlain. To this Order each man of said table was appointed chief steward in his turn, which came round once a fortnight.[6] Now, this person had the duty of taking care that we were all well and honourably provided for. This was so well carried out that though the epicure of Paris often tell us that we had no *Rue aux Ours* [a famous Paris hotel of the time] . . . as a rule we made as good cheer as we could have in this same *Rue aux Ours*, and at less cost. For there was no one who, two days before his turn came, failed to go hunting or fishing to bring back some delicacy in addition to our ordinary fare. . . . The same was repeated at dessert, though not always with so much pomp. And at night, before giving thanks to God, he handed over to his successor in the charge the collar of the Order, with a cup of wine, and they drank to each other.[7]

The jovial atmosphere created by these twice monthly get togethers went a long way toward their intended goal of lifting the men's spirits. There was also an unexpected, additional benefit. The natives were intrigued by the festivities and the settlers invited them to partake of the hospitality, thereby forging the first links in the bond that needed to be created between the natives and the Europeans.

Hebert and the others found the following winter (1606/07) very much easier to bear. Their new location was a considerable improvement because it was more protected from the elements. The men made sure that they ate nourishing food from their well-stocked provisions and the regular meetings of the Order of Good Cheer gave each man something definite in the immediate future to look forward to enjoying.

It was only in very quiet moments that Louis Hebert felt uncomfortable and somewhat unsettled. He knew he should have been happy. Here he was in the New World, where he'd always dreamed of being. It took him several weeks of thought before he was able to identify those feelings. Finally he realized what the problem was – he was simply lonely. Sadly, the realization only increased the isolation he felt, for he was well aware that there were simply no women available from whom he could choose a partner and so ease his loneliness. The only relief Hebert felt from the heartache came from work and sleep.

Champlain, de Monts and all the others around him may have noticed Hebert's increased dedication to his work and wondered about it. As they were all single men, unused to the comfort of a wife, it is likely, however, that they realized the young man was throwing himself into work to distract himself during the days and to ensure a sound sleep at night.

When the spring of 1607 came, the little camp was healthy and flourishing. The settlers must have been badly disappointed therefore when a ship arrived from France carrying orders for their immediate return to the mother land. With a heavy heart, Hebert packed his few belongings and as he made his way toward the ship that was to take him back to the confines of the city, he could not even bring himself to look back at the habitation he and the others had worked so hard to establish.

The men may have sulked all the way back across the ocean, but it would have been difficult for any but the most moody to remain disgruntled when they reached their final destination. They were greeted at the dock by peasants and aristocracy alike and immediately whisked off to the palace where they regaled all with stories of the success of their colony in the wilds of the New World.

The older men may have been used to such attention, but for Hebert it was all new and terribly exciting. Considering the loneliness he had suffered over the past few months, the efforts the young women made to attract his attention were especially exciting. Everyone wanted the honor of meeting the dashing adventurers.

At receptions he was invited to attend, Hebert often noticed the same beautiful girl. He found her very attractive and was always disappointed when, by the end of the evening, he still had not been introduced to her. At one gathering, when it had become apparent once again that no one was going to introduce the two young people to one another, Hebert took matters into his own hands. He approached the young woman and introduced himself.

"I know who you are," she replied simply.

"Then you have an unfair advantage over me for I do not know who you are," Hebert countered.

"My name is Marie Rollet and I am here with some of my family," she explained. "And if I may be so brash as to share some feelings with you, I must say I'm intrigued by the stories of all your adventures. It seems unfair to me that women have no chance to partake of these experiences."

With that last statement Hebert's head spun. Could this beautiful woman really have such a sense of adventure that she would want to give up her life here in Paris and travel to the New World, knowing the hardships she would have to endure? If so, he might just have met the woman of his dreams.

The two young people talked together for the balance of the evening and Hebert sought her out again the next day. It didn't take him long to accept that Marie Rollet was not like the other girls he'd been introduced to since his return to France. Although they too wanted to get to know the apothecary, their plans for their futures only included marrying someone who could provide them with a comfortable life and perhaps the added benefit of some increased prestige.

Marie Rollet was not like that. She was certainly a pretty woman, but she was also strong, robust and full of life, ready to take on any challenge presented to her. Louis Hebert's adventuring heart was captured and the two were soon married.

None of the colonists who had been ordered back to France were content to remain there. They petitioned the courts for funding to return to the New World. Eventually their persistent reasoning paid off and in the first few weeks of 1610 their ship left France and all its inherent comforts. This time it was understood by all that the settlement would be a permanent one. Toward that end and despite her family's heated protestations, the former Marie Rollet, now Madame Louis Hebert, was aboard, as was Poutrincourt's wife.

The voyage was horrendous. It took more than 13 weeks and, as a result, supplies of food and water ran perilously low. The seas were so rough that at one point all aboard were convinced their graves would be found directly below in the icy murky depths of the ocean. Father Joseph Le Caron, a priest travelling to the New World, was so sure they could not survive that he offered the terrified passengers their final blessings.

When they finally did sight the shoreline and the previously abandoned camp, the immigrants were too weakened to have much of a reaction. As soon as she had rested sufficiently to restore her energy, however, Marie Hebert decorated the altar with wild flowers and gave thanks for their safe arrival.

The following winter was nearly as harsh as it had been that first fatal year. By spring, Poutrincourt's wife insisted that he take her home to Paris. Marie Hebert, however, remained adamant that this is where she wanted to be. She worked alongside her husband and the couple soon won the respect, not only of their fellow colonists, but of the natives who often came to the Hebert's home looking for the herbs and plants necessary to make needed remedies. In turn, the natives taught the Heberts what they knew about disease prevention – some of which would have taken the Europeans decades to discover on their own. Had the natives not shared their knowledge of the annedda tree's green shoots being effective against scurvy, many more Europeans might have died.

Inevitably, children began to arrive in the Hebert household and by the spring of 1613 the family consisted of two daughters, Anne and Marie Guillemette, as well as a son, Guillaume.

One of the pleasures of being isolated from France was being excluded from the continual battles that raged between England and France. Both Heberts, being pacifists at heart, enjoyed this aspect of their seclusion as a blessing. The segregation, however, also served to increase the element of horrible surprise when a party of Englishmen from Virginia sailed into the Bay of Fundy intent on capturing the burgeoning French community for the English king.

Within hours the French settlers watched in anguish as the colony they had worked so hard to established was leveled by fires the English had set. The once-determined group from France were badly outnumbered. Battling back would only have increased their hardships. Quietly and with as much dignity as they could muster they admitted defeat – their colony had been overtaken.

Little is known of the retreat to Paris. Perhaps it was uneventful or perhaps the overpowered colonists were so distraught by losing their homes that they were unable to record the events of the next few months. We do not find the Heberts again until they have set up a chemist's shop on a side street in Paris. Just as they had been in the New World, Louis and Marie Hebert were working here side by side. They loved each other dearly and took comfort in being together, even if it wasn't where they wanted to be.

Paris, the city where they'd both been born and raised, now seemed confining and depressing. The rainy and comparatively mild winters seemed crueler than the blizzards they'd endured for the last few winters in the New World. Their pristine gardens and ponds were mere memories now. The privilege of working the soil or drinking pure, clean water from crystal clear streams were things of the past. Even food, for which Paris was renowned, tasted bland compared to some of the feasts they enjoyed with the camaraderie offered by the Order of Good Cheer.

They toiled away in the dingy store, only taking pleasure in each other, the children and their shared memories. And so it was until the day in 1617, when their old friend Samuel de Champlain sought them out. Presuming that the cartographer brought news from the New World, Louis hurried to the back of the store so that Marie could share in the excitement of their guest. They knew from previous visits with other former colonists, Champlain's call would give them happy fodder for conversation for months to come.

Marie Hebert squeezed her beloved Louis' arm as she came through the doorway and saw the distinguished-looking man standing in their shop.

"I hope you bring us news from the New World," she prodded.

"Of a sort, I suppose I do," the older man answered. "I bring you an invitation to accompany me there once again. This time we will settle farther inland at the place they call New France."

Champlain paused to give the couple a chance to respond. He could see, however, that the shock of his announcement had rendered them speechless and so he continued.

"There is a fur trading post established there already and so over the past few years we have won the natives' allegiance. Many of the hardships we endured in Port Royal would not exist in this new land."

Still there was no reply from either Louis or Marie Hebert. Their children had joined their parents and were also listening intently.

"There is only one factor about this particular settlement that you must understand fully before you accept any offers to travel there." Champlain spoke slowly and carefully. He did not want to risk being misunderstood. "This time we will definitely be staying in the New World for good. We will be settling there permanently and such a settlement needs exactly what you two and your children can provide – skills and stability."

The man's last few words were drowned out by gleeful shouts from the Heberts. All five were dancing and hugging one another in excitement. Champlain smiled broadly as he waited for the initial reaction to abate. If possible, he was even more pleased than they were by the turn of events.

No one wasted time preparing for the voyage and by spring of 1617, the Heberts and their children, along with dozens of other would-be colonists, set sail once again. Immediately upon their arrival it was evident that not all the advantages Champlain had enumerated still existed. The Indians had been treated very badly by some fur-traders and so were hostile toward the Europeans when they first arrived. The Hebert children charmed the natives first, but when a strange illness befell a young native man of their tribe, the others watched in admiration and appreciation as Louis and Marie Hebert took turns sitting with the brave and treating him until he was well again. From then on there was harmony between the two groups.

The land assigned to the Heberts sat atop the cliff where Upper Town Quebec stands today. The view must have been unparalleled, but still the couple's hearts must have plunged in desperation when they realized how much work would be necessary before they would be able to plant their garden or build their home. Fortunately they were united, not only in their goal, but in their relief at being back in the New World. With the children helping as best they were able, Louis and Marie Hebert began to make their dream of a permanent home in New France a reality.

The single men in the colony were fascinated by Madame Hebert. In France a woman would not have worked alongside her husband at such heavy tasks. Nor in France would a man have trusted his wife with such responsibility as dispensing medicines as Louis Hebert did. The husband and wife were rarely idle and even more rarely apart. They soon became the talk of the colony, for everyone enjoyed and admired the husband and wife.

Before long they had enough land cleared to begin constructing their home – the first permanent home built in New France by Europeans.

Because those who had come across the ocean on this voyage all intended to stay in what would one day become Canada, they had brought building supplies with them. Marie Hebert was determined to have a fine home in this fine new country and she did. The house was oblong in shape, built of stone and wood with proper gables, doors, windows and even a chimney.[8]

Before they left France, the Hebert's had sold most of their belongings, but despite her husband's teasing, Marie Hebert had brought her most cherished possessions with her from France – a few chairs, some dishes and pewter drinking cups. Soon the family's home looked so cozy and appealing that not only their fellow colonists found excuses to visit, but even the natives frequently dropped in for no real reason except to enjoy the home and share in its warmth and love.

In spite of the amount of work necessary just to survive in this harsh new environment, Marie Hebert was determined to have a little cultivated beauty around her home. She planted flower gardens and her roses became a real attraction in the community. Next she and Louis planted orchards. The fruits from these trees not only helped to nourish her family and the surrounding community, but every spring when they were in blossom, the land surrounding her beloved home looked as beautiful as it smelled.

In the evenings Louis and Marie Hebert often sought to be alone, for despite the years and adventures the two had shared, they were still very passionate in their feelings for one another and liked nothing more than to be alone together.

Perhaps seeing how happy the Heberts were in their new home, Champlain set out across the ocean once more – this time to bring his own wife back so that he might be able to have a little of the happiness that his old friend Hebert obviously enjoyed. There is much disagreement about the age of Champlain's bride.[9] It is possible that she was only 12 years of age when she married the man and 22 when he brought her to Canada. Whatever the actual statistics might have been, Helene Boulle Champlain did not adapt well to the country and insisted on leaving again after only a short stay. Champlain, sadly, was never able to capture for himself what he so admired in the apothecary and his wife.

When Champlain returned to New France next time, he brought young men with him to be employed as laborers and help with some of the work ahead. They proved a great disappointment and were soon sent back home. Their benefactor described his reasons for their expulsion most colorfully. "They have not cleared one bit of land, doing nothing but giving themselves a good time hunting, fishing, sleeping and getting drunk."[10]

Fortunately, other colonists proved to be suitable. Abraham and Marguerite Martin raised their daughters Anne and Marguerite in New France, as did Pierre and Françoise Desportes raise their daughter Helen, and Nicholas and Marguerite Pivert raised their niece. There was also Adrien Duchesne and his wife, whose name has been lost to history.

As the years progressed, the Hebert children grew to adulthood and because of the way they had been raised, were every bit as capable and positive as their parents were. The girls, therefore, had many suitors to choose from. When Anne Hebert married Etienne Jonquest from the settlement below the cliff where the Hebert's house sat, the parents were delighted. The ceremony was performed by Father Joseph and was the first marriage in Canada to be celebrated by Catholic Church rituals.

Happiness turned to all-encompassing grief the following year, however, when Anne Hebert died in childbirth. Presumably the child died as well and sadly, the young husband whom the Heberts had invited into their family like a son also died very young. Despite their grief, Louis and Marie labored on for the sake of their love for their new homeland. The Hebert's efforts did not go unnoticed. In 1623 they were granted title to their land in addition to another parcel of land along the River St. Charles. Louis Hebert was given the title Sieur d'Espinay and later, when a justice system was established in New France, Champlain wisely chose Hebert to hold a position of authority.[11]

On August 26, 1621, Hebert's younger daughter, Marie-Guillemette, extended the family by marrying a well-respected carpenter whose stay in Quebec actually predated that of the Heberts. The young couple became the parents of a healthy baby girl – the first French child born on Canadian soil.

The Heberts' lives in New France were such that none of them ever looked back with question on their decision to leave the dark chemist's shop of Paris for the abundance that this new land provided. There was every indication now that Louis and Marie Hebert would live out their lives in the well-deserved contentment they had earned for themselves through all their hard work.

Tragically, that was not to be. Early in January 1627, Louis Hebert suffered a fall. He never recovered from his injuries, but did linger long enough to speak of his great love for his wife, his children and the lives they had been blessed to lead. The well-loved and respected man died in his wife's arms on January 25.

The entire community mourned the loss. "The death of Sieur Hebert was a calamity to all of us,"[12] a resident priest explained. The natives had respected his kindness and knowledge, the French colonists had always looked upon Hebert as a leader, but in addition they greatly admired the contribution he and his wife had made to the community. And that fact that alone implied another imminent loss to the community, for no one was so deeply shocked by Louis Hebert's sudden passing as was his dear wife and partner, the former Marie Rollet. Whatever would she do? Many presumed they would lose Marie too, that the woman would return to her home in France. The Widow Hebert knew, though, that her home was

*Louis Hebert monument in Quebec. (Photo courtesy of Harry Palmer Gallery)*

no longer in Paris, France, but now in New France and that it was here that she would live out the rest of her days trying to heal from the loss of her dear Louis.

Later that year a second tragedy struck the colony when supply ships heading toward them with provisions were sunk en route. Champlain knew that the colony could not maintain itself throughout the coming winter on the stocks at hand. He had no choice but to start to load ships with colonists and send them back to France, at least for the coming months. He fully expected that Marie Hebert would have wanted to be among those leaving. When she declined the opportunity, Champlain was not surprised. He knew of the woman's love for her newly adopted country. He was, however, pleased, for to him the woman's decision spoke volumes for the permanency of the habitation he had established.

Just as the settlers in Port Royal so many years before had been ill-equipped to put up a fight when the English threatened to take over their settlement, the few who chose to remain in New France were no match for the English raiding party that visited the settlement in the winter of 1627. This time, though, the conquerors had no interest in burning buildings or chasing the settlers off their land. The British merely raised their own flag and encouraged the colonists to go about their business.

During his lifetime, and even now hundreds of years later, Louis Hebert's accomplishments have been effectively overshadowed by those of his more flamboyant cohort, Samuel de Champlain. Because history's traditional focus has been patriarchal, Marie Hebert's vital contributions to the development of Canada have received even fewer notations. As a result we have pitifully few direct references to this dedicated couple.

Of the little that has been recorded about these pioneers, much is contradictory.[13] Despite the lack of agreement or acknowledgment the Heberts have received in the history books, their devotion to one another and to their shared dream of establishing a permanent colony in New France could never be questioned.

These omissions represent a very real loss to the collection of stories that form Canada's past, for several of my sources noted that the legacy of this romantic pioneering tale did not stop when they died. Hebert descendants have gone on to make important contributions to the country's well-being.

A monument in honor of Louis Hebert stands in Quebec.

## *Endnotes*

[1]Roughly defined, an apothecary was the predecessor of today's pharmacist. Because the field of medicine has changed so profoundly in the past 400 years, many of the functions an apothecary performed would not be included on a pharmacist's duty roster. He (or she) did, however, prepare and dispense medications.

[2]*Champlain, The Life Of Fortitude*, Morris Bishop, Alfred A. Knopf, New York, 1948, page 94.

[3]*Louis Hebert, The First Canadian Farmer*, Julia Jarvis, Ryerson Press, Toronto, 1929, page 6.

[4]*Wilderness Explorer, The Story of Samuel de Champlain*, Charles Morrow Wilson, Hawthorn Books Incorporated, New York, 1963, page 80.

[5]*Louis Hebert, The First Canadian Farmer*, page 8.

[6]*Wilderness Explorer, The Story of Samuel de Champlain*, indicates on page 85 that the Order met every week – this seems unreasonable.

[7]*Louis Hebert, The First Canadian Farmer*, page 10.

[8]some sources indicate the house measured 38' x 19', other sources give the dimensions as 33' x 19'.

[9]*He Went With Champlain*, Louis Andrews Kent, Houghton Mifflin Company, Boston, 1959, page 127 and *Louis Hebert, The First Canadian Farmer*, page 20.

[10]*Champlain, The Life Of Fortitude*, page 183.

[11]*Louis Hebert, The First Canadian Farmer*, page 21.

[12]Ibid., page 22.

[13]When I came across such conflicts in researching the re-telling of the Hebert love story, I've chosen to use either the most frequently subscribed to version of a point, or if that was not possible, the most reasonable given the facts at hand. Occasionally too, it was necessary to extrapolate from what is known.

# John Brownlee
# & Vivian Macmillan

On Wednesday, the 24th of May, 1933, Alberta's premier, John Brownlee, became the subject of a claim filed jointly by Vivian MacMillan, a clerk in the attorney-general's office, and Allan MacMillan, her father. Brownlee immediately filed a counterclaim against Miss MacMillan and her boyfriend, John Caldwell.[1]

The trial, which fascinated a nation, and the appeals, which ultimately travelled all the way to England's Privy Council for resolution, lasted six stressful years. The love affair leading to these legal complexities lasted only half that time – and began in much less exalted surroundings.

Like so many other love stories, it probably began with one person's infatuation and another's arrogance. Or did it ever happen at all?

John Brownlee came to his position as leader of Alberta under unusual and rather distasteful circumstances. In 1921, Albertans had elected their fourth Premier. Herbert Greenfield represented the newly formed United Farmers of Alberta and his leadership was expected to bring great things to the young province. Unfortunately, by 1925, the party deemed Greenfield incompetent and demanded his resignation. Lieutenant-Governor William Egbert appointed John Brownlee to replace the disgraced politician.

Brownlee took the post reluctantly, and apparently only out of a sincere desire to serve. And serve he did.

On a frigid December evening in 1929, the people of Alberta turned out to give their Premier a hero's welcome. He was returning from a trip to the nation's capital, where he had successfully negotiated an agreement with the Dominion government. The province would now retain all the rights and profits from its natural resources. For people badly in need of some economic hope, the news was not only fiscally heartening, but also a sign that the 14-year-old province was gaining equality with older, more established provinces. Brownlee's political coup served as the basis for what would become Alberta's substantially endowed Heritage Trust Fund.

Born and raised in small town Ontario, John Brownlee originally trained as a teacher. His career at the front of the classroom was apparently short-lived, because by 1908 he had graduated from the University of Toronto and moved to Calgary. Here he articled with various law firms and was admitted to the Alberta bar in 1912.

That same year, Allan and Maude MacMillan, of Edson, Alberta (200 kilometres west of Edmonton), rejoiced over the birth of a daughter. They had all but given up hope of having another child. Maude, especially, had found it hard not to become absorbed in their fruitless quest to create a proper-sized family. She viewed this second pregnancy as a miracle. At last their son, Allan Jr., would have a little sister. And what a tiny beauty she was. The proud parents looked upon their daughter as a divine gift and named her Vivian, meaning "to live."

Shortly after his admission to the bar, John Brownlee became involved in the legal intricacies of a farmers' co-operative, a group which eventually became the very influential United Grain Growers. By 1919, Brownlee was both the general solicitor and general manager of the United Grain Growers, as well as being the lawyer for the United Farmers of Alberta (UFA), a burgeoning political party.

After the UFA's victory at the polls in 1921, Brownlee was asked to accept the position of provincial Attorney General.[2] In order to serve in this capacity, he needed a seat in the Legislative Assembly. Percival Baker, the elected representative in the small farming community of Ponoka, had recently died in an accident and Brownlee gained the deceased man's political position by acclamation.

In Edson, Vivian MacMillan continued to bring joy to all those around her. The girl wasn't much of a student, but that didn't concern her parents in the least. They preferred that she devote herself to the piano – for Vivian dreamed of a career on the world's stages as a concert pianist.

Holding such an exotic ambition was viewed by the MacMillans' neighbors as being decidedly odd. No one else in that rural railroad settlement had ever aspired to such heights. But then, Allan MacMillan's time as the town's mayor had already set the family somewhat apart and slightly above the rest of the community.

The MacMillans did not consider the lack of camaraderie a hardship. By her teenage years, Vivian would never have considered mixing with the other young people in Edson. They were simply beneath her dignity. She especially disliked the boys in town, whom she deemed to be childish.

While still in her teens, Viv had turned down an eager marriage proposal from Carl Snell, one of her high school teachers. Although her parents thought Snell[3] might have made a good son-in-law, Vivian would not even entertain the thought. She protested that she was far too young. In reality, Vivian merely wanted to wait and choose her mate from the enormous selection of sophisticated and worldly men in the cities she knew she'd travel to as a concert pianist.

Premier John Brownlee, the popular leader, and Vivian MacMillan, the aspiring concert pianist, met one August day in 1930. The 46-year-old Premier, unaccompanied by his wife and two sons, drove to Edson. The man may never have sought to hold political office, but once there he executed the duties of the Premier's office with diligence. If his obligations in the provincial capital allowed him to, Brownlee often travelled to political meetings in the small towns scattered throughout the sparsely populated province.

*J.E. Brownlee. (photo courtesy of the Provincial Archives of Alberta, A-433)*

*Vivian Macmillan. (photo courtesy of the Provincial Archives of Alberta, A-8005)*

And that was exactly what took him to Vivian's home town that fine summer day, where he first met briefly with Allan MacMillan and other dignitaries in the town. From there, the group planned to make their way to the coal mining town of Luscar. The railroad which ran through Edson existed largely to ship coal to markets. Voters in the area had not forgotten that Brownlee's tactics in Ottawa had favorably affected the revenues from mining. Brownlee was, in short, a well-liked and respected man in the area.

While the Premier enjoyed the drive from Edmonton to Edson in his luxurious, government supplied, Studebaker, he did not want to drive the car on to Luscar. With considerable justification, he worried that arriving at a coal mining town in the opulent automobile would have a detrimental effect on his popularity. And so it was arranged that 18-year-old Vivian MacMillan would take a break from her music in order to pick her father and the Premier up in the MacMillan's more practical Model A Ford.

She maneuvered the motorcar to the curb in front of the town's meeting hall. Moments later a group of men emerged. Vivian spotted her father immediately and smiled with pride. He was certainly the most handsome man in Edson. It was important to the man that he look his best at all times and so he didn't mind the added expense of having his suits tailored. Maude MacMillan enjoyed her husband's exalted status in the town and she always made sure her husband's clothes were clean and smartly pressed. As a result, he cut an impressive figure, especially beside the railroad workers who formed the bulk of Edson's population.

But this time Allan MacMillan was not the nattiest dressed of the men standing about on the town hall porch. Beside him stood a bespectacled man fairly oozing an air of dignity. As the knot of men dispersed, Vivian watched as the impressive-looking man walked along beside her father.

Seconds later, the Premier approached the driver's side of the car. Knowing that her father would never allow her to drive all the way to Luscar, Vivian jumped out of the car and stood between the two men. Brownlee reached to open the Ford's back door for Vivian as her father introduced the two.

"I'm delighted to meet you, my dear," the older man exclaimed with apparent sincerity. "Thank you for bringing your father's car to us here. I hope you'll be able to accompany us on the trip to the next town. I have heard a little about your musical talents and am anxious to hear more."

Vivian could feel the blood rising to her cheeks. She felt lightheaded and when she tried to speak found she could not. Brownlee might have guessed the reactions his words had caused, but all he saw was an extraordinarily pretty young woman blushing slightly and smiling sweetly.

He was charmed – and so was she. Once Vivian regained her voice, the two chatted happily throughout the trip. Brownlee was the antithesis of the pimply-faced, gawky adolescent males around Edson. He was older, sophisticated, charming, intelligent and best of all he was paying a great deal of attention to her.

In retrospect, that ride to the political rally in Luscar, Alberta, marked the beginning of John Brownlee's tumble from political grace.

The next day, fairly squealing with delight, Vivian told her mother that Premier Brownlee had invited her to go Edmonton. "He said he could get me a job and everything," the teenager gushed, apparently forgetting the lure of the stage.

Mrs. MacMillan gave the only answer she could, considering her position in life. "We'll discuss it with your father when he comes home from work this evening."

Vivian knew there was no point in fighting such a pronouncement. Dreamily, she returned to the piano where she continued perfecting the complicated fingering patterns required by Beethoven's D-Major Sonata.

That night Allan MacMillan's booming voice shook the windows of the frame cottage which he and his family called home. "If you're too young to marry a perfectly respectable local man when he asks you, then you're too young to leave home. Carl Snell could have provided you with a comfortable life here in Edson, but no, you had to turn down his marriage proposal," he exhorted.

"But Daddy," the teenager protested. "He was my science teacher. He's old. I don't want to marry an old man and live the rest of my life here in town. I want to see the world and Edmonton's a start."

"I'm not in the habit of repeating myself, Vivian. I have told you what my answer is to your outlandish idea. There won't be another word spoken about the matter."

A few weeks after her father's tirade, he succumbed to the pressure of Vivian's nagging and contradicted himself by reversing his decision. Vivian boarded an eastbound passenger train the next day, and following the Premier's recommendation, she enrolled in an Edmonton secretarial school.

Vivian's first few weeks away from home were as miserable as most are for a newly independent youngster. She was lonely and homesick. In the city no one treated her as anything special, the way they had in Edson. The privileged position of cherished only daughter seemed a lifetime away. At home Vivian had been excused from anything approaching a domestic duty, lest she somehow damage her musically-gifted hands. In the city she attended school with a common group of girls and, despite her obvious superiority to them, no one doted on her. Worse, she was virtually ignored by both staff and students. Her classmates found her cold and aloof and her teachers quickly became frustrated with her complete lack of both ability and effort.

Vivian's accommodation didn't ease her loneliness. She'd found a room at the YWCA in downtown Edmonton. It had the advantage of being near the school she was attending, but it certainly wasn't a homey environment. A room at the "Y" included meals and in Vivian's opinion they were awful. Nothing like the delicious food her mother always served. Vivian stopped eating.

Today, an interested party might recognize stress-induced anorexia nervosa. Then, little was known about psychosomatic illnesses and besides, no one had much interest in the pathetic young woman's plight. Even the Premier, it seemed, was ignoring her presence in Edmonton.

It was Brownlee's apparent snub that hurt Vivian the most. In the estrogen-inspired daydreams she'd treated herself to all through the summer of 1930, John, as she dared to call him in her fantasies, would already have left his wife and married Vivian.

After one month at secretarial school, Vivian was doing abysmally, both at school and socially. She had not touched even one of her beloved 88 black and white keys since she'd been in Edmonton. How was it that one so accomplished on a piano keyboard could find mastering a typewriter keyboard completely beyond her abilities? The question was merely rhetorical.

Vivian had already decided to place a long distance call to her mother. The only solution to her misery was to go home and return to the life she'd been leading before all this upheaval. She'd have to wait until Monday to place the call though. Otherwise her father would be home and that would only add unpleasant complications to the situation.

That afternoon, as Vivian lay sulking on her bed, the YWCA matron knocked on her door.

"A telephone call for you, Miss MacMillan," the woman advised.

Shocked, Vivian jumped up quickly, too quickly. She held on to the handle of her still-closed bedroom door as a wave of nausea and dizziness abated. Lack of nourishment had made sudden movements tricky. "A call for me?" she queried doubtfully.

"Yes, Miss MacMillan," the older woman verified impatiently.

Vivian stared at the matron as the older woman led the way downstairs to the phone in the front hall.

"Hello," she said tentatively into the heavy black receiver.

"Vivian, this is Premier Brownlee calling. How are you, my dear?"

Vivian's body lurched in reaction to the familiar booming voice.

"Vivian? Vivian? Are you there, Vivian?"

"Yes, Mr. Brownlee, I'm here," she finally replied.

"I checked with your school yesterday. You're not doing at all well there, Vivian. What is the problem?"

Oh no, he knew. He'd never hire her now. It was just as well she'd already made up her mind to go back to Edson. This was never going to work out. She wracked her brain for a reply. A strongly developed sense of social propriety combined with Vivian's frequently rehearsed fantasies dictated that she'd have to tell Mr. Brownlee exactly what he wanted to hear.

"I'll try to do better, sir," she replied.

"Perhaps you're just a little lonely, dear, what with being here alone and away from home for the first time. I'll pick you up tomorrow afternoon in my car and bring you here to my home for a visit. That will set everything right, I'm sure," Brownlee paused for Vivian's reply but there was none so he continued. "I'll meet you in front of your building at one tomorrow afternoon then. Wait for me outside on the sidewalk."

Again Brownlee paused and again the invitation for Vivian to speak was met with silence.

"Until tomorrow then, Vivian," the man concluded and then the line went dead.

Her legs barely holding her, Vivian made her way back to her room. Sitting on her bed she let the welcome series of events sink into her mind.

"He called me 'dear,'" she repeated over and over again to herself.

After a few minutes she'd calmed down enough to first wash her face and then put on her coat. An invitation to the Premier's home required a trip to the Johnstone and Walker shop on Jasper Avenue. She'd treat herself to the dress she'd been admiring in their window. Vivian's sudden weight loss meant that none of the pretty dresses she'd brought with her from Edson were at all becoming any longer. She wanted to look her best for "John."

As she tried on the dress, Vivian's imagination took full flight.

"He's already left his wife," she decided. "That's why it took him so long to call me. He was making arrangements for her. After all, it isn't his poor wife's fault that he's been hopelessly smitten and if dear John is anything, he's a gentleman."

Vivian had seen that right from the start. Why, look at the way he held he car door for her that day in Edson.

Several hours later, thoroughly pleased with the new addition to her wardrobe, Vivian was far too excited and happy to return to her drab room. She decided to treat herself to a movie at the Capitol. *Sunny Side*

*Up* with Janet Gaynor and Charles Farrell was playing and from overheard conversations both at school and around the communal supper table at the "Y," Vivian determined that she'd enjoy seeing the picture. And she wouldn't have to be concerned about the money necessary for the admission. In a very short time concerns about budgets would, once again, be a thing of the past for Viv. She and the Premier would likely be married before too long and she'd be living a carefree life in his grand home.

That night Vivian surprised herself by sleeping soundly. She woke up Sunday morning feeling refreshed and happier than she'd been in weeks. She thought briefly of going to church. She knew she really should, but the thought didn't hold much appeal. Instead, Vivian bathed and dressed carefully and then went out for a long walk. No self-respecting girl would ever sully her cheeks or lips with rouge, despite the admittedly attractive result. Fortunately, you could accomplish the same thing by taking a brisk walk and biting your lips a bit and that is just what Vivian set out to do.

First noting the time, Vivian headed west. She had more than an hour before Mr. Brownlee was expected so if she walked west for half an hour and then turned around and walked back she should be out in front of the YWCA, as he had instructed she should be, when he pulled up.

As she started out on her cosmetically-motivated walk, Vivian giggled to herself. Just thinking of riding in such a luxurious automobile sent a delicious shiver down her spine. Vivian let her mind wander aimlessly as she walked along the tree-lined avenue.

When she'd gone a few blocks she recalled a conversation she'd overheard while waiting for a class to begin. Two of her classmates had spoken of a fancy apartment building along 100th Avenue. She thought she remembered one girl saying it was called Lemarchand Mansion. Even the name sounded glamorous, although Vivian doubted that the building was quite as opulent as her classmates had described. They'd even said it had an elevator, an automatic lift – imagine. Of course there were elevators in some office buildings here in the city but in an apartment house? That would really be something to see. Besides it would give her a destination for her walk.

Another block along she spotted the imposing three storey building in the distance. It certainly did look magnificent the way it dwarfed the nearby houses. Perhaps she and John would take a flat there and leave Mrs. Brownlee in her home. People would see the sacrifice as noble, Vivian was sure. She saw herself drinking tea in the dining room while looking out over the North Saskatchewan River valley and pondering deep thoughts.

Boisterous sounds from a group of children jolted her from her daydreaming. Vivian checked her tiny Omega wristwatch, an 18th birthday gift from her parents earlier in the year. She'd have to hurry to get back to the "Y" in time to meet her dear John.

Somewhat out of breath, Vivian opened the building's front doors with five minutes to spare. She rushed upstairs to her room to check the results of her walk. She smiled at her reflection, her cheeks were pleasingly pink and the moment spent looking into the mirror had given her breathing a chance to return to normal after the exertion. Being out of breath when the Premier arrived certainly wouldn't help to give the sophisticated impression she was determined to make.

Holding her head high and at an ever-so-slight angle, Vivian stepped out of the building and onto the sidewalk. She was so convinced that Brownlee's impressive car would be waiting there for her at the curb that she stared blankly, uncomprehendingly, at the empty roadway.

Checking her watch again Vivian panicked. She was almost five minutes late. Well, maybe more like three minutes. Surely he hadn't been here and left already. Vivian's stomach heaved, she felt faint. The walk had been good for her but even on her young and previously pampered body, the emotional upheaval and lack of nourishment had taken its toll. She went back into the building and sat down on the uncomfortable, straight-backed chair by the telephone. She'd watch for his car from here.

Twenty minutes later Vivian had made several trips out to the sidewalk to confirm what she knew full well. She could see Brownlee's car arrive as readily from the lobby as she could from the sidewalk and he had clearly not arrived yet.

Badly disappointed, Vivian decided that either the Premier had meant he'd pick her up the following Sunday or some pressing political business had kept him from her. She undid her coat and began to climb the stairs to her room when she heard a raucous blare from the road.

"He's here," she thought with utter delight. She turned on the stairs so quickly she almost lost her balance.

Vivian forced herself to walk slowly toward the enormous motor car. Should she wait until he got out and opened the door for her? Brownlee remained behind the steering wheel, not making a move to get out of the car. Should she open the door herself, and if so, which door should she use? Would he think she was brash if she got in the front seat beside him or would he think she was aloof if she got into the back seat? Finally, the man's impatient hand signals directed her into the front seat.

"Where have you been?" he demanded. "I hate to be kept waiting."

"I'm sorry," Vivian replied quietly.

She was shocked, confused, hurt. Hadn't he been the one to keep her waiting? Shouldn't he be the one to apologize?

They drove in silence.

Moments later the car pulled up in front of a nondescript house not far from the university campus. Vivian wondered why they would be stopping there. With a jolt, she read the carefully hand-lettered sign halfway between the house and the road. It told her the address was 11151 88 Avenue. The owner's name appeared under the numbers. "Brownlee." For a moment the romantic youngster had trouble righting this reality with her dreams. She suddenly remembered, though, that it didn't matter a whit. She and John would leave his wife and sons in the house when they took up residence in that beautiful apartment building.

Brownlee came around and opened the car door for Vivian.

"If only he weren't so unbearably handsome," she thought as she stepped out on to the driveway.

Standing there beside the car, Brownlee finally spoke. "You look very lovely this afternoon, my dear."

With that he escorted her up the stairs to the front door of his family home. Once inside Brownlee introduced Vivian to his wife as "the girl from Edson" and then disappeared into his study where he remained until a light meal was served. He ate quickly and returned behind the closed door as soon as his plate was empty. Confused, Vivian spent virtually the entire visit in silence. At five-thirty John Brownlee emerged from his study once again, this time with Vivian's coat over his arm.

"I'll take you back to your room now," he announced, answering Vivian's unasked questions about whether or not she'd be expected to spend the evening with the family. Evidently the invitation only offered an afternoon's visit and refreshments. Vivian put on her coat unassisted, thanked Mrs. Brownlee for her hospitality, and got back into the Studebaker. Riding in it didn't seem nearly as exciting as it had earlier in the afternoon.

Again Brownlee drove in silence. As they pulled up in front of the YWCA residence he finally spoke.

"My wife is not well, Vivian. I try to be kind and you must too. I am strong but sometimes it is just too much to bear. Her illness places a terrible burden on me. It would on any man."

"I'm sorry," Vivian said, too confused to think of any other answer.

"Good night," the man said, clearly signaling the end of the bizarre visit. This time he made no move to get out of the car and open Vivian's door for her.

Wordlessly, the youngster fled the car and for the first time was grateful to be back inside the ugly residence. She bolted up the stairs to her room and closed the door firmly behind her. For a moment she just stood and stared. Shaky legs soon forced her to her bed. She sat numbly on the edge of the bed for a long time. Nothing in Vivian MacMillan's indulged and self-centered life had prepared her for the bizarre circumstances she'd become involved in.

Although Vivian attended her classes the next week, she absorbed nothing. Her mind was not on keyboard drills or shorthand exercises – it was on the Brownlees. Mrs. Brownlee certainly didn't appear to be ill. Being ill meant you had to stay in bed and take medicines. The woman seemed to Vivian to be strong and vibrant – virtually the picture of health.

By the end of the week, Vivian was no closer to sorting out the issue than she had been when she'd fled from Brownlee's Studebaker the previous Sunday. By Friday, the mental and emotional energy she'd spent on the problem left her drained. She looked forward to resting in her room and going to sleep early. Perhaps with a fresh start Saturday and no classes to attend she could piece it all together and decide what to do.

Still in her slip and stockings, Vivian was drifting off to sleep when a harsh voice from the other side of the closed door called her name.

"Vivian, do you have someone in there with you?" the house matron called through the door.

"No, ma'am, no of course not," Vivian replied, startled. She must have been talking in her sleep.

"Well, open the door, then. Besides you have a phone call downstairs. I wish you young women would show some consideration instead of just letting your friends phone at all hours of the night and day disturbing me. You could give some thought to me now and again, you know. I'm not as young as I used to be, you know. Climbing these stairs with phone messages for the lot of you will be the death of me yet, you mark my words."

The last few phrases of the matron's speech were lost in the air between the first and second floors of the building for Vivian had already run down to see who could be phoning her.

"Do you like car rides, dear?" a male voice asked as soon as she picked up the receiver and said, "Hello."

A moment of terror oddly combined with exaltation ran through Vivian's thin body. "Why yes," she replied with as much composure as she could muster.

"Good, I thought you might. I shall pick you up at eight o'clock this evening," Premier Brownlee said before disconnecting.

Vivian stood with the lifeless telephone receiver in her hand. Knowing she'd be waiting on the sidewalk before eight o'clock stirred even more emotions in her but she wasn't able to identify them.

Vivian was standing in the dark at the curb 10 minutes ahead of the appointed time. It had started to snow early in the afternoon and so far showed no signs of letting up. She'd chosen her winter boots with fashion in mind rather than warmth and for the first time it occurred to Vivian that she might have been wise to have been a little more practical. Cold feet, however, would not be enough to shake Vivian's determination tonight.

"This time I'll wait right here no matter how long it takes," she told herself.

She didn't have to wait long. A few minutes before he'd said he would, John Brownlee, Premier of the province of Alberta, pulled his car to a stop along 100th Avenue, in front of the YWCA building.

Neither one said anything as the car sped westbound along Jasper Avenue. As he drove, the businesses lining the road gave way first to homes, then to a few shacks and finally to farmers' fields. Without warning, John Brownlee pulled the car over to the side of the road and turned off the ignition.

"Vivian, my dear, I love you," he informed the frightened youngster. "I have loved you from the moment I cast eyes on you. I must have you. My wife is ill, I already explained that to you. She hasn't truly been a wife to me in years. You have no idea what a burden that is for a man. Sometimes it is more than I can bear. You are the only one who can ease this suffering for me."

Terrified, Vivian pressed herself up against the car's door. The handle gouged painfully into her ribs as she put as much distance between herself and her captor as possible. She tried to turn her head away and press her face to the glass, but the man's ham-like hands painfully forced her cheeks from the smooth, cool glass of the car's window. Suddenly his mouth was against hers. She thought she might vomit, although she'd eaten next to nothing for several days.

"What is he doing? What if he gets angry and pushes me out of the car?" Vivian wondered, bewildered and frightened. She glanced out the car window. The steady snowfall blew into thousands of tiny blizzards across empty fields.

"I'll die out here in the cold and the snow. They wouldn't find my body until spring," she thought dramatically.

Animal-like sounds distracted her thinking and for a moment she stopped trying to squirm away from the groping man. "My God, it's him. Those sounds are coming from him. He's making that noise. He's having a heart attack. Maybe he's going to die. What if he dies? I could never drive this car back to the city and even if I could they'd think I killed him."

Just when Vivian's terror gave away to blind panic, the sounds stopped. A satisfied Brownlee slumped back against the seat beside Vivian, his wire-rim glasses hanging at an angle across his face and spittle dribbling from the side of his mouth.

Incorrectly convinced that her fears had become reality, Vivian half stood in the car, shrieking and shaking her assailant's shoulders. He stared straight ahead, then expelling something between a moan and a sigh. Brownlee fumbled for his glasses, paused for a moment, cleared his throat and spoke, "You must never say anything about this to anyone. It is all my wife's fault. If she were truly a wife to me this would never have occurred."

Confused, but relieved that whatever had just happened was finally over, Vivian concentrated on getting her breathing patterns to return to normal. The car's engine jumped to life. Brownlee steered the huge automobile in a half circle and headed back toward the city.

Again they drove in silence and even when he pulled up in front of her rooming house, neither person spoke. Vivian fled from the car as soon as it came to a stop, painfully twisting her ankle against the curb which was hidden now under several inches of snow. By the time she reached the safety of her bedroom, her only thought was of gratitude that the whole ugly experience was behind her – she thought.

For now, the once-pampered little Vivian MacMillan from Edson lay shaking and badly confused on a narrow cot in a small room in a strange city. Regaining her breath, Vivian allowed herself to reflect on the incident. "I'm ruined, I know I am," she sobbed over and over again.

When the crying stopped Vivian sat up and looked around her drab room. It looked so bleak that any alternative seemed an improvement.

"Of course, he did say that he loved me and he needed me," she reminded herself hopefully. "And he's so handsome and important."

For just a moment, the memory of Brownlee's behavior and appearance in the car surfaced in Vivian's memory. She pushed the mental image aside as quickly as she could and considered the many torments those heroines in her romantic novels had had to suffer in the name of love. Vivian MacMillan may have been an overprotected teenager from a small town, but she had read voraciously and knew for a fact that true love always involved suffering. Why, if this was to be her lot, it was a joy compared to some others she'd read in stories.

This thought eased the girl's anguish considerably and within a month, the rides in the Studebaker had become routine. By then Vivian MacMillan was no longer a virgin, but the loss didn't disturb her nearly as much as her mother alluded it would.

Slowly, Vivian became aware that, although she held a distinctly subservient position in the pairing, there were aspects of power within her grasp. She realized she was supplying a service the man depended on and apparently was not able to find elsewhere.

A few days before the annual Thanksgiving celebration in 1930, Vivian decided to see if she could benefit from re-structuring the relationship just a bit. During the next session in the government-owned car, she unenthusiastically let Brownlee have his way with her. That accomplished, she decided to try to have her way.

"Please," she began. "When I take the job with the government I don't want to have to type. I hate typing."

188 Passion & Scandal

"I'm afraid, my dear, that you'll have to take whatever job's available at the time," he answered as he gave his clothes a final adjustment and turned the car's starter.

Far from disheartened by that apparent failure to tip the balance of power, Vivian was anxious to create an opportunity to modify the scheme and try again.

"It's Saturday," she reminded him. "Can we go for another little drive tomorrow?"

Brownlee smiled and glanced over at his young passenger. "I suppose we could work something out, my dear. Shall I pick you up around three tomorrow afternoon, then?"

"I'll look forward to that," she said with sincerity.

Less than 24 hours later the Studebaker and its two anxious occupants arrived at their now familiar, secluded spot west of the city. Brownlee immediately turned to her, ready to satisfy his desires as expediently as possible.

"No, John," she told him firmly. She'd never used his first name before. She'd never called him anything to his face before. The tone of her voice and the brash use of his given name startled the impassioned man into attention. He tried to speak, to quieten the youngster so he could get on with his lustful agenda, but annoyingly, she persisted.

"No, John. You'll not have me right now. Right now you'll only listen to me and then you'll promise to do what I ask," she stated flatly. "I'm tired of school. I'll never learn to type and my money is running out. Last summer you said you could find me a job. Well, that's what I want. One where I won't have to type. You're the Premier, surely you can make the arrangements easily. I can be ready to start work this week."

Once the words were out of her mouth, Vivian felt like a fool. Not for saying them, but for not saying them sooner. She could have saved herself several weeks of sitting in a stuffy classroom. She could have been walking up the enormous stone steps of the Legislative Building and into a glamorous office if she'd only figured out the timing pattern a little earlier.

"Yes, Vivian, of course. I'll do that first thing after the holiday weekend. I'll have my secretary call you at noon on Tuesday and let you know where and when to report," Brownlee assured her. The plan actually made a lot of sense, now that he thought of it. He'd be free of the necessity of these weekend drives in the country. Vivian would be right there for him whenever he wanted her.

"Come, now, my dear. Come to your John and tell me again how I'm your first and only lover."

Having accomplished her purpose, Vivian knew she'd have to accomplish his too. She set about her duty while trying to puzzle out why he had to be told over and over again that he had been the first to have her. Did he forget from one time to the next, she wondered. Old people's memories, she knew, sometimes weren't as good as they should be, but still – every time! She hoped she never got as old as him.

When he dropped her off at the YWCA, Vivian reminded Brownlee of his promise to her.

"Yes, yes, Vivian," he answered impatiently. "I've told you I'll make the arrangements and I will."

She didn't mind his impatience. He was always abrupt with her when they drove back into the city and at least this time there had been a pay-off for Vivian. To celebrate both her accomplishment and the holiday tomorrow she'd treat herself to sleeping late and an afternoon of reading romance stories.

On Tuesday morning Viv didn't bother to let the secretarial school know she'd be withdrawing. Her efforts in class and her marks were so poor it's likely that the school officials barely noticed her absence. Instead, she set out to do the shopping necessary to make her wardrobe fit her new station in life. She picked out several new outfits and charged them to her father's name in Edson.

Carrying three paper shopping bags by their brown cord handles, Vivian made her way south from Jasper Avenue and toward her residence. It wasn't quite 11:00 a.m., so she expected to be in plenty of time to receive the phone call from Brownlee's secretary. She barely got the door to the residence building open before the matron was calling to her.

"Miss MacMillan, Miss MacMillan," the shrill voice reverberated against the panels in the hallway. "Miss MacMillan, there was a call for you. I thought you were at school but now I see you weren't."

Vivian glowered. She was annoyed at both the woman's screeching and having missed the important phone call. Juggling the packages into her right hand, Vivian checked her watch. It wasn't even 11:30. She wasn't late at all, the call had come early.

"Did you take a message for me?" Vivian inquired somewhat peevishly.

"Why, yes, of course I did," the woman replied with as much self-righteousness as she could muster. "I had an upbringing, you know. Besides, it was a call from the Attorney General's department down there at the Legislative Building. I've been there once, you know. Last year on New Year's Day they offered tours right through the whole place and me and my friend we took one . . ."

"May I have my message please," Vivian interrupted. As the woman rattled on about all the splendor she'd seen during her visit to the "Ledge," Vivian put down her parcels and began to dial the phone.

"Hello, this is Vivian MacMillan calling," she said.

There was a pause at the other end of the line before she was informed that she was expected at room 201, in the Legislative Building, the next morning by nine o'clock.

"Yes, of course I'll be there," Vivian informed the unidentified female voice.

She said good-bye quickly, picked up her parcels and ran up the stairs, a very unladylike two at a time. The matron stood at the bottom of the flight still describing the glorious sights she and her nameless friend had been privy to this past January 1.

Vivian unpacked her new clothes with great care. She chose an outfit to wear the next day and then lay down on her bed. She slept soundly for several hours and woke up feeling better than she had for months. Even dinner in the noisy dining hall with its bland, lukewarm food was tolerable. When she spoke pleasantly to the young woman seated next to her, the two girls across the table burst into giggles.

"Look at that!" one exclaimed to the other. "There must be a blue moon in the sky. First Miss Priss lowers herself to eat with us and next she's even speaking. Now, isn't that the limit?"

Vivian ignored the girl's childishness, knowing she'd never have to be friends with anyone in the room. Starting tomorrow she'd be associating with sophisticated women, not uncouth youngsters like these.

Wednesday morning Vivian arose early. She bathed and dressed with care, put on her coat and began the pleasant walk to her new life. She knew she'd be received warmly. Brownlee would have seen to that.

"You're early," a middle-aged woman sitting behind the desk in room 201 replied when Vivian knocked on the open door and identified herself.

"Yes, a little, I guess," Vivian replied, wondering whether or not her punctuality was viewed as a good thing.

"Well, you might as well get your coat off and get started, then. There's lots to be done. You'll be doing all the filing for this department."

"All right, yes, that will be fine. But perhaps I should see Mr. Brownlee before I begin?" she said, raising her voice to indicate this was meant as a question.

"Mr. Brownlee?" the woman behind the desk repeated before dissolving into laughter. "You want to see Mr. Brownlee before you start work? You're a corker, you are. Mr. Brownlee is the Premier of the province, are you aware of that? Besides he's in Ottawa this week."

Vivian had no idea her John was away, but she made a mental note to tell him about it if this woman's disrespectful attitude toward her continued.

"Here's the basket of filing that needs to be done and here are the cabinets. The files are all alphabetical, so I'd say that any clerk who thinks she should see the Premier should have it all looked after by noon."

Vivian found herself alone in a small, narrow room lined with metal chests of drawers. It was just behind the older woman's desk and she could hear her on the phone.

"Gladys, is that you? Wait till lunch time. I've got to tell you the funniest thing. Meet me in the rotunda at twelve."

Vivian hadn't thought it was possible to be more miserable than she had been at secretarial school, but her first three days as the file clerk for the Attorney General of Alberta was far, far worse than any experience in the school. She was miserable and determined to move back to the comforts of her parents' home. Viv left the cramped file room on Friday afternoon with nothing to look forward to but an empty weekend followed by another horrid five day stretch of stuffing documents into folders.

As she started down the steps of the "Ledge," she noticed a young woman about her own age standing on a step near the sidewalk. The girl appeared to be staring at Vivian as she descended the stairs. When the two were on the same step, the girl spoke to Vivian.

"Hello, my name's Agnes. You're the new girl in the A.G.'s office, aren't you?"

It took Vivian a minute to realize it was she who was being spoken to.

"Yes, I guess I am," she replied.

"Ooh, that's rough. That means you're working for the battle axe. We'll hate her. Try to get out of there as soon as you can but, until you do, you can at least come and have your lunch outside with us. It's a bit cold by now but even so, it sure beats sitting at your desk, don't you think?"

The girl chatted on and Vivian was surprised at how very grateful she felt for the obvious offer of camaraderie. Agnes began walking beside her and so Vivian presumed the girl must also live north of the Legislative Building.

"There's a group of us going to the movies tonight," Agnes informed Vivian. "Would you like to come with us? *The Vagabond King* is playing and they say its a dream."

"Why, yes," Vivian replied. "I would like that, I'd like that very much. Shall I meet you at the theatre?"

"No, that's all right. I'll come by for you at the 'Y.' It's on my way anyway. How's seven o'clock sound?"

"Fine. Seven o'clock sounds fine," Vivian told her new friend, not yet curious about how the girl would know where she lived.

As good as her word, Agnes arrived at the door of the residence right at seven o'clock.

"A nice change from waiting in the cold for John," Vivian thought as she started down the walk to meet the group of girls about her own age waiting at the curb.

Agnes introduced her to everyone but, try as she might, Vivian couldn't keep all the girls' names straight with their faces. Jean's wearing the little fur hat, she told herself trying to remember at least one or two. But, no, that was Anne in the hat and Jean was bareheaded, but had a smashing red coat on. Then, which one was Helen? Oh, well, it didn't matter all that much for tonight, Vivian supposed. What mattered was that they were all friendly and seemed to enjoy having her along.

At the end of the evening they made plans to go walking together after church on Sunday. It was clear that Viv was included in those plans. By Monday morning Vivian was less determined to flee for home. She had a nice group of friends to do things with when John wasn't available and, besides, she was sure he'd leave his wife by Christmas time at the latest.

A stray thought crept into Vivian MacMillan's mind occasionally, but every time it did, she pushed it away. Still, the thought niggled through – why did she feel happier with her new girlfriends than she did when she was with John? Fortunately, all those confusing concerns would be gone shortly – once she and John were married.

The next week flew past for Vivian. Her dreary days among the file cabinets were so much easier to bear with lunchtimes and walks home with friends to look forward to each day.

Thursday afternoon, Agnes informed Vivian that the movie at the Roxy had changed and the same group of girls would be going the next night. Vivian gratefully accepted the implied invitation and hoped that soon her inclusion in their weekend adventures would be expected.

In the evening, while getting her clothes ready for work the next day, Vivian was called to the phone. It was Brownlee.

"I'm home from Ottawa. Stay late at the office tomorrow afternoon. I'll come down and get you when everyone else has gone."

He hung up without giving her a chance to explain that she already had plans. Somehow his self-centered manner didn't seem important. Vivian knew she wouldn't have said anything about her arrangements even if he'd asked. Which he certainly hadn't.

Torn between disappointment at having to miss an outing with her new friends and anticipation at seeing Brownlee, Vivian returned to her room. She'd have to think of an excuse to give Agnes. She could hardly tell the truth, not yet, anyway. Perhaps it would be tomorrow night that John would inform her he was leaving his wife and preparing to share his life with her. She hoped he'd had enough time to make all the arrangements by now.

Vivian worried all through her work day. She'd never had a group of friends before and now the thought of having to lie to them was causing her considerable angst. She'd have to tell Agnes something ordinary enough to be believable and yet extraordinary enough to explain staying at work late, especially on a Friday. By five o'clock the situation itself had created the excuse.

"Aren't you ready yet?" Agnes called to Vivian from the entrance to the filing room.

"Oh, Agnes, no, I'm not. I don't know where my mind's been all day and I'm still in a horrible muddle here. I'm going to stay and fix it up as best I can. There are files that people will need first thing on Monday morning and I'm nowhere near getting to all of them yet."

The words spilled out of Vivian's mouth far more readily than she expected they would, perhaps because she wasn't really lying. She had, indeed, been working very inefficiently and was well behind on her routine duties.

"Will you join us at the cinema, then? The show doesn't start until eight o'clock," Agnes inquired.

Vivian hesitated. She hated to miss the opportunity to take in a movie with her new friends, but she had no idea what John's plans were.

"Thanks, Agnes, but I think I'll go straight home and get to bed early tonight," she replied wistfully. "I've had a headache this afternoon."

Again the explanation came more readily than Vivian had imagined it would, but again it also contained a nugget of truth. She certainly did have a pounding headache.

"Gee, Viv, I'm sorry about that," Agnes responded with sincere sympathy in her voice. "I'll try to stop by your building sometime on Saturday to see how you're doing."

The young woman's friendly offer brought a lump to Vivian's throat. She was surprised to realize how very much she enjoyed being with Agnes and the others. Worse, a dreadful realization crept to the surface of Vivian MacMillan's consciousness. She knew now that she dreaded, almost beyond endurance, the thought of another brutal encounter on the seat of John Brownlee's Studebaker.

With Agnes gone and the hallway empty, Vivian relaxed enough to take a few deep, cleansing breaths.

"What can I do?" she wondered helplessly and began to sob softly, her head against a cold, hard file cabinet. Wallowing in her powerlessness and misery, holding government documents in one hand and a very damp hankie in the other, Vivian finally let the anxiety flood over her.

Somewhere in the distance she heard a phone ringing. It rang and rang and rang. Strange, the secretary rarely let the telephone go unanswered for more than two rings. Finally, the sound impinged on Vivian's injured psyche. The secretary would not be answering the phone because she had left some time ago. There was probably no one else in this part of the building except her and that call was, no doubt, her summons to the Premier's office.

Not answering the phone wasn't an option and so Vivian made her way from the filing room, across the hall to the secretary's desk and lifted the receiver from its cradle.

"Where have you been?" Brownlee bellowed into the mouthpiece of his telephone two floors above.

"Here," the young woman replied monosyllabically.

"Well, you're through work for the day now. Come up and see me. Do you know how to find my office?"

"Yes," she told him.

"Well, then up you come," he said, lightening his tone slightly. "But take the side stairway in case there's anyone else still in the building."

Instead of the seat of the car, this tryst took place on a large green leather arm chair in Premier John Brownlee's office. The change of venue did nothing to relieve Vivian's feelings of revulsion and humiliation. As always, as soon as the act was completed, both Brownlee and MacMillan hurried to straighten their minimally disturbed appearances. Only those articles of clothing that would have directly impeded the act were ever removed.

"Are you doing a good job downstairs?" the man inquired.

He had sensed a change in Vivian's attitude and was trying to demonstrate interest in the girl's life. His ploy was unsuccessful. Vivian heard the coldness in his voice and assumed his question was a reprimand. She defended herself as best she was able.

"I was doing fine until today," she replied. "If you've heard anything different you shouldn't believe it. It may be only that secretary saying things about me. She talks about all the girls. You can ask anyone."

Brownlee threw back his head and laughed. The reaction completely confused the youngster and she stared in disbelief, waiting for the outburst to end.

"Do you really think I'm about to talk to clerks in the Attorney General's office?" he snorted through deep guffaws. "I hardly think so, my dear. I am the Premier after all, I merely meant to indicate an interest in your well-being and I'm glad to hear that on the whole you think you're doing a credible job. I'm sure you are. Now that that's settled, Vivian, perhaps we can discuss your living arrangements."

Vivian's heart gave an extra beat. She looked up at the man pacing back and forth in front of her. At last he'd decided to ask her to live with him.

"I've already told you, Vivian, that my wife is not well."

Vivian nodded in agreement, although from what she'd seen so far, Mrs. Brownlee appeared to be in perfect health.

"I'd like to make arrangements to have you move in to my home," Brownlee continued to Vivian's utter amazement. "Would that be agreeable to you?"

"Yes, yes, of course it would," Vivian replied, trying, but not quite succeeding, in using the man's name.

"There's a good girl, then," the man went on. "You'll still be coming to work here during the days but in the evenings and on the weekends you'll be available to help Mrs. Brownlee in any way you can."

Vivian stared at the man, uncomprehendingly.

"Mrs. Brownlee will be there?" she stammered.

"Of course Mrs. Brownlee will be there. She's my wife. Where did you think she would be, my beautiful, slow-witted child?"

Vivian couldn't reply.

"Get yourself home to your room now and first thing tomorrow morning let the matron know you'll be moving at the end of the month. Oh, and don't worry about finances. I know your wages are low, so I won't charge you any more than you're paying now to live in residence. You're a very lucky girl, Vivian. I hope you appreciate the offer I'm making to you and I hope you'll remember to repay all my kindness with service to my wife. Away you go now, I still have work to catch up on and I'd like to get home in time to see my sons before their bedtimes."

Vivian wandered slowly through Edmonton's darkening streets. Whatever had she done to cause all of this? Whatever could she do to escape it? She could not see an answer to either.

"Perhaps by morning it will make more sense to me," Vivian told herself as she climbed in between the cold, white sheets of her cot that evening.

But it didn't. Nor did anything make any more sense by the following weekend when she packed her suitcase in preparation to settle in at the Brownlee's home. Vivian MacMillan's long awaited move from her spartan room at the YWCA was not the joyful occasion she'd expected it to be. Suppressing every emotion she could, Vivian rode the streetcar across the High Level Bridge. The suitcase at her feet slapped against her shins with each bump. In a perverse way, Vivian enjoyed the slight pain it caused.

"I'll have a bruise there tomorrow," she thought, and then proceeded to focus all her attention on that simple thought. It was the only reality in her life which Vivian MacMillan could deal with at present.

Vivian's mind stayed numb throughout her first weekend in the Brownlee home. She saw little of Brownlee himself during the day, and despite his assertions that his wife was not well, the woman rarely seemed to need or want Vivian's assistance. She was merely pleasant to her new boarder on the few occasions their lives intersected. Had Vivian been thinking more clearly, she might have realized that the older woman was as surprised and confused by the girl's presence in the Premier's home as Vivian was herself.

Not sure what areas of the house she'd be welcome in, Vivian spent much of her free time lying on her bed reading romance magazines. Her bedroom was not much larger than a closet and held only the bare minimum of furniture. It was situated at the back of the house, away from the two main bedrooms. Clearly, it had been intended to serve as the maid's room, if the Brownlees could have afforded such a luxury.

On the evening of Vivian's first, unhappy night on Edmonton's south side, John Brownlee came out of his main floor study. He approached the girl as she was preparing to wash the family's supper dishes.

"Tonight, after everyone has gone to bed I want you to stay awake. Listen for the toilet to flush. That will be your signal that I'm sure everyone else in the house is asleep. When you hear the flush, get up immediately and walk to the bathroom door. The noise of the toilet will cover your footsteps. Then we'll walk together, step by step, into my bedroom. If anyone hears us it will sound like only one person walking back from the bathroom and no one's suspicions will be aroused. Then you can come to my bed and be my own precious girl and it will be just like it was when you had me that very first time."

Vivian stifled a gasp at the suggestion. Her heart raced in fear as she noticed beads of perspiration forming on the man's forehead. How could she lie with him in his own bed? Wouldn't his wife be right there beside them? The girl stood at the sink shivering in terror. She needed time to think. After tidying the kitchen, Vivian took her hat, coat and boots from the front hall closet and announced to no one in particular, "I'm going for a walk."

She'd remembered seeing a telephone kiosk on her way to the Brownlee's house the day before. She'd place a collect call to her mother and soon she'd be on the train back to the security of her home in Edson. Walking quickly, Vivian checked over her shoulder several times to see if she was being followed. The sidewalk behind her remained empty. Breathlessly she asked the operator to connect her call.

"Mama?" she asked after her mother agreed to accept the charges for the call. "Mama, thank you. I'm sorry to have to call this way but it's important. I need to tell you something."

Sensing the urgency in her daughter's voice the older woman urged her daughter to explain herself. "You see, I've moved from my room at the YWCA residence and I'm living at the Brownlee's house now."

"Why Vivian, that's wonderful news. I'm so glad you called. You're right. That is important news. Just wait until your father hears. He'll be so pleased," the girl's mother gushed.

The woman's ill-placed enthusiasm took Vivian completely by surprise. She could not think what to say next.

"And you still have that job in the Attorney General's office, don't you?" Mrs. MacMillan continued. "We're so proud of you dear. You certainly made the right decision when you struck out for Edmonton. I should ring off now dear, but I do thank you for calling with such good news. Bye for now."

Vivian's last hope for salvation from the bizarre circumstances she'd found herself in evaporated with the sound of a dial tone in her ear. She left the public telephone booth and slowly made her way back to Brownlee's home. An all-pervasive depression settled over her mind and body.

Only because she could not think of anything else to do, Vivian prepared for bed as soon as she got back to the house. Staring sleeplessly at the ceiling, Vivian imagined the exciting weekend her new-found friends would have had, going to shows, out for tea and for long walks together, their arms affectionately linked. How ever could she explain her absence from the group's activities this past weekend? Agnes would be full of questions at lunch on Monday. She'd have to think of some convincing story, because it seemed doubtful to Vivian that she'd ever again be free to enjoy the slice of normalcy she'd barely glimpsed.

Vivian may have drifted off to sleep in spite of herself, because the sound of the nearby toilet flushing jolted her into consciousness. Was that the signal she wondered, or was that merely a result of one of the family's bedtime preparations? She had no clock in her tiny room and she couldn't see the hands on her wristwatch in the dark. Vivian lay paralyzed by confusion and fright until she heard the toilet flush a second time. She jumped to her feet, turned on the bedroom light and opened the door just a crack.

There, at the bathroom doorway stood Alberta's premier, his thin, bare legs protruding from a tartan dressing gown. Despite her fear, a small portion of Vivian enjoyed how absolutely ridiculous the man looked. He had taken off his glasses and his face was distorted by his squinting attempt to see down the darkened hallway. He waved excitedly to her to come to him and when she did the two matched their steps for the remaining distance to Brownlee's bed.

Vivian was surprised and relieved to find it was not a double bed with Mrs. Brownlee asleep on the other side. Brownlee slept in one of two single beds in the front bedroom. His older son slept peacefully in the other.

"Where were you?" he demanded in an angry whisper. "If this arrangement is to work you'll have to do better than that."

Vivian said nothing. She lay as still as possible beside the man. Having him pawing at her body while they were both at least partially clothed had become barely tolerable, but feeling his soft flesh against hers was almost more than the girl's stomach could endure. She fought encroaching nausea with all the strength she could summon.

The man accomplished his purpose expediently, after which Vivian left his bed immediately. Seconds later the toilet in the Brownlee house flushed again. And again. And again. This time the sound didn't cover retreating footsteps, but the pathetic heaving sounds coming from Vivian's body as she vomited time and time again. She returned to her bed and slept as though in a coma.

Sunrise and the effects of her deep sleep combined to lighten Vivian's mood somewhat. She dressed quickly and rode the streetcar to the stop nearest the Legislative Building. Agnes stood waiting for her at the entrance to the women's cloak room.

"Where did you get to all weekend?" Vivian's young friend asked in an excited voice. "We missed you. Do you have a wonderfully romantic story to share with me over lunch?"

Vivian laughed for the first time in several days.

"I missed all of you too," she began easily. To her amazement the rest of the story followed with equal ease, because, with a few omissions, it was the truth.

"I don't know when I'll be able to join you again. You see, I've gone to live at the Premier's house in order to help his ailing wife. He and my father are close and I really see this as my duty. The poor soul, his wife, she has very little time left. I'll certainly do what I can to lessen her suffering."

Agnes's facial expression indicated she was suitably impressed with the limited information she'd been made privy to.

"Oh," she exclaimed. "That's just the most romantic thing I've ever heard. Vivian, you're such a good person but you're a lucky one too. I'd give anything to be in your position."

Vivian sincerely doubted that, but she said nothing to dissuade her friend's delusions. Oddly, as she continued her fabrication of the recent events in her life, Vivian became quite enraptured of her own plotline. Explaining a skewed version of the truth gave her insight she'd not been blessed with before.

If she was in a position of power while Brownlee was satisfying himself with her at the side of a rural road, surely this current arrangement only increased the potential. Vivian hung up her coat, arranged to meet Agnes at lunchtime and sauntered into the file room with a small smile on her lips.

Brownlee was out of town the next week and so the opportunity to experiment with her new strength had to be delayed. The deferment only served to fortify her resolve.

His first night back in Edmonton, Brownlee once again signaled his desires by flushing the toilet. A very changed Vivian MacMillan met him in the hallway and accompanied him, step for step, to the bed beside his sleeping son.

"Your wife's not ill. Not that I can see anyway. Why do you want me here?" she inquired.

It took Brownlee a minute to respond. He'd expected Vivian to be completely silent when she came to his bed.

"Why for me, of course, you silly girl," he answered, while attempting to begin what euphemistically might have been referred to as love-making. "I want you here because I love you. I told you before I have loved you from the first time I saw you. You must try to understand about my wife's illness. It is not something I should be discussing with you except to say you must realize she can't truly be a wife to me. If she could, she would be lying here beside me, not you."

"If you love me and your wife can't be a wife to you, when are you going to leave her and marry me?" Vivian asked.

"I could never do such a thing, my dear. I could never leave my wife just as you must never leave me. You are the only bright spot in my life."

Vivian didn't answer. She thought to herself, "But that 'bright spot' makes you very vulnerable. The voters would not think you were so wonderful if they knew the truth – that you are an adulterer."

Moments later they were both satisfied. He, physically, and she by the added information she'd compiled. Vivian quietly made her way out of the man's bed. She could hear his soft snores before she even reached the door.

The next day, Brownlee offered the girl a ride to work.

"I'll be going out with my friends next weekend," she announced as soon as they pulled onto the roadway.

"What?" he retorted.

"My friends. I've made some friends at work and we like to do things together on the weekends. I'll be joining them again, starting this weekend," Vivian informed the man.

"Oh, well, all right then, I guess," he replied. "I'm going to be in Calgary anyway. Just be sure to help my wife if she needs a hand."

"Your wife manages just fine and you know it," Vivian assured him. Then, buoyed by her perceived success, Vivian, with a pleasant smile on her face, launched into another demand. "I don't want to make any room and board payments while I'm living in your house. I earn my keep there, I must say, and I need the extra money to buy new clothes for myself."

Knowing he had no bargaining power, Brownlee merely nodded. They drove along in silence until they'd gone north of the building where they both worked.

"Where are you going, John?" Vivian asked, worried that he may have some retribution lined up for her.

"Nowhere," he said. "But we can hardly arrive at the Legislative Building together. I'll drop you off up ahead and you can walk back. I'll have parked my car and be in the building before you're near the grounds."

The ruse seemed ridiculous to Vivian. Most of the women who worked in the building knew that she was staying with the Premier. She said nothing to him, however, and got out of the car where he indicated she should. Neither said good-bye.

Feeling that a deal had been struck, Vivian strode the few blocks back to the beautiful Legislative grounds. A further thought struck her as she walked up the marble steps – she'd take the day off. Leaving her coat on, Vivian made her way to her superior's desk.

"I'm not feeling well, ma'am," she began. "I wasn't feeling well when I woke up this morning, but I thought a walk in the fresh air would help me to feel better but it didn't. I feel worse now. I think I should just go home."

The older woman nodded knowingly. She'd been supervising young women for a number of years and she could tell a pregnant girl when she saw one. Her assumption might actually have been right, if it hadn't been for the awful tasting dark liquid that John made Vivian drink every month.[4] As it was, the "not feeling well" story was merely that – a story. Vivian only wanted a day free to shop for some new clothes. She could certainly afford to now that there'd be no room and board payment to budget for.

After making her way to Edmonton's main street, Vivian realized she hadn't eaten breakfast. She remembered a cafe just along the block. She and Agnes and the others had gone there for tea after the movies. As soon as Vivian opened the door to the little restaurant, the aromas of coffee, exotic teas and tobacco pleasantly assaulted her nostrils. She ordered a pot of tea and some biscuits and settled into a booth near the window. Watching the world go by like this is a bit like watching a movie, Vivian thought contentedly.

Only the proprietor's boisterous call of, "Come in boys, come in," disturbed her reverie. She watched as three handsome young men noisily entered the restaurant and sat down at a table near her. Vivian stared at them unselfconsciously, for she was still enjoying the strangely detached sensation of watching a movie.

The young man closest to Vivian had his back to her. Every now and then he'd turn his head to the side. His handsome features were not lost on Viv, however, she didn't guess that he was altering his position mostly to catch a glimpse of her sitting behind him. Suddenly, he swung around fully in her direction.

"Oh, hello," he said in a quieter voice. "Are my mates and I bothering you? If so, I apologize. We've just come from a political rally and we're all a little agitated. We don't usually behave like animals, I assure you."

His short speech took Vivian completely by surprise. She felt her cheeks flush. She averted her eyes, but said nothing to the young man.

"Hey, I've seen you before," he continued, not discouraged in the least by Vivian's lack of response. "You live by the university. I've seen you out walking, I think you must take the streetcar to work. I'm right, aren't I?"

Completely out of her element, Vivian MacMillan had no idea what an appropriate response to this man might be. She merely nodded, confirming that his assumptions were correct. By now he had turned his chair away from where his friends sat and moved it toward Vivian's table.

"My name is John Caldwell," the friendly young man explained while extending his hand to Vivian. "I'm a student at the university. That's why I've seen you. I live on the campus, in the interns' residence. We're all students. I'm in medicine but the others are studying law."

Vivian nodded.

"I do hope we didn't frighten you. We just get a little worked up about this stupid government. It's nothing more than a bunch of agrarian hicks and the cities in this province will continue to suffer until we can get them out of office."

Again Vivian nodded. Despite the fact she was the Premier's mistress, the girl had no understanding of provincial or any other kind of politics. To Vivian, governments were something other people were involved in. She had neither interest in, nor knowledge of, any political party, whether their leaning be toward the city dwellers or the farmers.

As the other young men in the group got up noisily from their table, John turned and saw they were leaving. For a moment he debated staying to chat with this beautiful, silent young woman, but decided she'd probably think him far too brash. Besides, with all the confidence of youth working for him, John Caldwell, medical student, deduced that if he'd seen the girl before, he'd see her again.

"I guess we're on our way now," he told Vivian. "It's been nice talking to you. I'm sure we'll see each other around. May I ask your name?"

"Vivian," the young woman heard herself say as she watched the men leave and John hurry to catch up with them. Temporarily paralyzed with pleasure, Vivian MacMillan stared after the retreating group. Slightly flushed cheeks and a small smile lightened her face attractively.

The girl's reverie was broken by a harsh sound nearby. She glanced toward the raucous noise and saw it came from the waitress who'd served her the tea. The woman stared at Vivian from a face distorted by something approaching a grin.

"Honey, you been smitten bad," she informed the embarrassed youngster. "I been around the block a few times and I never seen such a case as yours," she continued, as she resumed wiping the mirrored surface behind the counter.

Hurriedly, Vivian plucked a quarter from her change purse, slipped it under the saucer in front of her and left the restaurant. Once she was out on the sidewalk, away from the ignorant woman's crass assessment, the crisp fall air erased the painful humiliation of the crude comments.

By the time John Brownlee returned to Edmonton, young Caldwell's prediction that he and Vivian would see each other again had proved to be accurate. Although Vivian naively thought the second meeting was purely coincidental, John Caldwell knew better. He'd been waiting on a nearby park bench for Vivian to walk down 111 Street. As she did, he jumped up, hurried to the sidewalk and exclaimed in mock surprise as, a few steps later, their paths crossed.

Hoping that the element of carefully concocted surprise would create an advantage for him, Caldwell asked Vivian to join him for tea the following Sunday afternoon. Astonished that the fates would put such a handsome young man in her life, Vivian just nodded her assent and blushed prettily.

Vivian's resolve where the Premier was concerned strengthened through this new friendship. Enjoying Caldwell's attentions and having Brownlee out of sight combined to help Viv push the clandestine affair far from her mind. She was actually beginning to forget about John Brownlee and, although she knew when he was due back in Edmonton, his return came as a surprise to her. The first glimpse she had of him came as he was standing in the rotunda, ostensibly watching the civil servants' lunch hour activity. As she passed him on her way to collect her coat and lunch from the cloak room, he caught her eye and spoke quietly to her. He hoped it would look as though he was merely mingling, thoughtfully, with the lower echelons.

Vivian hesitated only a minute before replying, much too loudly for Brownlee's comfort, "That won't be convenient, sir. I have a date. I will be home by ten."

With the ground rules apparently altered once again, the liaison proceeded between the Premier and the file clerk in the Attorney General's office. For the next two and a half years, Vivian MacMillan lived at the Brownlee's home, worked in the provincial government offices, saw her friends during her spare time and regularly rose from her bed at the sound of the toilet flushing.

In 1933, while John Brownlee was in Ottawa attending sessions of the Royal Commission on Banking and Currency, his relationship with Vivian changed again. Vivian and her father, Allan MacMillan, launched a civil suit against the Premier. The MacMillans chose an obscure point of law which read, in part,

"The father . . . of any unmarried female who has been seduced and for whose seduction the father . . . could maintain an action in case such unmarried female was at the time dwelling under his . . . protection may maintain an action for the seduction, notwithstanding such unmarried female was at the time of her seduction serving or residing with another person upon hire or otherwise.

"Notwithstanding anything in this act, an action for seduction may be maintained by any unmarried female who has been seduced in her own name, in the same manner as an action for any other tort and in any such action she shall be entitled to such damages as may be awarded."[5]

In simple terms, this meant that if a young woman had been seduced, and therefore presumably had lost her "virtue and honor" (both of which were located in the hymen in that era), her father was also considered to be a victim.

And that is the story, from clandestine beginning to dramatically public end, of the 'love' affair between John E. Brownlee, Premier of Alberta, and Vivian MacMillan, once aspiring concert pianist.

Or is it?

Although Vivian and her father first visited Edmonton lawyer Neil Maclean, K.C., early in August 1933, to make the necessary arrangements, the lawyer did nothing to launch the suit until Friday, September 22, 1933. The delay was not by chance. Maclean, a staunch Liberal supporter and known Brownlee detractor, was well aware of the Premier's schedule. John Brownlee, the ever-dedicated politician, was in Ottawa when Neil Maclean chose to enter the action in Alberta's provincial court.

In Edmonton, Brownlee's closest advisors gathered to place a long distance phone call. After apologizing for disturbing his visit to the nation's capital, the men launched directly into the reason for their call. They knew the story would make the front pages of the local paper the next day and be picked up quickly by news services all over the country. This was undeniably a hot news item.

Brownlee gave no reaction when he was informed of the situation. That is, no reaction that was discernible to his callers.

"I cannot return to Alberta right now," Brownlee informed his staff. "These hearings are set to continue for another week. I've committed myself to attending and I shall keep my word."

Somewhat shocked at their leader's response to what they viewed as a very serious circumstance, the men exchanged looks.

"Perhaps a few hours to compose your thoughts would help," the caller suggested.

"Yes, perhaps. I'll call you back later this afternoon. I'm sure by then I'll have some questions I need you to answer for me and you may have additional information. For now there seems little to say."

With that, the Premier hung up the phone and paced about the office assigned to him for his stay in Ottawa. He realized that, no matter what additional information his advisors might gather, he'd need the services of a lawyer. Brownlee placed a long distance call to his solicitor in Calgary.

Marshall Porter had already heard rumors of the action even though he was 300 kilometres south of the courthouse and the claim had been registered only hours before. He'd reacted with shocked disbelief and was pleased to hear from Brownlee himself.

"You have twenty-five days to file your defense," the lawyer explained.

"Fine then," Brownlee said. "What about my wife? Is she aware?"

"I don't know, sir. Would you like me to call her?"

"No, that's all right, I'll do it myself. But what of the girl? Where is she? She had been working in the Attorney General's office."

"I've heard that she's left Edmonton, taken her annual leave, and is at her parents' home in Hinton," the Porter said.

"Edson," Brownlee corrected.

"What's that, sir?"

"Edson, the girl's home is in Edson, not Hinton, Porter," Brownlee clarified.

"I see sir," the other man answered, puzzled at the Premier's attention to a seemingly inconsequential detail. "You're wanting me to act on your behalf throughout this, I take it, John?"

"Yes, please do take care of it for me."

"I'll begin right away. I suspect there's more to this than meets the eye," Porter said.

"You may be right. I'll leave you to find that out and now I'll call my wife. She and my sons would do well to go away for a few days."

The conversation left Porter unnerved. Nothing like this had ever happened before, that he could recall. And now it was his job to defend this much admired leader's dignity. It was not a mantle a lawyer could wear lightly.

In Edmonton, John Brownlee's wife was also feeling pressured by the breaking story. Reporters from radio stations, newspapers and magazines had beaten a path to her door. As Neil Maclean knew it would, word of his carefully timed actions spread quickly.

Weeks before, on her lawyer's advice, Vivian had arranged her holidays from work to coincide with Brownlee's trip to Ottawa. She was safely in Edson. It would take hours for the ripples caused by the rising uproar to reach her home. And when they did, those ripples would stop dead at the front door.

Vivian MacMillan and her parents were three of only half a dozen people in the province prepared for the events at hand. What's more, Allan MacMillan, Vivian's father, was ready to take on all comers. No one would disturb his daughter's isolation. She had already been through enough. He'd have no hesitation leveling trespassing charges against anyone who approached his home uninvited. Once you've begun legal action against the Premier of the province, it's not much of a feat to throw a few newshounds in jail.

By the time the story hit the newspapers, the key players had their initial strategies mapped out. Brownlee would not interrupt his duties in Ottawa but would return, as planned, immediately following the closing meeting on October 1. His lawyer pointed out to the press that as defendants they had more than three weeks in which to file his defence.[6]

Vivian remained with her parents, in seclusion. She spent most of her time at the keyboard polishing her now rusty musical skills. Even Maclean, Vivian's lawyer, continued his practice pretty much undisturbed. Most of his work for this case had already been done and done well. He'd rarely felt so confident about winning an action. The case was as clear-cut as it was sensational. Winning this case would surely be one of the most satisfying highlights of his career.[7]

Meanwhile, in Calgary, Porter knew he would need help in order to get through everything which would require his attention in the next few weeks. He asked his colleague Arthur Smith to assist him. It would take the two of them, working at a feverish pace, to organize Brownlee's defence and hopefully find ammunition for a countersuit.

By the time Brownlee returned to Edmonton, Vivian had mailed a letter of resignation to her supervisor at the provincial government offices. On Monday, October 3, 1933, John Brownlee entered the Legislative Building for the first time since the story broke. Clearly not willing to discuss the matter, he issued a terse, one sentence statement.

"I do not feel free to discuss it now [as] it is in the courts."[8]

Vivian's former co-workers certainly didn't share the Premier's reluctance to discuss the news. Employee absenteeism reached an all time low at the provincial government offices that day. Clerks, stenographers and aides hurried to their desks ready to share and listen to any or all gossip and opinions. Those in authority were predictably tight-lipped.

By early November in 1933, the fuel for gossip ran low. On November 14, a seven-sentence, page one, report in the *Edmonton Journal* re-stocked the rumor mongers' ammunition caches. The headline, which took up almost as much space as the story itself, read, "Counterclaim Is Served – Service in Brownlee Case Has Been Made – STEPS COMPLETED – Trial Considered Unlikely to Come Until New Year."

The body of the piece held the fodder.

Service of Premier Brownlee's counterclaim [accusing Vivian, et al of attempted extortion] was made Monday on John Caldwell, medical student, and Miss Vivian MacMillan, formerly of the attorney-general's department.

Caldwell was served in this city by bailiff's officers while the counterclaim against Miss MacMillan, who is at her house in Edson was accepted by the office of Neil D. Maclean, K.C., her solicitor.

The next step then will be the examinations for discovery, which are expected to take some time.

Date of the trial then will be set by a supreme court judge, sitting in chambers, providing there are no other delays.

Judging by opinions expressed Tuesday, the cases may not come to trial before some time in the new year.[9]

Everyone in the province and most people in the country had an opinion. The story provided a new and inviting subject for tongues previously limited to enumerating the horrors of the Great Depression. This latest twist invited even further comment.

On November 18, 1933, the legal battle and the prurient interest in it, heated up considerably. Newspapers reported that one John Caldwell, along with Vivian MacMillan, had filed a defence against the Premier's counterclaim. The two asserted they had not "conspired with each other or with any other person to obtain money from the plaintiff . . . and deny that either of them made any threats of any nature or kind in default of payment either as alleged in the counterclaim or at all."

In a case of classic legalese redundancy, the statement went on for another six paragraphs, virtually repeating the opening sentence. The document ended with, "Wherefore the defendants by counterclaim [John Caldwell and Vivian MacMillan] ask that this counterclaim be dismissed with costs."[10]

Despite its high profile, the cases had to wait their turn as the wheels of justice slowly ground out previously registered suits. Applications for adjournments made the wait even longer. By Friday, April 13, 1934, the case of MacMillan versus Brownlee had been postponed three times.[11]

Lawyer Arthur Smith, Marshal Porter's partner in defending the Premier, backed his request for a further adjournment with the following explanation:

> I seek this adjournment because the defendant is the prime minister [sic]of this province, the legislature is still in session and he is the leader of the government. . . . Leading a government is something that takes the most of one's time to say the least. I will give an undertaking that I will be ready to go ahead as soon as the legislature is over.[12]

Neil Maclean, lawyer for the plaintiff, agreed and the judge ruled that the case be adjourned for an additional two weeks.

Still, the Premier himself was mute on the issue and continued to attend to the day-to-day tasks necessary for running a province. Despite Brownlee's apparent inattention to the matter, he, and all of the others involved, wanted the case to be heard before the summer recess. And it was.

Vivian MacMillan was the first witness to be called. Her calm and quiet recounting of the bizarre relationship she shared with John E. Brownlee had the courtroom abuzz with excitement. She told of her nightly trips down the hallway in the Brownlee's home, her footsteps muffled by the Premier's signal to her – a flushing toilet.

Much to the delight of the reporters present, the pretty young witness summed up the situation with the statement, "He played with me like a cat plays with a mouse." Copy this colorful was a dividend in an already significant news story.

John Caldwell also took the stand. As a medical student and the son of a minister, Caldwell made a highly believable witness. He told how he and Vivian had met, that they began to see one another socially and soon began to date. The young man explained that he realized very early in the relationship that he was in love with Vivian, but that he kept his feelings to himself for well over a year, feeling that explaining the intensity of his affections for Vivian might frighten her away.

"Why did you presume that?" Neil Maclean asked the handsome young man.

"Miss MacMillan was always extremely reserved, almost to the point of appearing afraid during any discussion of feelings," Caldwell responded.

"Did you ever tell Miss MacMillan how you felt about her?" the lawyer probed.

"Yes," the young man replied before explaining that when he admitted his love for her to Vivian, she responded with an emotional outburst.

"She didn't really ever answer me. As soon as I told her I loved her and asked her to marry me she began to weep uncontrollably. After sometime she regained control and confessed that she, too, loved me but because of a situation beyond her control, she'd never be free to marry."

"Did you accept her explanation without question?" Maclean asked.

"No, I didn't. I wanted to know about any situation, whether it was beyond her control or not, that would stop the two of us from sharing the rest of our lives," Caldwell continued. "After much probing, Vivian confessed that she'd been as much as a sex slave to the Premier of this province for the past several years."

"Did you believe Miss MacMillan's story?"

"Of course," Caldwell snapped angrily at the lawyer. "It wasn't a story. It was the truth. The possibility of not believing Vivian MacMillan never entered my mind."

Caldwell went on to explain that once he had a thorough understanding of the bizarre situation, he counseled Vivian to move out of the Brownlees' residence at once. He related that she agreed to do as he suggested and she had rented a small apartment close to her work.

"You could see her relief from the very first. She was so happy to finally be free," he testified. "She was so content that it took me weeks to convince her that she had suffered grievous harm that was in no way her fault. When she finally saw that this was so, we took the train to Edson and Vivian told her parents everything. This was very difficult for her to do and she broke down many times during the conversation. She and her mother went off to another room after less than half an hour."

Caldwell explained that he and Mr. MacMillan then discussed what should be done. Mr. MacMillan apparently agreed with the young medical student that Vivian would need a lawyer, but as a former mayor he felt somewhat self-conscious about seeking legal counsel in Edson.

"Because of that it was agreed that I should pursue the matter in Edmonton and I arranged for the initial appointment at your office," Caldwell stated.

"Has anyone approached either you or Miss MacMillan regarding the case since then?"

"Yes, a young woman visited Miss MacMillan's apartment. She said she was sent by someone high up who had the money and the authority to offer Vivian a substantial reward in return for dropping the charges against Mr. Brownlee."

"I see, and did Miss MacMillan ask this woman who had sent her?"

"No, Miss MacMillan didn't. She was surprised and caught off guard. Fortunately, I had been on my way over to pick Vivian up for a date. I arrived just as the woman was leaving. I had her repeat the message she'd given to Vivian and then I asked her what her position in all of this was.

She explained that she'd been given this message by her boss, Harry Brace."

"And please tell the court, Mr. Caldwell, who is Harry Brace."

"He's the provincial fire commissioner and superintendent of insurance. The woman who came to visit Vivian was merely a stenographer in his department," Caldwell concluded.

"Thank you, Mr. Caldwell, those are all my questions but please stay on the witness stand. I'm sure my learned colleague, Mr. Porter of Calgary, will have some questions to ask you."

"You presume correctly, Mr. Maclean," the defense lawyer confirmed, rising from his chair beside the Premier. "Mr. Caldwell, I submit to you that the entire scenario on which this case is based was trumped up by you in a criminal attempt to ease your own financial troubles."

"That is a lie!" Caldwell protested loudly.

"Please, Mr. Caldwell there is absolutely no need to raise your voice," Judge Ives scolded the young man.

"I'm sorry, sir, but Mr. Porter's allegations are preposterous. My father is a minister and he has been supporting me through medical school and once I have graduated I will be able to earn a substantial income."

"That's fine, but you must remember to uphold the dignity of this court at all times when you are in my courtroom," the judge admonished.

John Caldwell nodded and turned his attention back to Brownlee's lawyer.

"That may be so, Mr. Caldwell but I suggest that, like many young people today, the price tag on your tastes exceeds your financial well-being."

Caldwell started to reply, but was silenced by a signal from Porter's hand.

"I do not make this suggestion lightly, Mr. Caldwell. I propose to you that on several occasions just before you approached my learned colleague, Mr. Maclean, regarding this case, you attempted to borrow substantial sums of money from various Edmontonians. I further submit to you that you offered as collateral for those loans, the reassurance that because you were behind a big and potentially profitable suit you would soon be in a position to easily re-pay the debt."

"That is absolutely untrue," John Caldwell stated flatly while staring at John Brownlee as if to bore right through the man.

"Is it not true, Mr. Caldwell, that in order to help finance your expenses at medical school you had arranged with a Mr. Harold Davies, of Maclean's Publishing, to sell subscriptions to that magazine? And is it not true, Mr. Caldwell that several days after you made those arrangements you canceled them? Did you not turn down that sales position with Maclean's publishing saying you had found an alternative way to make money? I believe, Mr. Caldwell, that I can offer an exact quote of the words you used while turning down this position, I believe you said, 'It's not a nice way to make money but there's $25 000 in it.' Is that not true, Mr. Caldwell?"

"No," came the monosyllabic answer.

Premier Brownlee sat motionless to the end of John Caldwell's testimony, only occasionally returning the young man's gaze. Brownlee was entirely comfortable in courtrooms. Comfortable and confident. He was used to being victorious in any courtroom and his manner that first day in the defendant's chair didn't appear to be an exception. If he felt at all nervous or agitated by what he'd heard, Brownlee didn't let it show.

He even retained the cool, calm demeanor while on the witness stand.

"I have no idea where this young lady's story may have come from. I categorically deny ever making any untoward advances to her. My wife, as you can see by her presence here today, unquestioningly accepts my word." Brownlee addressed the courtroom in carefully measured tones.

Over the years he'd learned how important inflection could be to a witness's credibility. Carefully continuing to use authoritarian tones, the Premier disclosed that both he and his wife had gone out of their way, over the past few years, to be kind to young Vivian MacMillan. He postulated that this kindness may have been mistaken, both by Miss MacMillan and Mr. Caldwell, as vulnerability.

"Their suit against me is nothing more than an attempt at extortion. Fortunately, I have enough faith in the workings of the Canadian court system to be confident that they will not succeed in their culpable endeavour."

Oddly, both the defence and the prosecution felt satisfied by the events of the trial's opening day. All the lawyers and their clients were confident that their version of the truth would ultimately be revealed.

The trial added vicarious color and excitement to the bleak lives of ordinary citizens caught in the grasp of the worst economic downturn the world had ever known. Mere survival occupied most people's minds most of the time. An event like this was sure to keep them entertained for weeks. A few Edmontonians were even fortunate enough to be able to sit in on the trial. The rest of Canada had to wait to either hear reports on the radio or read them in the next day's news.

Journalists were ecstatic. They had a huge story to cover and sales of their newspapers were sure to increase. The case had developed a enormous following across the country.

The strongly Liberal *Edmonton Bulletin* had an especially good time in reporting the day's events. The paper was known to be the more sensationalist of the city's two dailies. Not content to print any testimony verbatim, a reporter paraphrased the proceedings for his readers as, "love-torn sex crazed victim of passion and jealousy."

Free copies of the *Bulletin* were supplied to the town of Ponoka. The community was well outside the newspaper's usual distribution area, but the Liberal supporters felt that, as this was Brownlee's home riding, the additional expense and inconvenience would prove to have been an investment come election time.

Defense lawyers Smith and Porter were in no position to sit back and be entertained by the goings on. They needed more ammunition in their fight to save the Premier. Accordingly, they sent an investigator looking for one Carl Snell, high school teacher. They found him in a small Nova Scotia town. It was Snell who had proposed marriage to Vivian MacMillan while she still resided in Edson with her parents. If the teacher would testify that he and the MacMillan girl had indulged in a physical relationship, then her credibility would, effectively, be reduced to zero. Porter was delighted to have this ace up his sleeve.

Snell agreed to testify and was brought to Edmonton. A few days later, he mysteriously changed his mind and abruptly left Edmonton. Brownlee's lawyers did not pursue the matter.

On Friday, June 29, the trial ended. Or seemed to end. After deliberating five hours, the jurors returned a verdict of "guilty" in the original lawsuit brought against Premier Brownlee. The *Edmonton Journal* carried the complete story under the headline

FLASH

The jury recommended an award of $10,000 be paid to Vivian MacMillan. An additional $5,000, they advised, should be paid to Allan MacMillan, her father as compensation for "interference with a daughter's services."

Judge Ives issued an unusual closing statement that foreshadowed the legal entanglements to come. In reply to the jury's statement he said, "Gentlemen, I can only say that I strongly disagree with you."[13] The full implication of that highly unusual sentence remained a mystery for several days.

Despite this inferred and potentially influential support, Brownlee immediately dropped the counter suit against John Caldwell and Vivian MacMillan and resigned as Premier.

The Wednesday following the jury decision, Mr. Justice Ives made another announcement. Although he didn't have the power to reverse the jury's verdict, he could and did cancel their recommendation for monetary compensation. He also ordered the MacMillans to pay costs to John Brownlee. These costs were enumerated at between $1200 and $1500.[14]

Ives' decision was distinctly unpopular with the majority of everyday citizens. They viewed those in power, such as politicians and judges, as being responsible for the current economic hardships. A fund to help the MacMillans finance an appeal trial sprang to life. Ironically, the address given for the fund headquarters was on the same block as Brownlee's home.

One week later, on July 11, Neil Maclean, lawyer for the plaintiff, announced his intention to appeal the judge's ruling.

"I'll take this case to the foot of the crown if I have to," he announced dramatically, referring to the Privy Council in London, England, the highest court of appeal available to Canadians.[15]

He cited a total of eight reasons for the appeal action. Accordingly, the case was heard again in January of 1935. On February 2, the same year, the Alberta court of appeal came to the same verdict that Justice Ives had – that neither Vivian nor Allan MacMillan suffered any damages due to the actions of John Brownlee.

The Canadian Newspaper Editors' Association voted the case to be the second biggest news story of the previous year. Only the Dionne quintuplets' birth in rural Ontario in May, 1934, was thought to have been bigger.

That summer, the media again carried Vivian MacMillan's name. Apparently the young woman's relationship with John Caldwell had ended, for the papers proclaimed her forthcoming marriage to Henry Sorenson, a pharmacist in Edson, Alberta. The brief write-up explained they were married on August 7 and, after a short honeymoon in Edmonton, the couple would live near the groom's business in Vivian MacMillan's home town.

Neil Maclean, Vivian's lawyer, had less celebratory rituals on his mind. He was preparing to make good his promise to continue to appeal the case. His efforts were rewarded and on March 1, 1937, the Supreme Court of Canada reversed the rulings of the two lower courts. Brownlee was ordered to pay nothing to Allan MacMillan but $10,000 plus costs to Vivian.

Now it was defence lawyer Porter's turn to organize an appeal. And, as Maclean had intimated it eventually might, the Privy Council in London, England, heard the case. On June 4, 1940, presiding judge Sir Lyman Duff dismissed the appeal and upheld the Supreme Court of Canada's monetary award to Vivian.

And so, almost six years after the issue came to trial, Vivian MacMillan Sorenson emerged the final winner. There is no record, however, of her ever having received the financial restitution she was awarded. Vivian MacMillan Sorenson and John Caldwell went on to live their lives in separate obscurities.

The UFA party, without Brownlee as its leader, lost the next election. It was widely rumored that the charges against the man had merely been an attempt of the part of the Liberal party to discredit the once popular Brownlee. From today's perspective, however, that possibility doesn't seem likely. Even if it were true, the ploy failed miserably at enhancing the Liberal's popularity. The Social Credit party won a landslide victory in the 1935 provincial election, effectively wiping out the other political parties. The charismatic, energetic William Aberhart, "Bible Bill," riding a wave of popularity that even exceeded John Brownlee's five years before, took over as Premier of Alberta.

Brownlee returned to his position as the United Grain Growers of Alberta's lawyer, where he remained employed until his retirement in 1961. He died a few weeks later.

Vivian MacMillan Sorenson died in 1980.

Only those two people ever knew the truth about the bizarre love story that brought down Alberta's provincial government. As their versions of the story conflict with one another, the truth will forever remain a mystery.

## *Endnotes*

[1] Caldwell's name was occasionally spelled "Coldwell" in the press – *Alberta Report*, November 26, 1984.

[2] *Premiers of the Northwest Territories and Alberta,1897-1991*, D. Blake McDougall, Legislative Library, Edmonton, Alberta.

[3] In newspaper reports, Carl Snell's name is periodically given as "Carol."

[4] This could have been liquefied ground beaver testicles; source – Planned Parenthood

[5] *The Edmonton Journal*, Sept 23, 1933.

[6] Ibid.

[7] According to Dr. F.L. Foster's thesis, *John Edward Brownlee: A Biography*, 1981, Neil Maclean had been waiting for an opportunity to "get Brownlee." Maclean had apparently been involved in a motor vehicle mishap while intoxicated. The young lawyer had pleaded with then-Attorney General Brownlee to have the incident wiped from the records. Brownlee refused and from that day on Neil Maclean had been looking for an opportunity to exact his revenge.

[8] *The Edmonton Journal*, October 2, 1933.

[9] *The Edmonton Journal*, November 14, 1933.

[10] *The Edmonton Journal*, November 18, 1933.

[11] *The Edmonton Journal*, April 13, 1934.

[12] Ibid.

[13] *The Edmonton Journal*, June 29, 1934.

[14] *The Edmonton Journal*, June 30, 1934.

[15] *The Edmonton Journal*, July 11, 1934.

# Pauline Johnson
# & ?

## Prologue

A portion of this preamble to the most mysterious of all great Canadian love stories may seem familiar and that is as it should be. After all, the plot of Cinderella is known to us all. This version of the popular children's bedtime story, however, is not a work of fiction but rather a small, documented portion of Canadian history.

❦    ❦    ❦

In the early 1800s Upper Canada was a rapidly developing area of settlement. Pockets of harmony between the recently arrived Europeans and the "New World's" indigenous people had evolved and were an important factor in this growth. There were even occasional marriages between the two cultures. These unions, for the most part, promoted the already existing accord. One interracial marriage that took place in the first half of the 19th century was between Chief Sakayengwaraton and Helen Martin. The groom was a proud, full-blooded native and Helen Martin was the daughter of a white woman and a native father.

Despite her divided ancestry, Helen Martin only identified with the native half of her heritage. She refused to learn English, even though her native husband spoke the language fluently and got along well with the white immigrants to the area. Because the British found his name nearly impossible to pronounce, Chief Sakayengwaraton frequently went by his Anglicized name – John Johnson.[1] Sakayengwaraton, the name those white settlers found unpronounceable, meant "the haze that rises from the ground on an autumn morning and vanishes as the day advances."[2] This enchantingly descriptive phrase became simplified to the considerably less romantic single word, "smoke," and when the English wished to acknowledge Johnson's native ancestry, they included their translation of the word. As a result, Helen Martin, who tried to completely deny any biological association with white people, married a native man who was not commonly called by his native name and title, but was merely known as John Smoke Johnson.

The couple produced five children, including a boy who was born in the fall of 1816. They named this son George and as he grew up they encouraged him to pursue traditional skills. Accordingly, George became adept at canoeing, hunting and like activities, but he also demonstrated a real flare for the dramatic and a deep appreciation of words. He loved pageantry and romance. Congruent with those qualities, but in rather stark contrast to his Indian ancestry, George Johnson became fascinated with Napoleon Bonaparte. This interest endured throughout George's life, frequently verging on obsession, as evidenced by the fact that he wanted to name his first son after the French general and did choose his last child's name to honor the tiny leader's sister.

Complementing George Johnson's love of the spectacular was his natural propensity for foreign languages. As a youngster, in addition to his native tongue, George became conversant in the languages of the tribes surrounding his home territory. He learned to speak English from his father, but because John Smoke Johnson never learned to read or write, he sent George to school to complete his education.

As a young man George was appointed to serve as an interpreter for a new missionary in the community, Reverend Adam Elliott. Elliott's wife, the former Eliza Howells, had been one of eight children born to a harsh Quaker father and an Anglican mother. Eliza's father had been banished from the Quaker church as punishment for marrying a non-Quaker woman. Despite having been rejected by the faith, he continued in strict adherence to the religion's orthodox dictates. Howells' wife died prematurely and in true story book fashion, Howells remarried, choosing a woman with no interest in her new husband's children.

The children left home as quickly as they could after their father's re-marriage. Eliza, one of the first to make the break, did so by marrying Reverend Adam Elliott. The duties inherent in being the Reverend's wife, coupled soon after with child-rearing responsibilities, meant that Eliza needed help around the house. Only her youngest sister, Emily, remained in their father and step-mother's home. Sending for the younger woman seemed like an obvious solution to both their dilemmas. Emily, who presumed that in accepting the offer she was merely extending her tenure as an unpaid domestic help, was nonetheless grateful to be given the opportunity to escape the unpleasantness of her father's home. She knew, at least, that her sister would treat her with respect that would far exceed that which she'd been receiving in her father's house. And so it was that both George Johnson, age 29, and Emily Howells, age 21, came to be employed by the Adam Elliott family.

The Reverend depended heavily on his native interpreter and when the young man fell ill with typhoid fever, Elliott was devastated and asked Emily Howells to do all she could to nurse George back to health. Perhaps to ensure that the offer was accepted, the Reverend offered to buy Emily a new dress if she agreed to his request. Whether or not the dress was ever purchased is not recorded, but neither was it important, because by the time the young man was well again, he and his hastily appointed nurse-maid were deeply in love with one another and determined to marry. Cinderella had found her dashing and flamboyant Prince Charming. Being real life, however, and not a fairy story, their ride together off into the sunset to live happily ever after was littered with obstacles.

While Eliza and Adam Elliott were delighted with the pairing, George's half-white mother was aghast. She had spend most of her life repudiating the part of her ancestry that was not native. She was certainly not going to welcome more British blood into the clan. The older woman not only flatly forbade the marriage but, in an attempt to prevent the possibility of the idea ever being raised again, responded by arranging for a suitable – i.e., Mohawk – bride for her son.

Showing admirable diplomacy, George refused to marry the woman his mother had found for him, but he did agree to postpone the marriage to his beloved. In an age-old reaction to parental disapproval, George and Emily carried on an intensely romantic courtship while they were waiting out the delay to their marriage.

Both young people were highly literate and a large part of their courtship involved a rather complex but very proper ruse of hiding notes for one another in a tree on the Elliot's property. And it is likely that this was as intimate as the two became for many years while they attempted to wait out George's mother's objections to their planned marriage.

After waiting four years, however, the young people's patience ran out. They decided to ignore the older woman's objections and marry anyway. Just as that decision had been made, Emily's sister, the Reverend Elliot's wife, developed tuberculosis and Emily's full attentions were diverted to nursing Eliza. Sadly, the disease was fatal and she died the following year. Before anyone had recovered from that death, three of Eliza's children also died.

By the time Emily and George were finally able to get back to making wedding plans, it was 1853. George's mother was still no closer to accepting Emily as a daughter-in-law, but the couple began to plan for the long-awaited day anyway. Preparations for the wedding were no sooner underway when scattered relatives on Emily's side decided they, too, had objections to the union. Despite it all, the 36-year-old groom, wearing a new black suit, lavender waistcoat and carrying grey gloves[3] and the bride, a comparative matron at 29, were married on August 27, 1853.[4]

Realizing that his bride had already suffered as a result of the interracial aspect of their union, George pledged to give his beloved Emily everything she would have had if she'd married a white man. George's standing in the community, which had always been high, had increased in the intervening years, as had his wealth. As a result, George Johnson was able to purchase 200 acres of prime land abutting the Grand River. On this enormous property he built a home, the likes of which had not before been seen in the area. He named the new family estate, his Cinderella's palace, "Chiefswood."

The continuing adoration of the couple for one another was even evidenced in the layout of the house. The back and front of the house were identical. Some deemed that quirk to be symbolic of the couple's acceptance of visitors from both their cultures. Another theory ran that they could not agree whether the front of the house should be oriented toward the river bank or the forest. In order that they should each be equally pleased with the house, it was built, effectively, with two front doors.[5]

And so this poignant little love story has a happy ending. George and Emily Johnson, having surmounted tremendous obstacles, had finally come to the part of their story where they would live "happily ever after."

Less than two weeks before her death, Emily Pauline Johnson, youngest child of George and Emily Johnson, wrote her will. In it she avowed that her remains should rest as near as possible to the city of Vancouver and that she be "dressed in my grey cloth evening cloak, with my small gold shield-shaped locket (containing the photograph of a young boy) fastened round my neck by the small gold chain."[6]

Those who undertook to carry out Pauline Johnson's final wishes did not open the locket to examine and possibly identify the photograph it contained. Only one person, a woman named Elizabeth Rogers, ever came forward to say she had been privy to seeing the picture in the locket. *When* she saw it, however, is a significant and controversial factor. *The Broadview Book of Canadian Anecdotes* indicates it was "[y]ears earlier,"[7] while Betty Keller, Johnson's most recent biographer maintains Elizabeth Rogers saw the photograph only "some weeks earlier."[8] If the former is correct, it is reasonable to think that by the time she wrote her will, Pauline Johnson might have changed the picture she kept in the locket. If Rogers saw it only "weeks" before the will was penned, then it is considerably less likely that the picture had been changed. Whether or not a new picture had been inserted becomes important, because some 30 years after Johnson's death, Rogers is quoted as distinctly remembering not the photo of a "young boy," but of a man.[9] She claimed not to have recognized the man nor have asked Pauline Johnson about his identity.

By now, of course, no one has any way of knowing whose picture the locket contained, so one of Canada's most prolific and popular poets has gone to her grave keeping her love story a mystery. In 1988, Johnson's biographer Betty Keller speculated on a long list of males who were important in the poet's life. She concluded that the "only one cannot be ruled completely out" is in that position "partly because so little is known about him."[10]

To examine this mysterious love story, we must go back to the palatial "Chiefswood," just a few years after the story's prologue ended.

A boy named Henry and a girl named Helen had already been born to Emily and George Johnson by the time the grand mansion Chiefswood was ready for occupancy. The little family continued to grow, however, and two years later another son arrived. Three years after that on the second Sunday of March in the year 1861, Emily Pauline Johnson was born.

This youngest child was named Emily after her mother but always called Pauline – a name chosen by her father to honor his hero Napoleon Bonaparte. (Pauline being the name of Napoleon's sister.) The little girl was a sickly child who required a great deal of care and attention, and so was sheltered and pampered by her concerned mother.

Unlike Pauline's paternal grandmother, both her parents identified strongly with the white culture around them. The Johnson children led a considerably more cultured life than all but a few of their native counterparts. As a result, they had few friends from the reserve.

Their white neighbors beyond the grounds of the reserve regarded the Johnsons as an oddity. The family regularly received internationally important visitors to their magnificent home. Standards of conduct demanded from all the Johnson family members were stringent. The attire and behavior expected both inside and outside Chiefswood were absolutely consistent, whether the occasion was a routine family meal or a social affair attended by royalty.

These peculiarities combined to drastically limit the number of friends the children were able to make in the white community. By default, therefore, the four children were, for a long time, not accepted in either culture. Consequently, they learned to depend almost entirely on their parents as role models and on one another for companionship. Although their unusual heritage undoubtedly caused their isolation, they viewed their mixed ancestry as a very positive aspect of their lives. As children, Henry, Helen (who was always called Eva), Allen and Pauline Johnson all looked upon their unique background with pride.

Little Pauline's delicate health was an additional factor in the isolation. She spent so much time with her mother that the older woman's values, to a large degree, became Pauline's values. It was her mother who imparted to Pauline the single greatest gift she was ever to receive – literacy. Without the ability to write, Pauline Johnson would have been unbearably frustrated. "My verses sang themselves in my head until I had to write them down."[11] The depth of joy revealed in that simple but profound statement approaches actual physical relief.

But it was Pauline's father, George Johnson, whom the youngster truly adored and perhaps this is why Pauline found her identity as an Indian. Johnson told marvelous tales from both the white and the native cultures while his youngest child sat spellbound, equally enthralled by the legends of her ancestors Hiawatha and Tecumseh as she was by her father's inclusion at a dinner party hosted by Alexander Graham Bell, the inventor of the telephone. Pauline also thoroughly enjoyed the frequent presence of dignitaries at Chiefswood.

And so, in this privileged, if segregated, environment, Pauline Johnson grew into a young woman. She and her parents no doubt assumed that the path of Pauline's life would see her married to a suitable man and settled into a comfortable existence similar to that of her mother. Life, however, was not to run nearly that smoothly for the young maiden. On February 19, 1884,[12] when she was a decidedly immature 23 years of age, Pauline Johnson's adored father died.

"Whatever shall we do now?" the Johnson sisters asked each other in whispered voices so tense they failed to belie the panic the two young women felt. Not only had a pivotal emotional support been removed from their lives but, practically speaking, they knew they could no longer afford to live in their extravagant home – the only home Pauline had ever known.

"Perhaps our brothers could help. Allen might come home from Hamilton or Henry from Montreal," they speculated optimistically, knowing that there wasn't a job anywhere that either of them could even hope to apply for that would bring in the amount of money necessary to operate the enormous property. With George Johnson's death, the land and beautiful home that sat upon it became a white elephant. The former object of community envy was now a terrible burden.

The sisters knew they could not turn to their mother for either guidance or assistance. The recently widowed woman had responded to her husband's death by withdrawing completely from the world and closeting herself into her bedroom at Chiefswood. Pauline and Eva at least had each other and although they often opposed one another, dealing with this frightening new situation together must have brought each one of them some consolation. Eva's presence in the equation also provided the trio with their only source of income, for she was employed at the Indian superintendent's office.

The fact that Eva was working and therefore able to contribute financially to looking after her mother and sister was not something that had been part of Eva's plans for her life. At an acceptable age she had become engaged, but roughly five years prior to her father's death an unrecorded event occurred that sealed the woman's fate as a spinster. Whether or not her fiancee died at that time is not known. We are only told that something tragic happened and that there were no longer plans for a wedding.

Although Eva's wages would support her mother for the rest of the older woman's life, that income could not come near the amount of money necessary to run Chiefswood. And so, as was inevitable after the prescribed year of mourning, the three Johnson women accepted the fact that they must seek more economical accommodation and that their beloved home for nearly 30 years would have to be leased out to strangers.

By the time the three were settled in their much more practical rented house in the town of Brantford, Pauline was approaching her 25th birthday. Many young women of that time and place were still single at that age, because convention dictated that their future husbands be well established in careers before taking on the additional responsibilities that taking a wife and starting a family would bring. Generally though, by the time women were Pauline's age, if they were not formally engaged, they were seeing a particular young man on an exclusive basis. For Pauline this was not the case. Although she had, in her late teens, cultivated many warm friendships with both boys and girls, the younger Johnson off-spring did not have anything approaching a prospective husband in her life. The formerly-pampered-child understood well that her days of being catered to were over and that she was now in an extremely vulnerable position.

The only inherent interest or talent Pauline ever demonstrated that even approached being a marketable skill was her ability as a poet. There exists a delightful legend surrounding Pauline Johnson's childhood love of poetry. One version has it that prior to making the 12 mile trip into Brantford one day, Pauline's mother asked the child what she would like as a gift upon her mother's return. Without hesitation the little girl replied, "Verses please."[13] Another, slightly more colorful variation of the story has the query coming from a friend of her father's, but including an option of candy. Pauline declined the latter choice, saying that she preferred verses.[14] Another transformation of the small but apparently significant interaction determines that Pauline replied, "Poems please," when asked by a guest at Chiefswood what he could bring her as a gift when he next visited the parents' home.[15] A modification of that rendering indicates that while a friend of Pauline's father's was visiting the Johnson home, he explained that he would soon be travelling to a distant city. He asked if there was anything he could bring back to Chiefswood upon his return. Pauline replied to the inquiry without hesitation, "Verses please."[16]

Alterations are inevitable with any anecdote that is re-told as frequently as that one has been. The noted changes are trivial; the gist of the story, however, is telling – from earliest childhood Pauline Johnson had a deep and abiding love of poetry.

The poems were initially crafted simply for her own amusement, but later she shared some of them by reading aloud to her parents and brothers and sister. Later she began to write poetry to give to her friends as gifts. This widening of the application of her talent eventually led not only to her career, but effectively the immortality of E. Pauline Johnson, The Mohawk Princess.

For the first year the three women lived together in town, Eva continued to go to work each day while Pauline kept the house. During that year there she consciously scaled down her social life. When the family had lived at Chiefswood, everyone in the family proudly invited guests to enjoy the luxurious hospitality of the impressive home. Now that they lived in rather spartan conditions, Pauline was no longer comfortable inviting friends to her home. Fittingly, then, she began, one by one, to refuse people's invitations to their homes. Clearly, in her mind, if she couldn't reciprocate then she couldn't accept either.

This did not mean that Pauline returned to her childhood state of seclusion. She merely disassociated herself from her former companions and made new friends within the town of Brantford. These people tended to be accustomed to less themselves and had never glimpsed the splendor that was Chiefswood. They expected nothing more than Pauline now had to offer.

Once the considerably reduced Johnson family adjusted itself somewhat to its forced incarnation, Pauline again began to write poetry, this time with an eye toward selling her verses to publishers. She had already had some success in that regard, having sold half a dozen or so poems to various publications by the year 1885. Success with publication continued at about that pace until autumn of 1886 and the unveiling of a monument in Brantford commemorating the great native hero Joseph Brant.

It was an enormous celebration involving speeches by visiting dignitaries, special editions of the newspapers, parades and the like. One of those addressing the crowd was a local business man who, after citing young Pauline as the poet responsible for the verse, read "Ode to Brant." The audience's reaction was swift and sure. They loved the poem and would accept nothing less than Pauline's mounting the stage to acknowledge their commendations.

The next day the newspapers were filled with reports about all the Brant-related events, but most particularly about the wonderful new talent that the occasion had revealed. Here, in their midst, was a poet of extraordinary ability.

"My goodness, Pauline, look here in the newspaper. They've written nearly as much about your poem as they have about the great Brant himself," her mother pointed out with great maternal pride.

Pauline merely smiled prettily and blushed, but there was no denying she was extremely pleased to be the recipient of so much positive attention. Eva only glanced at the sheet her mother indicated before noisily getting up from the breakfast table in order to get ready for another workday.

"I provide the only regular income for this family but it's my sister who wins the praise," she thought with deeply wounded pride.

Eva had grown up realizing, although certainly not appreciating, her mother's obvious preference for Pauline. Since becoming a widow, it was apparent that her younger daughter's accomplishments were the only joyful aspect to their mother's life. Although she did enjoy seeing her mother happy, Eva was nonetheless relieved when all the fuss about her younger sister's poetry died down and they were able to resume their normal family life. After all, it wasn't as though the unexpected meeting with fame had brought anything really positive Pauline's way. There hadn't been suitors extending marriage proposals nor publishers with contracts they hoped Pauline would sign, so really the whole thing was rather foolish. A smart return to normalcy would be best for everyone.

And for a number of years that is effectively what occurred. Pauline enjoyed herself with an amateur theatre group in the winter and canoeing with friends in the warmer weather. Her life was much like that of other women her age, who were filling in the years before the inevitable marriage. The only perceptible difference was that Pauline continued to write and occasionally sell poetry.

One of those poems was included in an anthology entitled, *Songs of the Great Dominion*.[17] Shortly after the book was published, Frank Yeigh, a former school chum of Pauline's, happened to see it. He remembered Pauline fondly, especially having seen her perform with the group of amateur actors she belonged to. For his day, the man was a "mover and a shaker." He joined many organizations and often quickly fell into leadership roles within these groups. With Pauline's published poem in mind, he had recently promised the Young Liberals that he would arrange an evening of Canadian literature for their entertainment.

"An old friend has written a most interesting letter to me, mother," Pauline indicating the piece of notepaper. "It's Frank Yeigh. He wants me to recite some of my poetry on stage at a meeting of a group he's involved with."

"Yeigh? I don't recall hearing the name. Do we know his people?" the older woman queried.

Pauline smiled at her mother's predictable response and quickly assured her, "I do Mother. He is engaged to marry Kate Westlake. She edits the *Fireside Weekly*. It would be great fun to accept his invitation, but I really have nothing to wear to such an occasion."

Perhaps relieved that she would apparently not have to share the joy of her life with anyone else even for one evening, Emily Howells Johnson declined to make any possible wardrobe suggestions to her daughter and Pauline replied to Yeigh's invitation in typically feminine fashion, saying that she could not accept, even though she'd have enjoyed the occasion, she was sure. He must understand she simply had nothing suitable to wear.

Frank Yeigh's enthusiasm for his own project would not be put off nearly that easily and he replied that he was glad she liked the idea and that an outfit of "Indian togs" would be eminently suitable for the occasion. The passage of nearly 100 years has created great confusion over the description of the outfit Pauline Johnson finally did choose to wear for her first recitation on stage. Depending who is reporting on the evening, she wore either a "striking Indian costume," "a simple white dress" which had been made specifically for the occasion or "a grey silk dress" that already existed in her wardrobe.[18]

There is no disagreement, however, on the success of Pauline's debut. Moreover, it was not a success that was easily earned. The evening's entertainment had begun to go badly by the time it was the young poet's time to perform. Fortunately, for Yeigh and his reputation as an organizer, Pauline performed spectacularly, winning not only the affection and admiration of the crowd, but an encore to boot. She didn't know it at the time, but finally, at the age of 31, Emily Pauline Johnson had found the medium by which she would earn her living.

Yeigh was anxious to take as much credit for the audience's enjoyment as he possibly could. After all, he had arranged for the performance. By the time the curtain fell at the Liberal Club's meeting on January 16, 1892,[19] he was already making plans to capitalize on the success.

As a journalist, he was in a natural position to offer his talented young friend a great deal of publicity. This, coupled with word of mouth, soon spread people's interest in seeing and hearing this appealing Indian maiden on stage. With Frank Yeigh as her manager, Pauline Johnson was suddenly in demand as a performer.

Pauline was torn by the popularity that had been thrust upon her. On the one hand, in addition to thoroughly enjoying all the attention, she knew that this was a way for her to earn some badly needed money. Not only did she feel responsible to contribute toward the family's support, but having some money of her own would help to support her while she wrote enough poetry to publish as a book. On the other hand, she knew that recitalists were generally held in esteem so low as to be barely above that of actors and she was well aware that stooping to such a level would be completely beyond her mother's acceptance.

The dilemma was a classic one for Pauline who, all her life, would struggle to find a balance between the romantic and pragmatic sides of

*E. Pauline Johnson. (photo courtesy of the Provincial Archives of Alberta, #B-967)*

her nature. Finally she settled on embracing the life of a recitalist while maintaining the air of an aristocrat.

With Yeigh acting as her manager and publicist, Pauline's career soon took off. Unknown only weeks before, she now played several times a week to full houses all over southern Ontario. The routine was grueling, but the young woman appeared to thrive on the hectic schedule. She was constantly adapting and enhancing her performances, much to the delight of, not only the audiences, but the critics.

Shortly after the death of Pauline's paternal grandfather, John Smoke Johnson, she had adopted his father's Indian name, Tekahionwake as an addition to her own distinctly British name. When asked for an explanation regarding the new name, Pauline asserted that if her family name had not been Anglicized she would have been known as Miss Tekahionwake anyway. That assertion was incorrect, as the word "Tekahionwake" had actually been a title awarded to the older man and not the equivalent of a surname that his descendants would inherit.

Despite this inconsistency, the newly adopted moniker no doubt suited Pauline's needs in a number of ways. It certainly drew attention to her native ancestry, in addition to making her billing as a recitalist more attention grabbing. Many people attended Pauline's performances when they would not have thought of spending their evening in any other concert hall. The reason? She gave them their first opportunity to cast their eyes upon a flesh and blood "savage."

Frank Yeigh quickly identified this added advantage and began to book Pauline as the "Mohawk Princess." He did this with Pauline's consent, even though neither word was correctly applied in her case. Emily Pauline Johnson was only one quarter native and not a princess. Despite the inaccuracies, the title succeeded in its purpose and, probably because Pauline consistently promoted its use, stayed with her throughout her life.

It is likely not coincidental that this period of changes in her life also marked a shift in Pauline's sense of identity. Previously proud of the uniqueness of her status of her racially mixed background, she now began to credit anything worthwhile about herself as being a direct result of her native ancestry. Like any generality, this assertion was far too sweeping to be accurate, but in one important regard she may have been right. The native culture embraces the oral tradition and Pauline certainly excelled in that area.

However well it tied in, this shift in emphasis might have been damaging to Pauline's relationship with her mother but, as Emily cherished her daughter's similarities to the deeply missed husband, George Johnson, the potentially hurtful point of identity never became an issue. Sadly, at about this time, whether by default or decision, the rest of her family acted as though Pauline's success had somehow undermined their relationship with them. Neither of her brothers nor her sister made the effort to attend a performance to which they'd been specifically invited.

Here Pauline's practical side won out and despite the familial snub, she continued along her career path. Both Pauline and Yeigh, her self-appointed manager, realized they were onto a money-making proposition and, whether consciously or unconsciously, they both began to sculpt their product to the audiences expectations. Recitals and recitalists were hugely popular forms of entertainment in the 1890s. The performances followed a predictable format and toward this end, Yeigh soon teamed his "Mohawk Princess" with a young man named Owen Smily.

"Pauline, you'll enjoy Smily I'm sure," Frank Yeigh predicted. "He's a pleasant young chap and, considering his age, is well experienced on the stage."

Yeigh's prediction was correct and the partnership was an immediate success in all ways. Smily and Johnson not only complemented each other on stage, but Pauline picked up valuable skills from the young veteran of the stage. Perhaps even more importantly to the potential longevity of both their careers, Owen Smily and Pauline Johnson provided one another with companionship. The life of an itinerant performer on the circuit must have been an agonizingly lonely existence, consisting of one dreary hotel room after another in cities that would surely all begin to look alike. For a solo performer, the isolation alone could have led, prematurely, to the end of either of their careers.

The forced intimacy implicit in such an arrangement must, at first, have been extremely difficult for Pauline to cope with. What she had been raised to consider proper behavior was likely quite different from Smily's upbringing, but even if he too would have preferred a more restrictive atmosphere, maintaining anything approaching a strict code of propriety simply wouldn't have been feasible within the confines they operated.

And so, with her eventual goal of getting a book of her poetry published and, in all likelihood marrying, Pauline Johnson continued to pursue her wildly successful career on Canada's various stages.

"Owen, I have a question to ask you," Pauline announced just as they'd settled into their seats aboard the passenger coach of a westbound train.

"Then ask away," the man prompted.

"Can you spare me for a few months? Yeigh has nothing further booked for us after this next month and I'd like to finally make that trip to London."

"This means you must be ready to begin looking for a publisher, then doesn't it, Pauline?"

The woman merely smiled and nodded. She was so thoroughly pleased and hopeful about the forthcoming trip that she found it difficult to talk about. She wanted to return to the little house in Brantford, not so much to say good-bye to her mother and sister, but to make the final arrangements necessary to pursue this pivotally important step on the road to her goal of becoming an author.

Perhaps because this trip was a significant step toward terminating her stage career, Pauline's mother, brother Allen and sister Eva helped to organize a bon voyage party for the youngest member of their family. The next day, Friday April 27, 1894, they and many others were on hand to see her off on the train that would take her to the New York harbor where she would board a ship to Britain.

It is an interesting contradiction that while Pauline Johnson consistently promoted her identity as a native Canadian, she sought a British publisher for her poetry. As there were publishers in Canada by that time, she might also have been motivated to make the trip by there being a considerably greater possibility of acquiring a patron in London, England, than there was in London, Ontario. Biographer Betty Keller describes the role of a patron as including "buy[ing] out the house on opening night, be[ing] conspicuously present, and bring[ing] all his friends." Keller further described, hopefully with some tongue in cheek, that an artist's patron "could also arrange *little* suppers of *several hundred* influential people"[20] [emphasis mine].

Although Pauline failed to obtain a patron, she did arrive back at the doorstep of her mother's and sister's home, exactly three months after the farewell party, with a publishing contract. Four days later she was away again, embarking on another tour with Owen Smily.

When the two reunited in Toronto, they each had important news they were anxious to share with their partner.

"Owen, I did it. I found a publisher and my book should be released next year," she reported with evident pride.

Smily, of course, was not surprised. He had been sure that a woman as talented and determined as Pauline would not have returned from her trip with anything else.

"That's wonderful, Pauline, and I have some news for you. Frank Yeigh's had to devote himself solely to his own career and so I've arranged for us to work with Ernest Shipman."

Pauline's face fell with the news. Frank had been a good friend to her since adolescence and he'd done admirably well managing her blossoming career. Seeing the woman's reaction, Owen quickly explained the new manager's impressive credentials and although that might have satisfied Pauline at the time, the new business arrangement was not a positive one. Despite this complication, Smily and Johnson continued to play to full houses and positive reviews.

The demands of their schedule meant the two lived in virtual isolation. For Pauline this was a pattern she would have fallen into fairly naturally. It would not have been a great change from the interdependency that existed among her siblings and herself during their isolated upbringing at Chiefswood.

Of course life was not all rigorous touring. The pair did take breaks during which Pauline would go on canoeing expeditions with old friends or temporarily return home for a visit with her mother. Sadly, though, the base from which Pauline derived family support was shrinking. She and Eva, her only sister, had never appreciated one another's qualities. The only motivation they shared was a great fondness for and desire to protect their mother.

Henry, their older brother, who had been living and working in the United States, died in 1894. His death was premature and completely unexpected. The man had long ago become estranged from the little household in Brantford and he harbored ill feelings toward his mother for the way they all had been raised.

The changes through time in brother Allen were perhaps the most difficult for Pauline to bear. She and Allen were closest emotionally as well as in age. She had always depended on and admired Allen. They shared many personality characteristics including, initially, great pride in their Indian ancestry. Sadly, after taking part in the public performance of a native dance, Allen had been fired from his job – a job he very much enjoyed and counted on. From that moment on his enthusiasm for his exotic background altered considerably.[21]

Professionally, Pauline's life continued to flourish. Her first book of poetry, released in the summer of 1895, was well received and supplied her career with a timely injection of new life. She was, by now, likely very aware of how important her career would be to her. It was becoming increasingly evident that writing and performing poetry was not destined to be merely something she did while awaiting marriage to the right man. By that time she was approaching middle age and so far there had been no serious marriage prospects. It was increasingly apparent that Pauline Johnson would always be responsible for her own support.

She must have had that pragmatic thought in mind when she returned from England. A series of one night concert stands in small towns must have seemed decidedly uninspiring after the sophistication she'd grown accustomed to on her trip abroad, but these performances clearly netted the highest financial return. Earning more money for each stint had now become important to Pauline as the additional funds allowed her time away from the stage – time that could be spent writing poetry. Her first book was being well received and she hoped to eventually release a second volume of poetry.

Toward this end she and Smily took their show into the United States. The reactions from American audiences were disappointing to Pauline. The trip also served to mark the beginning of the end for the once pleasant and popular partnership. By the autumn of 1897, the relationship had ended, although exactly why, where, when or how is not known.

Although she still visited her mother and sister in Brantford, Pauline by now called Winnipeg home and it was here that she met her next performance partner – J. Walter McRaye, a 21-year-old "humorous and dramatic reader."[22] J. Walter McRaye was actually a recent incarnation. The young man had been christened Walter Jackson McCrea, a name he obviously felt was not glamorous enough for a career on the stage.

What he lacked in talent, McRaye more than made up for in self-confidence. Despite consistently bad reviews of his performances, McRaye's attitude to his stage career was undaunted.

On December 29, 1897, on an evening when he had no performance of his own to give, J. Walter McRaye and a friend attended an evening of entertainment given by Pauline Johnson. He was struck either by the woman's skill on stage, by the audience's appreciation for her or possibly by both. Whatever it was, McRaye knew instantly that he wanted to be associated with her. As the curtain fell, he rushed to her dressing room in hopes of immediately cementing a business relationship with the Mohawk Princess. He found the entrance to her dressing room blocked by a man not much older than himself. The man at the door introduced himself as Charles Drayton before adding that he was Pauline Johnson's fiancee and that she would not be receiving guests after the show, as she had to prepare herself for a party he was hosting in her honor.

McRaye's confidence did not allow him to be discouraged. He merely slipped into the social gathering uninvited and came away with the beginnings of a partnership that was to last for many years. The longevity of this business relationship between McRaye and Johnson was in direct contrast to the romantic relationship between Johnson and her fiancee/host/dressing room door guard, Charles Drayton.

Their engagement was officially announced early in 1897. As marriage was what she'd wanted all along, Pauline must have been as happy then as at any other time in her adult life. That elation, however, was short lived, for Allen's telegram advising of their mother's imminent death was waiting for her when she arrived at a prairie city just weeks later. Pauline left immediately, arriving at her mother's bedside less than an hour before her mother died.[23]

In July of the same year, Drayton's mother also died. Pauline attended the funeral, marking the first time the "engaged couple" had seen one another in more than half a year. The next reference to the relationship came almost exactly a year after the engagement had been announced. The text of this report emphasized an upcoming performance of Pauline's before reminding her fans that as her marriage was forthcoming and at that time the recitalist would, of course, be retiring. Great confusion arose when that announcement was followed immediately by another that indicated she would be touring extensively in the near future. Greater confusion still resulted when the month in which she and Drayton were supposed to marry passed without the two being in the same city, but with Pauline embarking on a tour very different than the one described by the press.

Despite the lack of evidence, Pauline Johnson's friends and fans continued to refer to the upcoming nuptials for months after the scheduled event had failed to occur. Pauline's health and her performances both began to deteriorate from the stress. She was undeniably devastated by having been jilted by Drayton and, of course, by the death of her mother. For the first time in her career, Pauline Johnson was regularly receiving poor reviews and, although she and McRaye had done a short, successful tour together, they were not performing together through this difficult time. Pauline Johnson may not have been used to having a lot of company, but she was equally unused to being as entirely alone.

To this point there had been no closure surrounding the abortive "engagement" to Drayton. In January 1899, nearly two years from the day their engagement had been announced, Drayton finally met with Johnson and officially asked that the engagement be terminated – he wished to be free to make other plans. Those plans included marriage. His future wife was a woman his family felt was a more suitable candidate to join their family. It's a safe bet that in this case the phrase "more suitable" included a heritage other than part Indian and a background that did not include stage performances.

No record exists of her reaction to Drayton's request, however, much can be inferred from events that followed, the most significant of which occurred in June of 1902 when Charles Drayton married a woman named Lydia Howland.[24] Presumably to save face, Pauline never directly acknowledged the painful and humiliating rejection, but her patterns of behavior did change dramatically at that point. Drayton's change of heart was responsible, both directly and indirectly, for this change.

Pauline Johnson was at her lowest ebb, having suffered through the death of her brother and mother as well as the crushing disappointment of her failed engagement. Not surprisingly, she became ill and so for awhile was unable to perform. When she recuperated sufficiently and was able to return to the stage, the vibrancy that her adoring audiences had counted on from their favorite recitalist had faded.

Coinciding with these downturns, Johnson met a man who was destined have a negative effect all aspects of her life. Charles Wurz was an opportunist in the most negative sense of the word. Easily sensing her state of vulnerability, Wurz attached himself to Pauline not only as her stage manager but also, it can be deduced, as her lover. Even the poetry she wrote during this time changed considerably. Never before had her works alluded to physical love. Now the references were unmistakable. For over a year it is likely the two enjoyed a whirlwind relationship. They spent a great deal of money, money that Pauline had borrowed to finance a trip to Australia – a trip that never got much past the stages of initial planning.

Until she met Wurz, Johnson probably led a chaste life. There had never been any indication of a physical relationship with any of the men in her life. This likely didn't reveal any great amount of discretion on her part, but rather simply reflected the fact that she still hoped to marry. Given the era and her station in life, retaining her virginity would have been an important component of her offerings to the future groom. By the time she and Wurz began their affair, she was very nearly 40 and Pauline had probably set aside those aspirations. The need to remain celibate would have been removed.

The fling with Wurz likely lasted a little more than a year. When it was over Pauline Johnson found herself bitterly alone, broke and broken. Just at that time the ever-confident J. Walter McRaye arrived back on the scene. The two had done that one tour together back in January of 1898, when Pauline was glowing with excitement about her engagement.

Dates for the reunion of Johnson and McRaye differ depending on whose version of the truth is examined. Pauline's sister, Eva, had despised Walter McRaye right from the start. The woman's embarrassment over her younger sister's behavior during the affair with Wurz, however, enabled her to override those feelings sufficiently to ask McRaye to lie about when his performing partnership with Pauline had begun. If he told people that it began earlier than it actually did, those embarrassing months with Wurz could be covered over. It must have been difficult for Eva to lower herself to ask a favor that included dishonesty of a man she felt distinctly superior to, but it was not much of a stretch for McRaye to accommodate her. McRaye had a very easy-going relationship with the truth and often fitted it to whatever his needs were at the time. Despite the elaborate attempts at cover up and enhancement, it can safely be stated that the McRaye-Johnson partnership officially began late in the year 1901.

McRaye and Johnson were such an odd pair that they complemented one another. McRaye loved the stage and yet had reconciled himself to the fact that he would never be a "headliner." Johnson, who was one of the era's biggest stars, was on stage ostensibly to support herself while she wrote poetry. Despite the fact that McRaye was 15 years younger than Pauline, he was a veteran trouper who knew his way around the worst of itinerant performing, knew his place and as a bonus he had a pleasant disposition.

With McRaye as her partner, over time a bit of spirit began to creep back into Pauline Johnson's performances and into her life. This despite a serious bout of illness. For the first time since her partnership with Owen Smily many years before, Pauline was once again forced to be in the company of one man nearly constantly. This time, however, she must have found it much less stressful. She was not the naive young woman she had been during the period she'd been travelling with Smily. Further, McRaye proved himself to be a most amusing travel companion. The pair created an ever-growing entourage of whimsical, imaginary friends who travelled with them on the endless train rides between performance venues. Each one of these fanciful and fictitious characters was endowed with a distinct form and personality. Johnson and McRaye whiled away the formerly grueling hours of train travel creating and enjoying the misadventures of their invisible companions.

This little bit of fun in Pauline Johnson's life likely helped to keep her emotions from hardening entirely. She was by now not the delightful, starry-eyed young woman who had shyly begun a career on the stage. She was a worldly-wise woman whose experiences had made her not only more pragmatic, but by now profoundly embittered. McRaye's lighthearted influence provided much-needed relief in her life.

It was during this time that Pauline Johnson finally began work, in earnest, on her second book of poetry. Although the original book had been neither a critical nor a commercial success, the interminable touring with McRaye was paying off handsomely and by spring of 1906, the pair were off to perform in London, England. The trip was successful beyond the pair's wildest expectations and in one particular way that neither of them could have predicted. J. Walter McRaye met the woman he would marry.

Pauline Johnson made a point to introduce her partner to Lucy Webling while they were in London. The Weblings had lived in England for many years by that time, but Pauline remembered the family from the years they had all spent in Brantford. McRaye was smitten immediately. Not only was Lucy the perfect companion socially, but she was a seasoned performer and therefore had great potential to become his next partner.

It is not known whether Pauline and McRaye ever discussed her eventual retirement from the stage but, given her age (mid-40s) and increasingly frequent bouts of ill-health, it was inevitable that she would be ready to quit many years before he would. The implications of this new union, therefore, were clear and probably slightly threatening to Pauline. Fortunately, the intensity of McRaye's relationship with the pretty Miss Webling developed at a pace that gave everyone ample opportunity to adjust as the changes occurred.

Upon their return to Canada, the Johnson-McRaye team took some time off and each visited family. Pauline's writing output changed at this time too. Perhaps because of the poor reception her second book of poems had also received, she began concentrating on short stories and pieces of nonfiction prose. Although this writing style was certainly not her first choice, she was successful at it and it was undeniably more immediately profitable than her poetry had ever been.

Also toward the end of financial security, Pauline and McRaye began to tour the United States. By now Pauline was actively planning to retire. In 1907 she embarked on a rather mysterious third trip to London, returning from it without any perceptible change in her life. It was not until the following year when, back in Canada, she checked in to the Hotel Vancouver for a prolonged rest that the reason for her recent solo trip to England became clear. Pauline Johnson was presumably looking for a hospitable place in which to live out her final years. She would have been aware by then that the lethal lump growing inside her right breast was advancing rapidly.

McRaye and Lucy Webling were married in August 1909. The joyful event marked another significant milestone as well – the end of the career as a touring recitalist for E. Pauline Johnson, Tekahionwake. Johnson settled herself in a Vancouver apartment and filled her days with walks, visits and writing. By the time she confided the news of her terminal illness to one of her friends, people had already begun to suspect she was not well. The cancer was eating away at her body. The figure that had once been striking, and recently even increased to matronly, was being consumed.[25] A visit to the doctor finally confirmed what she'd known intuitively. Pauline Johnson had breast cancer and would not live much longer.

One of the visitors to her Vancouver apartment was Chief Joe Capilano. Like Johnson, he had a terminal illness. Sharing this fate meant the two friends also shared a sense of urgency. He was by nature almost completely nonverbal, but overcame his natural tendencies to tell Johnson some of the legends of his people in order for her to record and publish them. Their combined purpose was accomplished when the *Legends of Vancouver* appeared, first as a series of newspaper articles and then compiled in book form.

Publication of the native stories had begun before the Chief died. As it had been desperately important to him that his people's stories not be lost, the timing was most gratifying. The fact that the series of legends had been enthusiastically received meant that the newspaper continued to be interested in serializing them and as those sales were virtually her only income, it meant the stories were even more important to Pauline.

Against all odds, Pauline Johnson stubbornly battled the cancer that was eating away at her body. Through 1912, she refused to give up her walks in Stanley Park and despite horrific pain in her right arm, she continued to write as much as she was able. Displaying the qualities that kept her going through so many years and so much physical and emotional adversity, the dying Tekahionwake even gave the occasional presentation. By the first months of the new year, however, her strength had been depleted. It was all she could do to lie, sedated against the terrible pain, and wait to be released from life.

Death had been a long time coming and by now she was well prepared for it. Although she had never been able to manage money, Pauline Johnson had her affairs scrupulously well in order at the time of her death. She may also have left a posthumous practical joke or two.

The first may have come in the form of a triple-sealed "time capsule" which she left in Eva's care. The poet instructed that the package be held, unopened, until 25 years after her death. Did Pauline chose this time line in order to protect her two remaining siblings from any embarrassment that the contents might reflect upon them? This is certainly possible – Johnson was always conscious of the importance of keeping up the good family name. She must also have known that her behavior through certain periods of her life would not have preserved that family tradition.

In hindsight, however, leaving a time capsule may only have been a highly effective way of tormenting her sister – a way for Pauline to gain the last laugh on her older sister. The question of what the package might contain would be tantalizing enough, but the timeline would have added greatly to the surviving sister's sense of frustration. Given that Eva was seven years Pauline's elder she stood very little chance of living long enough to ever know what the parcel contained – if she abided by the decreed instructions.

Although Eva did live to the age of 81, the full 25 years had not elapsed. As a result the cache became part of her estate. She bequeathed Pauline Johnson's time capsule to a local benevolent group. They could have opened it a year after taking custody of the artifact, but for unrecorded reasons, it remained in their possession, unopened, tripled-sealed, for six years. On the day it was finally opened, the long-awaited time capsule was found to contain nothing of significance.

Had it ever contained anything significant? Had Eva gone through the contents long before her own death and removed articles that she thought might have the potential to tarnish her sister's image? Or had Pauline succeeded in master-minding a joke at Eva's expense by either having her worry for the balance of her life about nothing or by having her suffer a guilty conscience for the balance of her life over having violated one of Pauline's final wishes?

And what of the locket? Whose picture did Pauline Johnson insist on wearing as her body was cremated? Was it a man or was it "a young boy" as described in her will? The question is not whether or not she was ever in love with a man, for we know that she lost at love at least twice. The question is which one of the men in her life still meant enough to her to justify the request. Who could have meant so very much to her? Or, like the time capsule, was the locket story simply another hoax Johnson perpetrated?

The latter is highly unlikely if, in fact, it was just weeks and not years before her death that Johnson had so solemnly showed the photo to her friend Elizabeth Rogers. At the showing she did not explain whose picture it was nor did her friend inquire.

Johnson described the photograph as being of a "boy," which is interesting, because her friend remembered glancing at the likeness of a grown man. This discrepancy may only reflect terminology. Johnson had been known to refer to grown men somewhat younger than herself as "boys," even though she knew full well they were men.[26] Written in the will, however, she modified the general term "boy" with the adjective "young." Even taking into account the oddity of a person's speech habits, it's difficult to imagine anyone specifically referring to a man as "a *young* boy" [emphasis mine].

Could it have been a picture of her father, or grandfather or one of her brothers, perhaps taken during their youth? Some support for this theory can be extrapolated from historical record. Johnson held both her grandfather John Smoke Johnson (Chief Sakayengwaraton) and her father George Johnson (Chief Teyonnhehkewea) in the highest possible esteem. She was also extremely fond of her brother Allen. The only male relative who can be eliminated without question would be her eldest sibling, Henry. Even in childhood the two weren't as close as Allen and Pauline were; adulthood only served to widen the emotional gap that already existed.

Or is the answer considerably more impassioned in implication than merely familial love? Could Pauline still have held a torch for some man at the time of her death? If so, who?

J. Walter McRaye, Charles Drayton and Owen Smily were all significant men in Pauline Johnson's life and they were all younger than she, and therefore any one of them could be a likely contender as the solution to the riddle.

Her first biographer, Mrs. Garland Foster, declared, "The record of Pauline's friendships would fill a volume by themselves."[27] Many of those friendships were with men and, of course, her list of male acquaintances was even longer. From what is known of them and their relationship with Pauline Johnson, all of the acquaintances and many of the friends can be struck from the list of those whose picture the locket might have contained.

Effectively defeating the thesis that the person pictured in the locket was a relative is Elizabeth Rogers' description of the circumstances under which she was allowed to glimpse the photo. While the friend was visiting in the dying woman's apartment, Pauline described the contents of the locket as being a great secret that she would not feel comfortable sharing with anyone. Shortly after making that assertion she opened the tiny piece of jewellery and showed the picture to her visitor.[28] It is not reasonable to assume that there would be that much conspiratorial secrecy surrounding a photograph of a male relative.

❦ ❦ ❦

Frank Yeigh was undeniably an important figure throughout much of Pauline Johnson's life. The two were acquainted in their teens and we can presume that Yeigh remembered her with fondness or, at the very least, admiration. Surely he would otherwise not have risked asking Johnson, a complete unknown at the time, to perform during an event that held such importance for him. That evening, of course, changed the entire course of Pauline Johnson's life and led her directly to a successful career. Although it certainly had its difficulties, and was not the life Johnson had pictured herself leading, the woman's path might well have been bleak with poverty, decidedly unexciting and unsatisfying, if that first opportunity to recite her poems on stage had never presented itself. For this reason Johnson owed Yeigh at least a debt of gratitude.

Although Yeigh could certainly be accused of being an opportunist where Johnson was concerned, he did remain loyal to the woman throughout her life. This loyalty extended to her dying days, when there was nothing left for him to gain from his kindness to Pauline. By then she was simply a person he cared deeply for and who needed help.

But what of Johnson's feelings for Yeigh? There is no proof that she regarded him as anything other than a friend and she once poignantly expressed respect and admiration for his "safe, secure marriage."[29] It seems fair, therefore, to assume that it was not Frank Yeigh's picture in the necklace.

❦ ❦ ❦

Could her former partner, Owen Smily, be the face in the photo? He was reported to have been a clever and physically attractive man. Pauline would have found those qualities appealing. He was younger than she, but he could not automatically ruled out as a potential lover for that reason alone, as she was older than many of the men in her life.

Pauline learned a great deal from her association with Smily and those additional skills strengthened her presentation on stage. Giving a more polished performance, of course, enhanced her appeal as a performer, but it also caused her to agonize over the conflict between the financial necessity of spending time developing herself as a performer, when performing took away from time she could spend perfecting her poetry.

From Johnson's perspective, because their partnership came early on in her career, it's unlikely anything deeply emotional would have developed between the two. At that time Pauline viewed her career on stage as a temporary undertaking, a part of her life which she would happily cast aside as soon as she met her future husband. She was "saving herself for marriage" and Owen Smily was certainly not husband material. For one thing, Johnson considered him to be considerably below her station in life. A second and more important factor was also in play. Owen Smily was likely not the least bit interested in Pauline Johnson or any other woman in a romantic sense, as there are indications that Owen Smily was not heterosexual.[30]

As an addendum to the Owen Smily synopsis. Despite the influence the man had on Pauline's career, he is mentioned only twice in Mrs. Garland Foster's 1931 biography about her.[31]

"Miss Emily Pauline Johnson is to be married to Mr. Charles Drayton of Toronto."[32] The importance of such an announcement certainly cannot be overlooked when assessing the romantic interests in Pauline Johnson's life. It is extremely unlikely, however, that she would have continued to carry a flame for the man she was once engaged to. She would have had plenty of time to have recovered from her feelings for Drayton before he as much as asked that the engagement be called off. All indications point to Pauline's having successfully gotten on with her life after having been jilted by Drayton.

Interestingly, Charles Drayton is not mentioned at all in Foster's biography.

Johnson probably spent more hours alone with J. Walter McRaye than any other man. Despite this forced intimacy, there was never any indication of romantic involvement between the two. As in her relationship with Smily, Johnson always felt superior to McRaye. The fact that he met and married his wife while he and Johnson were a team indicates that he was without the constraints of an ongoing relationship during that time.

Biographer Betty Keller has determined that Charles Wurz is the only man who cannot be ruled out as being the man in the locket. She makes this assertion based not on information she unearthed through her research into the woman's life, but instead on the very lack of information that exists about either the man or his relationship with Johnson.[33] We know that Wurz took terrible advantage of Pauline Johnson and treated her poorly, but it is likely that he was her first and possibly only lover in a physical sense. This alone may have earned him an enduring place in her heart and coincidentally the spot in the locket.

There is also the possibility that Pauline had a relationship which no one knew about. Could a love affair have motivated that second, seemingly pointless trip to London, England? She made the round trip alone and at the time no one understood its purpose. Could she have met someone during a previous trip and gone back to see if a relationship would develop? Biographer Keller quickly and effectively dismisses that possibility by indicating that, by the time of the second trip Pauline Johnson was matronly, not only in appearance, but more importantly in attitude. The woman was just simply no longer looking for love by then.

Could the mystery of the picture in the locket merely have been the second of Pauline Johnson's posthumous jokes? While this theory cannot be completely eliminated, the seriousness of Johnson's attitude when she showed the photograph to her friend demonstrated a tremendous depth of emotion. It is hard to believe that someone fighting to prolong life would waste the energy necessary to perpetrate a hoax.

The solution to this mysterious love story can, by now, never be found. E. Pauline Johnson, Tekahionwake, the Mohawk Princess who was neither a full-blooded Mohawk nor a princess, successfully took the secret of her love story to the grave with her.

## Endnotes

[1]*Legends of Vancouver* gives his native name as Onwanonsyshon, page xi.

[2]*Pauline, A Biography of Pauline Johnson*, Betty Keller, Formac Publishing, Halifax, Nova Scotia, 1981, page 10.

[3]*Maclean's Magazine*, April 1, 1952; *The Passionate Princess*, Jack Scott.

[4]*Pauline, A Biography of Pauline Johnson*, page 16.

[5]Ibid., page 18 and previously mentioned issue of *Maclean's Magazine*

[6]*The Broadview Book of Canadian Anecdotes*, Douglas Fetherling, Ed., Broadview Press, Peterborough, 1988, page 64.

[7]Ibid., page 64.

[8]*Pauline, A Biography of Pauline Johnson*, page 268.

[9]*The Broadview Book of Canadian Anecdotes*, page 64.

[10]*Pauline, A Biography of Pauline Johnson*, page 268.

[11]Ibid., page 25.

[12]Ibid., page 40.

[13]*Maclean's Magazine*.

[14]*The Mohawk Princess*, Mrs. W. Garland Foster, Lions' Gate Publishing Company, Vancouver, 1931, page 27.

[15]*Pauline, The Indian Poet*, Lorraine Devorski, Canadian Library Association, Ottawa, 1986, page 4.

[16]*Flint and Feather, The Complete Poems of E. Pauline Johnson*, page xxiv; *Pauline, A Biography of Pauline Johnson*, page 57.

[17]Ibid., page 57.

[18]Ibid., page 77.

[19]Ibid., page 98.

[20]Ibid., page 77.

[21]Ibid., page 136.

[22]Ibid., page 179.

[23]Ibid., page 247.

[24]Ibid., pages 276 and 277.

[25]Ibid., page 173.

[26]*Mohawk Princess*, page 134.

[27]*Pauline, A Biography of Pauline Johnson*, page 268.

[28]Ibid., page 157.

[29]Ibid., page 68.

[30]*The Mohawk Princess*, index.

[31]*Pauline, The Indian Poet*, page 11.

[32]*Pauline, A Biography of Pauline Johnson*, page 132.

[33]Ibid., page 268.

# Eddie
## & Doreen Boyd

Little Eddie Boyd was the apple of his mother's eye. Even after his sister and two brothers came along, mother and eldest son enjoyed a very special relationship. They were both affectionate people, anxious for approval and they shared a common enemy – Thomas Boyd. Ed's father was a cold man who tried to control his family as though it was an extension of his beat as a Toronto cop.

Happily, Tom Boyd's job not only provided a comfortable living for his family, it also kept him out of the home a great deal of the time. When the man was home, his wife, Eleanor, catered to him in order to insure peace in the household, and the children did their best to stay out of the way. As soon as the elder Boyd left for work again, the boisterous, loving atmosphere of the home returned. While Mrs. Boyd may have longed for a more satisfying arrangement, the children happily accepted the imbalance and thrived in the loving atmosphere their mother created for them.

The younger siblings learned to count on Eddie for protection against such childhood evils as the inevitable schoolyard bully. In return they accepted and respected his privileged position in the family.

Eddie never showed much academic ability, but he didn't need to. He was a good looking, polite youngster, an accomplished athlete and an award-winning musician. He naively assumed that the rest of the world would find him as appealing as his mother did. By his mid-teens Ed looked forward to launching himself successfully into the adult world.

Then came the autumn of 1929. By the time the stock market crashed, heralding the Great Depression, Eddie Boyd's world had already collapsed – his mother had died.[1]

Just days after standing beside them, as they watched their beloved mother's casket being lowered into the ground, Tom Boyd scattered his children to four separate foster homes. It would be years before Eddie would feel secure again.

Almost overnight Boyd had lost everything on which his previous 15 years had been based. Without his mother's loving approval as a reward, there seemed to be no point in striving. Within days of her death, Eddie joined thousands of other young men riding the rails into the Great Depression. Four years later, still handsome, polite, agile and able to pick out a tune on a harmonica, he had served his first jail term – six weeks for vagrancy.[2]

The sentence was designed to punish Eddie and make him see the error of his ways, but it didn't do either. Eddie Boyd thoroughly enjoyed his period of incarceration. Years later he reminisced about the time as though recalling adolescent adventures at summer camp. That jail term, and Boyd's reaction to it, set the tone for the future. Like many of his fellow vagrants, Eddie spent much of the 1930s in and out of jail on charges ranging from vagrancy and petty theft to break and enter.[3]

The days and months and years built upon each other until the autumn of 1939. Then, almost exactly ten years after the first dramatic change in Eddie Boyd's life, there came a second transformation. The outbreak of the Second World War put a sudden stop to Boyd's career as a vagabond and petty criminal. He enlisted in the Army immediately and, only weeks later, happily found himself stationed in England.

Nothing could have suited Eddie better. Here he had all the camaraderie he enjoyed both in jail and in the hobo camps, combined with respect and a pay packet. What more could a young man ask for? Why a young woman, of course.

Fortunately, for Eddie's healthy libido, the English towns and countryside offered an exciting number of interesting and interested young lasses. Within a few weeks Eddie had applied to his commanding officer for permission to marry a delightful young woman, a school teacher by trade. Only the girl's fiancee, returning from his own service posting, changed those plans. Mildly disheartened, Ed sensibly decided that if he wanted to meet other women, and he did, he'd have to go to where they were. He enrolled in a dancing class which, indirectly, led him to meet his wife.[4]

After an evening's class in June of 1940, Boyd was driving back to his barracks. A steady rain fell. As the windshield wipers of his truck intermittently cleared and smudged the glass, he thought he caught sight of something on the road ahead. Rounding the next bend he could see more clearly, but it was too late. His truck hit the oncoming motorcycle and sent it flying into the gutter.[5] Eddie jumped from his vehicle and rushed to the motorcyclist's side.

"My gosh, fella, are you all right? I didn't see you till the last second."

The rider's reply gave Eddie almost as bad a start as the accident itself had. He expected a gruff and perhaps aggressive reply. Instead he heard a soft, well-modulated and distinctly feminine voice. Straining to see through the rain and the dark, Ed Boyd first glimpsed into the beautiful, brown eyes of his future bride.

"I'm all right, all muddy, though, I suppose," she said. "Is the motorcycle ruined?"

Eddie waded through the culvert to the twisted cycle some ten feet away.

"Yes, I think so," he replied honestly. "It doesn't look to me as though that bike's ever going anywhere again. Let me drive you back to your unit. They can send a truck out to pick up the wreck."

Doreen Mary Frances Thompson hesitated only a moment before accepting the offer – and altering her life forever.

Years later Eddie and Doreen disagreed on many details of their unusual meeting and even on the whirlwind days that followed. On one important point, however, they enthusiastically agreed – it was love at first sight.

Nothing in the pretty young woman's life had prepared her for meeting Edwin Alonzo Boyd.

"We were brought up staunch Catholics, all of us. There's my brother Bill, my sister Freda and then there's Joan and myself. We're twins. My father was a miner but Joan and I, we were brought up by my grandmother because my mother was sick after we were born," Doreen explained a dozen years later before adding, "My grandmother met Ed once. She liked him. She liked him a lot but she said to me, 'Doreen, you'll never know what that man is thinking. He's as deep as a drawn well.'"

"When I was fourteen I entered the convent – the Sisters of Charity. They were good to us, they taught me a lot. We had to choose to devote our lives either to prayer or work. I'd chosen work. My name was going to be Sister Bonaventure. Then, after four years of training and preparation, the Sisters gave us time to reconsider before we took our final vows. I decided I wanted to go out into the world again."[6]

Part of her training in the convent had included "homemaking arts" and before long, a more secular Doreen Boyd had found a job as a parlormaid for Lord Louis Mountbatten.[7] Not long afterward, the war broke out.

"I was the first of the family to enlist," Doreen related proudly. "I joined the auxiliary territorials as a dispatch rider. My father was a veteran of the first war, and he enlisted in the second. He served in Palestine and with the Eighth Army. My brother enlisted and my sister worked in munitions."[8]

The war meant an exciting increase in the numbers of single men inhabiting the small English towns. Better still, these boys weren't just your run-of-the-mill types that all the girls had grown up with. These fellows were Canadian – they were far from home, slightly exotic and extremely appealing.

"I met Norman Boyd, one of Ed's younger brothers, first. He told me all about his brother and I had [also] heard about Ed from the other fellows in his unit. They all liked and respected him. They said he was quiet, saved his money and didn't drink or smoke," Doreen explained before adding. "But that he was a good fellow all the same."[9]

Perhaps these glowing testimonials helped Doreen make up her mind quickly, because within two weeks they were married. Eddie expedited matters considerably by merely changing the name on his "application to marry" form still being held by his commanding officer. Substituting Doreen's name for the school teacher's greatly minimized the time necessary for paperwork.

They were young and in love and madly happy.

"We were married quietly in the registrar's office. I wore a pink dress under a grey coat, and I had no flowers. We had seven days leave in London then back to our units. When I'd be out on a [dispatch] run I used to take my speedometer off and go visit him. Later he used to drive fifty miles a night to see me. He was smart. He went from private to sergeant-major in no time at all. Then he was demoted to private again for coming to see me too often and over-staying his leave."[10]

Despite the rather unorthodox marital conditions, Doreen soon realized she was pregnant. Their first child, a son, was born in London during a heavy blitz.

"I didn't mind too much. Ed was there to hold my hand. He never left me. [After that we] lived in a series of flats over there until 1942 when Ed decided I should bring the baby and come to Canada. I lived with his parents [father and new wife] in Rosedale.[11] They seemed very religious, evangelical, I think."[12]

Shortly after arriving in Canada, Doreen gave birth to her second son. This time it was much harder. Her beloved Eddie was still in England, so she did not have his presence to comfort and support her.

The baby, whom she'd named Edwin, died in infancy. Both Doreen and Eddie were devastated, not only by the tragic loss, but by the fact that they couldn't be together to share their grief. Eddie wrote:

Your words tell me of your precious love for me and all about the heartbreak of having our baby son snatched away. However, darling, it was better that we hadn't a chance to get to know him as we knew our oldest boy, because it would have been harder that way. We still have our very deep love for each other.[13]

Doreen lived in Canada with her in-laws for the duration of the war. Love letters between the younger Mr. and Mrs. Boyd flew back and forth across the Atlantic until May, 1945, when the allies declared victory. At last, Eddie and thousands like him, made his way home.

"We took a small bungalow in north Toronto. When the twins came along Ed would think nothing of changing the twins' diapers or feeding them for me or helping with the dishes. He's always been thoughtful and helpful that way."[14]

Now, at the age of 31 and on "civvy street," the thoughtful, helpful and romantic Edwin Boyd was faced with a new challenge. He had to find his first steady job.

Both Boyd's brothers had gotten work with the Toronto Transit Commission and so Ed applied there too. They took him on immediately. Occasionally the three Boyd brothers worked together on tandem streetcars. Ed was the driver, Gordon was the conductor and Norman sat in the trailer. Some high-spirited pranks among the brothers helped pass the otherwise routine hours.

This, Ed's first "real job," was undeniably steady, clean work, but it lacked an element that had become important to Boyd over the past 15 years – excitement. He packed it in after only nine months.

For the next three years Edwin Boyd worked at a number of dead-end, low-paying jobs to support his adored Doreen and their three beloved children. All of these positions offered one quality in common with driving streetcars – they were boring. Ed became frustrated and bitter seeing men around him succeed while he seemed unable to find satisfying employment.

It wasn't that Eddie minded much for himself. He didn't. If he'd only had himself to be responsible for, he would merely have wandered off looking for adventure. But Doreen – she was so loving and patient with the children, so deserving of more. It warmed Ed's heart every time he thought of his wife. In his wildest imaginings he never for a moment thought he'd have the good fortune to marry a woman as wonderful as his mother but, just like the popular song of the time, he'd managed to find "a girl, just like the girl, who married . . . Dad" and he was fiercely determined to give her the devotion and respect his father had never given his mother.

Ed was considerably less concerned, however, about his attributes as an employee. He had few specific job-related skills, and showed absolutely no interest in developing any additional ones. He sincerely believed that he had served his country during the war and in return his country should now provide him with a comfortable living. When that comfortable living wasn't forthcoming, Ed became resentful and angry.

His attitude, however, was due to change. The last autumn of the decade was quickly approaching and as with 1929 and 1939, the autumn of 1949 marked a further turning point in Eddie's life. This time the personal watershed would affect many who, up to that point, had never heard of Edwin Alonzo Boyd.

"I was listening to the news on the radio one day and I heard about a bank robbery. That started me thinking. I thought and thought for days because it all seemed so simple. Too simple. Finally I decided I had nothing to lose. I didn't have to worry about buying a gun. I'd kept my pistol from the war, lots of us had. We'd report them lost and just pack them away in our locker," Boyd explained.

"Then I began to look around for the best bank to rob. It couldn't be in my own neighbourhood where I'd be recognized and it had to be on a main street so I could disappear quickly into the crowd once I had the loot. I wandered around the city looking for my first job. I didn't say anything to Doreen about what I was doing. I just told her I was looking for work, which, in a way was right."[15]

On the morning of Friday, September 9, 1949, Eddie Boyd waited somewhat impatiently for his wife and three children to leave for their morning playtime at the park. He kissed and hugged all four warmly and told Doreen not to hold lunch for him.

"I think I might be able to get a couple of window-washing contracts," he informed her dishonestly.

"You'll be home for dinner, though, won't you?" she inquired.

"Of course, my Brownie," he assured her. The diminutive referred to Doreen Boyd's dark brown eyes.

Once the house was empty, Eddie had second thoughts. Maybe he should just go out looking for window washing jobs. Maybe this robbing banks wasn't going to be as easy as it had first seemed. He wandered around the house blindly and in a quandary for half an hour. As he entered the cramped living room he looked about as though noticing the place for the first time.

In the living room a secondhand couch was sagging badly and even ripped in spots. On the table beside it lay a pile of unopened mail – bills. Eddie turned on his heel and walked quickly to the bedroom he and Doreen shared. He opened the top bureau drawer, the one where Doreen kept her makeup. Moments later he had darkened his face with rouge and stuffed half a dozen cotton balls into his mouth. The effect was dramatic. He not only looked very different but as a bonus, slightly intimidating.

From the outside Ed Boyd may have looked the way he wanted but he certainly wasn't feeling the way he needed to in order to commit his first bank robbery. He was vibrating with nervousness. Fortunately, he could fix that with one long, strong, slug of courage from a bottle which had sat untouched in the Boyds' kitchen since the Christmas before.

The unaccustomed taste still burned in Eddie Boyd's throat as he steered his truck toward Avenue Road. The trip seemed to take an inordinately long time and was punctuated by Boyd violently shaking his increasingly foggy head.

"I shouldn't have had that whiskey," he realized, about 15 minutes too late. "I guess I'll just have to keep going as best I can."

He drove his car to a residential street one block east and six blocks south of his intended target – the Armour Heights branch of the Bank of Montreal where the staff worked in blissful ignorance, their only shared concern was the anticipation of an exceptionally busy Friday, the Friday of the annual Labor Day weekend. It was 11:02 a.m.

By 11:04 a.m. Eddie Boyd had come and gone – with the equivalent of almost a year's pay. And the bank employees had a new story for their future grandchildren.

In retrospect, the heist had been easy – undeniably unnerving for all involved, but absolutely simple and straightforward. Once his heart had stopped pounding and Eddie was able to drive away to a more familiar neighborhood, in his familiar truck, the job, in his mind, became easier and easier.

"Why didn't I think of this sooner?" he asked himself, grabbing an old rag from a carton behind the driver's seat and wiping away his cosmetic disguise.

He didn't want to go home just yet. He needed more time to calm himself. Besides, he was rich now. He could afford to buy some gifts for his beloveds.

Eddie drove to Yonge and St. Clair where he treated himself to lunch at Fran's Restaurant before doing some shopping. He bought a new outfit for each of the children. They would be starting school again right after the holiday weekend and he didn't want his children to be shabbily dressed.

Then he chose a new dress for Doreen. He was particularly pleased with this purchase. It was so pretty even just hanging on the rack; pretty and very feminine in a quiet way – just like Doreen herself.

As anxious as Ed was to see his family's faces as he gave them their gifts, he timed his arrival home carefully. He could not let excitement blow his cover. He waited until he knew the twins would have gone back to the park to play, with the older boy as supervisor. Doreen had established the routine at the beginning of the summer in order to give her a chance each day to do housework.

This particular afternoon, however, the carpet sweeper stayed in the broom closet and the lunch dishes remained on the kitchen table. Taking advantage of the children's absence, the Boyds spent a very physical and satisfying afternoon. Made a little giddy by the unexpected interlude in her day, Doreen feigned annoyance.

"I'll never get anything accomplished this afternoon, with you carrying on like that," she informed her grinning husband. "We might as well sit and have a cup of tea, I suppose."

Eddie jumped from the bed, where he'd been reposing and captured his wife in his arms once again. To her cries of 'put me down, Ed, put me down' he swung the pretty woman around and sprinkled her face with kisses.

"You'll never have another thing to worry about, my dear Brownie," he predicted with considerably more enthusiasm than accuracy.

Doreen Boyd wondered what had gotten into her husband to make him talk and act so foolishly. She loved him too unselfishly though to think of spoiling his euphoria with her questions. And so for the time being, she remained in innocent ignorance of Ed's career change.

The Boyd family enjoyed summer's last long weekend and Tuesday morning Doreen watched as first her husband went off to work as a window washer and then her children happily headed off for the first day of their new school year.

"It's a good thing I have the whole day ahead to get the house clean. I need it after that episode Friday afternoon and then the long weekend," Doreen thought with a smile as she surveyed the little house.

Eddie found his window washing assignments much more tolerable now that he knew he wasn't financially dependent on them. When he worked, which he did irregularly at best, he did so with a grin. He had stashed away the balance of his take from the heist and was careful to bring it out only in believable allotments. Ed didn't want Doreen to become suspicious. He bought a new car and told her he was making monthly payments on it, when, in fact, he had paid for the vehicle with funds begrudgingly supplied by the Bank of Montreal.

Although he'd stolen the equivalent of a reasonable year's wage, the funds didn't stretch that far and within a few months Boyd was broke again. Not that you could fault the man for not budgeting more carefully – he knew there was plenty more cash where that first infusion came from – the banks. And so Eddie Boyd robbed his second and then his third bank.

Doreen noticed that occasionally Eddie would arrive home a bundle of nerves and testosterone. She wondered about these manic outbursts, but never for very long. Then one morning early in March of 1951, Doreen was listening to the radio as she prepared the children's lunch. She hummed along happily as the station played "Tennessee Waltz." Suddenly the radio announcer's harsh voice replaced Patty Page's melodic one.

"We interrupt this broadcast to bring you a news flash. Another Toronto bank has just been robbed at gun point. It is not known yet how much money the lone gunman made off with. No one was injured in the hold-up, although shots were fired."

Patty Page's voice picked up the beat again, almost as though she'd never been disturbed. Doreen's accompaniment did the same. She might never have given the news announcement another thought if the side door hadn't opened just at that moment.

"Hello, my beautiful Brownie!" Eddie called out from the doorway. She hadn't been expecting him home until evening. Suddenly Doreen Boyd knew. She watched her husband approach her, his eyes glistening and cheeks slightly flushed. He held out his arms to greet her, but she remained by the kitchen counter as though frozen in place

"I just heard on the radio about another bank robbery. It's you, isn't it, Ed?" she asked simply.

He nodded.

"Please, give me a moment," Doreen asked. "I have a lot to think about."

Without another word Eddie Boyd, bank robber extraordinaire, took over the lunch making chores and Doreen made her way to the living room where she sat in silence for just a few minutes. The sounds of the children arriving home from school for their noon meal broke her trance.

The chaos of the lunch hour at least allowed time for contemplation. By the time the twins and their older brother were on their way back to school, Doreen was over her initial shock. A tiny part of her mind had to admit that the scenario wasn't really a complete surprise. If she'd been completely honest with herself she might have recognized that she'd been repressing suspicions for some months now.

"Eddie, you're careful, aren't you?" was all she said.

He nodded reassuringly and embraced her warmly to show his appreciation for her concern and understanding. Their love making that afternoon was more subdued than it had been after the previous robberies. Years later she defended her acceptance of Eddie's activities by saying, "If it had been murder or rape, I might feel differently but Ed never hurt anybody, only the banks and they're heavily insured. They don't lose anything."[16]

Whether or not Doreen Mary Frances Thompson Boyd actually believed that convoluted sense of what was right is anyone's guess. She may have, or conversely, those somewhat warped ethics may have evolved through the years as a coping device.

Whatever the order of events, at least now Eddie was able to drop the "going to work" guise and freely discuss, with his wife, the trials and satisfactions of his new career.

By early summer of 1951, the influx of cash into the Boyd household, combined with a grant from the Department of Veterans' Affairs office, enabled Eddie and Doreen to realize the great Canadian dream – home ownership. They bought a small lot in Pickering, just east of Toronto, and began to build themselves a cement block bungalow.

Eddie did most of the work himself. Doreen supervised the children, who played happily in the surrounding fields, and helped her husband when he needed it. At first their living conditions were spartan, but still it was fun. This was the closest the Boyds had ever been to a normal domestic situation. Brick by brick the house began to take shape. Soon they had electricity and then running water. Ed liked to stay up-to-date on current events and so, as he worked away, he listened to the radio.

The news reports he heard concerning a gang of bank robbers operating in rural Ontario interested Eddie. He was a quick study and each time Ed pulled off a job, he had learned something from it. It would be even better if he could learn from the experience of others as well. Perhaps this "Numbers Mob," as the police had taken to calling the group of robbers, knew something he didn't. Maybe there would be more safety in a group.

Eddie's biggest concern during his hold-ups had always been control. Because he was badly outnumbered by bank staff it was difficult to keep watch over all of them. Disturbingly, often this had resulted in being shot at. So far, thanks only to poor bank staff marksmanship, he had escaped unharmed. But Eddie knew his luck wouldn't hold forever. Maybe he needed to take on a partner. If he chose the man carefully, Ed figured it would help to balance the ratio during a hold-up. One man could keep the bank staff covered with his gun, while the other cleaned out the tellers' cash drawers. But where to find the right accomplice?

In their book, *The Boyd Gang*, Marjorie Lamb and Barry Pearson explain – the perfect partner would be a man who was easily led, needed the money, had experience robbing banks, but was not necessarily too smart. With luck he would be fast on his feet and at ease with a weapon.[17]

Unfortunately, the man Boyd ultimately settled for had few of those characteristics. Howard Gault *was* familiar with weapons and he *did* need the money, but there the similarity to perfection ended. Despite this, Boyd took him on and his luck as a bank robber continued. The haul from their first joint robbery was poor. It netted each of them less than a thousand dollars, and caused Eddie to seriously re-think the wisdom of a partner. If he hadn't had to share the take, he and Doreen would have been sitting pretty for a much longer time.

Still, the theft had to be termed a success in the greater scheme of things. In addition to the cash, it had provided Gault with a new revolver, courtesy of the bank's administration, and better still, just days later, another man, Peter Marino, was arrested for the hold-up. Although he protested his innocence long and loud and even provided a witness who swore he was working in her store at the time of the hold-up, Marino was convicted of the crime Boyd and Gault committed and was sentenced to 10 years in Kingston Penitentiary.

What a dividend for our Eddie! Convinced they had the robberies solved, the police effectively closed the file. Boyd no longer had to be worried about them tracing the crimes to him. Fate had provided him with an extraordinary situation – he had all the advantages of starting fresh with the added benefit of experience.

By now both Eddie and Doreen fully accepted all the advantages and disadvantages of Ed's career choice. Doreen learned to budget household expenses around occasional lump sums of money rather than the weekly pay cheque that most of her peers had to work with. They both enjoyed the fact that they had considerably more time together than most couples.

Then on July 3, 1951, police arrested Leonard Jackson, suspected kingpin of the highly successful "Numbers Mob." Boyd was badly shaken by the news. He had greatly admired the gang and had thought they had all the angles figured. Apparently not.

Eddie set about finding out as much as he could about Jackson and the others. If he could learn from their successes, he had better also learn from their failures, he reasoned and on one point he was adamant. In Eddie's estimation, the Numbers Mob had been asking for trouble having their "molls," as the gangster women were called, drive the get-away cars. Combining women and bank robbery was a surefire route to trouble in Eddie's mind.

And really, there was no need to buy into the whole gangster image. You left yourself too vulnerable that way – flashy women, flashy clothes, flashy cars. These were the kinds of things the cops would be looking for when they were looking for bank robbers. Ed was comfortable being a nondescript kind of fellow who knew when he left for work in the afternoon his woman would be scanning the *Ladies Home Journal* for a new pot roast recipe.

All in all, Boyd was satisfied that he was on a long, lovely roll of good luck and that he was far too clever to ever face Jackson's fate. Ironically, Boyd planned his next bank job with even more confidence than usual.

Doreen knew where Ed was going when he left the house on October 16, 1951. She anticipated that her husband would be home just a few hours later, with that meaningful twinkle in his eye. She arranged for the children to play at a friend's house for awhile after school before setting about her routine housekeeping tasks.

By late afternoon Doreen was as concerned as most women are when their husbands are late getting home from work. First she was irritated at what she thought was his lack of consideration, and then worried that something out of the ordinary had happened. It had.

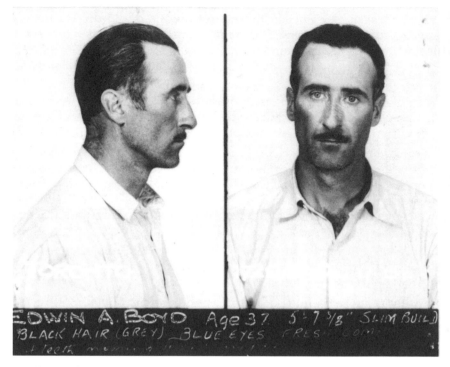

*Edwin Alonzo Boyd's mug shots. (photos courtesy of the Toronto Police Museum)*

Boyd had been right about the roll of good luck continuing – unfortunately it wasn't *his* luck that held. It was the luck of the Toronto police force that held. Less than three months after they'd captured Lennie Jackson, they collared Boyd and Gault. The three thieves were now locked away in a row of cells in the Don Jail. The arrangement was tailor-made for trouble.

Jackson had tried unsuccessfully to break out a month before. Steve Suchan, a member of the Numbers' Mob the police had missed in their round up, had done what he could to be of assistance, but their plan hadn't panned out. Now that the authorities had seen fit to add Eddie Boyd to Jackson's pool of resources, he knew they would both be back in business in no time.

On an unseasonably cold night in early November 1951, Edwin Boyd and Leonard Jackson excused themselves from the confines of the Don Jail via sawn bars and a rope constructed of prison-issue bed sheets. They escaped the jail yard undetected, taking a man named Willie Jackson (no relation to Lennie) with them. Willie was a likeable fellow and an accomplished petty thief whom Eddie and Lennie had befriended during their stay.

Eddie got a message to Doreen. As quickly as she could without drawing attention to herself, Doreen made her way from the cement block bungalow in Pickering to the bank robbers' hideaway at the Suchan home in central Toronto. The Boyds may have been reunited, but their days of normal family life were now behind them.

No one knows what Doreen Boyd's reaction to the remnants of the Numbers Mob was. Was she shocked by the molls, by their conduct and appearance? These women were just a few years younger than Doreen, but they were certainly more streetwise. Their jobs as "hostesses" at downtown bars provided them with life experiences not available to Doreen at the Sisters of Charity Convent.

Doreen may have been intrigued by these differences or she may have been appalled by them. Meeting Ann Roberts and Mary Mitchell at least allowed her a privilege she'd never had before. If she wished to do so, Doreen Boyd could now candidly discuss her husband's work-related problems with other women. There is no indication whether or not she took advantage of the opportunity.

There is evidence, however, of Eddie and Doreen's unwavering devotion to one another and their children.

"We spent that Christmas [1951] at the Sunnyside Motel," Doreen recalled. "It was a real family Christmas. The children were all there. We handed out the presents and even had a turkey dinner. The only thing we didn't manage was a Christmas tree.

"In the evening Ed and I went to the Famous Door and had supper there. It was nice but we both had the feeling we might be recognized at any minute and that doesn't make anyone in our position feel very comfortable.

"New Year's Eve we spent at home [in Pickering]. Ed bought a bottle of champagne and we toasted the New Year in – just the two of us. It wasn't the best New Year's we'd ever spent, but we both had high hopes for the future.

"[L]ater, just before the kids had to go back to school, Ed decided that we all needed a holiday. He took the kids and me over to Niagara Falls for the weekend. We stayed in a motel. For those few short days at Niagara it seemed as though we were a normal family again."[18]

Even escaped convicts have bills to pay and with two mortgages on his house, Eddie needed to find work. And he did. The Boyd Gang had pulled off two successful bank jobs within their first few months of existence. By early in 1952, Doreen moved back to the house she and Ed had so happily built. Her exposure to Ann and Mary's involvement with the gang only intensified Doreen's unrelenting desire for a normal family life. She told a newspaper reporter, "If it hadn't been for me he'd still be free. I led them to him, but I didn't know it. Why, he risked his life two or three times a week to see if I was all right. That was when we lived at Pickering. There was only one way in and one way out, through the lake but he came anyway."[19]

It is unlikely that Doreen was as much to blame as she feared. By the time Ed was captured, the little house was empty and Doreen was where she wanted to be – beside her husband. The children were in boarding school and the neighbors in Pickering believed Doreen had fled to her native England.

No, in reality, the end of Edwin Boyd's freedom was not brought on by anything Doreen did or didn't do. It was the actions of one of the other women in the mob that set the stage for that.

While Steve Suchan was enjoying a warm relationship with Mary Mitchell, Lennie Jackson's sister, he had also developed a close relationship with a woman named Anna Bosnich. So close, in fact, that Anna was pregnant with Steve Suchan's son.

One of the many advantages Steve gained through this relationship was access to Anna's expensive new car. Either to keep Steve away from Anna or as revenge for his infidelities, Mary informed Sergeant of Detectives Edmond Tong, on the Toronto Police Force, of Suchan's friendship with Anna. Mary even specified the other woman's address and added that if police spotted a dark colored 1949 Mercury Monarch, and a man was driving it, they would have Steve Suchan, former member of the Numbers Mob, now a pivotal player in the Boyd Gang.

On March 6, 1952, Tong and his partner, Roy Perry, were patrolling the area around the address Mary Mitchell had given them for Anna Bosnich. They caught sight of the Monarch. As Mary had predicted, Suchan was driving. Leonard Jackson was in the passenger's seat. A gun battle ensued. Both Tong and Perry were hit, Tong fatally. Jackson and Suchan fled, unharmed, in the Monarch.

Completely unaware of this serious turn of events, Eddie and Doreen spent the evening seeing a movie.

"We first heard of the shooting when we came out of the show," Doreen explained. "We had been to see *Another Man's Poison*. Ed saw the headlines and bought a *Telegram*. When he read the news we bought groceries for a week and went home. We stayed inside the house [not their own bungalow] for a week, never setting foot outside the door.

"The one room was so hard on Ed and me though, and we decided to move. That was when we went to the Heath Street house where Ed was captured."

She added, "Believe me, neither Ed nor I saw or heard from either Suchan or Jackson from the time of the shooting."[20]

Boyd was furious when he realized it was one of the "molls" who had led to the shooting. He'd known all along this would lead to disaster.

Eddie may have been a bank robber, but he would never have lowered himself to infidelity. He might be late getting home from work because he was being shot at or arrested, but never because he was in bed with another woman. Not only did he not need those complications in his life, but he was still very much in love with his wife. Doreen was simply everything he'd ever hoped to find in a woman.

Suchan and Jackson fled to Montreal. The next day, in a hail of bullets, Suchan was arrested.

Lennie remained holed up in an apartment across town. He had recently married the very beautiful Ann Roberts, one of the gang's molls. Ann was pregnant with Lennie's child. Once they heard of Steve's arrest, they knew it would only be a matter of days before the police would find them. Four days later, on March 11, 1952, Ann heard a commotion outside the apartment.

"They're here," she said simply.[21]

Like Suchan, Jackson chose to shoot it out. As police led the seriously injured Jackson away, he threatened to send Eddie Boyd after them. The threat further etched the image of a closely knit, high-living gang.

In fact, when they were arrested, Lennie and Ann had less than a dollar and a half to their names; Suchan had been existing on borrowed funds, and they had had little contact with Boyd for weeks.

The Boyds knew they would not have long now. The police had already been in touch with Eddie's brothers and were convinced the Boyds were still in Toronto. And that was where authorities intended to keep them. Roadblocks were set up at the city's exits. Effectively trapped, Eddie, Doreen and Norman Boyd posed as missionaries and rented an upstairs flat in a pleasant residential area.[22]

Doreen and Norman settled into the rooms first. That evening they brought a tired and dejected Ed Boyd to the new-found hideout. It was Friday, March 14, 1952.

"Why don't you take a leisurely bath, dear?" Doreen asked as soon as Ed was upstairs. She could see the terrible toll the last few days had taken on her husband.

"No," he said. "I'm too tired. There will be plenty of time in the morning."[23]

Although they didn't know it, the Boyds were already under close surveillance. Dozens of police officers were hiding in the house next door to the Boyds' rented rooms. Dozens more were waiting in a circle that cordoned off the block. All the men had been thoroughly briefed and knew what they had to do to pull off the arrest of Canada's Most Wanted Man, Edwin Alonzo Boyd.

Despite the unwavering intention of the Toronto Police Force to capture Eddie Boyd, a reminder had been issued to the officers involved.

Now look, boys, this comes straight from the boss. You're going into a very refined district. If all hell breaks loose up there, the chief says if there's any cursing or swearing on behalf of the members of this department, they will be charged.

One detective grumbled later, "The word was really laid down. You might have to kill some son-of-a-bitch, but be a gentleman about it."[24]

The plan was to phone Boyd just before daybreak, tell him he was surrounded and give him the chance to give himself up. Eight minutes before the call was to be made, the police holed up in the house next door began to move. Detective Dolph Payne led his men into the house at 42 Heath Street West and up the stairs. The first room they checked was empty. In the second room they found Norman Boyd. With his gun drawn Dolph Payne kicked open the third door.

"Boyd, it's Payne," he called out.

Doreen sat up in bed.

"The police are here," she said quietly.[25]

It was the Ides of March.

As the people in the "refined district" surrounding 42 Heath Street West began their day, it quickly became apparent that something very exciting was unfolding in their usually quiet neighborhood. The *Toronto Telegram* reported a "party atmosphere."[26] Everyone except Doreen Boyd and Dolph Payne joined in the festive mood. Doreen was angry and distraught. Not only was she made to dress in front of a bunch of policemen, but they took all her personal possessions. They wouldn't even let her have her toiletries. She left the house on the arm of a police matron. With her other hand she shielded her face from the onlookers and the press.

Dolph Payne was just too busy to join the others in their celebration. He was a thorough man and wanted to make sure he had all the evidence he needed before he left the house.

Eddie, however, seemed to have no such concerns. He hammed it up for the news photographers and even posed for pictures with Allan Lamport, Toronto's flamboyant mayor. "Shall I smile?" he asked the mayor.[27]

Boyd's banter that morning was merely a show. The unthinkable had happened. All of his efforts to provide for Doreen and the children had failed. Worse, his beloved family was now separated from one another. The children were in a boarding school, Doreen was in a cell for women and he was back behind the bars of the Don Jail. He had failed miserably. He had managed no better than his father had. Ed had never forgiven the older man and now he knew he could never forgive himself either. Utterly despondent, Eddie lay on his jail cot, motionless, for hours on end. He had been told of the police official's original plan to capture him and lamented the last minute change.

"I wished they would've phoned me first and told me the place was surrounded," Boyd said. "It would've been marvelous. I would've shot my way out. Actually, in my mind from the very beginning I figured that life wasn't really worth living. I never got any real enjoyment out of life until I started robbing banks. Then when they finally got me and the chips were right down I didn't care whether I lived or died. I didn't want to go to prison. I'd already had a little bit of a taste of that. Just a day-to-day hum-drum existence meeting with lots of people you really didn't want to mix with. I couldn't really see the years ahead as being that worthwhile, to be honest."[28]

Eddie Boyd was a changed man. Gone was the tender and loving man who married Doreen Mary Frances Thompson Boyd, and who pined whenever he was away from her and who doted on their children. The realization that he had fallen so far short of his intentions was unbearable to him. He began to hide in the "tough guy" image the press had created for him.

"There is no point in living," he decided.

Slowly, Eddie's suicidal depression lifted. He began to write letters to Doreen and the children. Every correspondence leaving the jail was censored and so he could not tell his family that he planned to see them very soon. He did, however, remind all four that he loved them.

The authorities were on guard against another of Boyd's escape attempts. Displaying almost awesome incompetence, they placed him in a high security cell block – right next to his former colleague, Willie Jackson. Eddie and Willie began a bizarre campaign of prayer – prayer directed at Satan. To their utter delight and amazement, it seemed to become effective. For one thing, Lennie and Steve were gaining strength everyday. They were already well enough to be transferred from a Montreal hospital to the Toronto jail. Soon they'd be well enough to help carry out the escape plan.

About this time fate (or the devil) sent Willie Jackson an unscrupulous lawyer. The man admitted there was little he could do for Willie in a courtroom, but perhaps there might be one or two things he could supply to Willie and his friends from the outside world. What a kind offer! There certainly was – a file would be a handy device and so would a small, thin sheet of metal. Thanks to these smuggled gifts early in the morning of September 8, 1952, the newly re-united Boyd Gang was ready to say farewell to the temporary hospitality the Don Jail had, once again, afforded them.

As the four desperadoes stood poised to drop from a second storey ledge outside their cells they suddenly froze. Directly beneath them was a policeman. They were trapped. From the corridor outside their cells, they could hear the early morning bed check beginning. In seconds their absence would be noted and the hunt would be on. Just as they were ready to give up, a door in the jail courtyard opened below them and someone waved the patrolman in. It was time for the man's coffee break. Their prayers had once again been answered and the Boyd Gang jumped to freedom.

As soon as she heard of their escape, Doreen Boyd also sprang into action. She contacted journalists. She assured them the Gang would rob "several banks in the Toronto area."[28] The entire city and much of the country was on edge. Maintaining she had no idea where her husband was, Doreen made regular appeals, through the media, for Eddie to give himself up. On September 9, 1952, her picture appeared on the front page of the *Toronto Telegram*. It was three years to the day since Edwin Boyd had robbed his first bank.

In a lengthy interview she had with *Telly* journalist Dorothy Howarth, Doreen proclaimed, "I wouldn't give him up for a million [dollars]. You know what it's like when you love a man."[29]

In keeping with the fashion-conscious times, Howarth included in the article details of Doreen's "smart red, white and blue purse," her "small, beautifully chased cigarette lighter of a foreign make in a monogrammed leather case." Even though several close up photographs accompanied the feature, Howarth described the woman's appearance in detail.

> The wife of Canada's "Master Bank Bandit" is a small woman, about five feet four, with very dark hair and snapping dark eyes. She has a wide attractive smile and a well-modulated English voice.[30]

Two days later, after Boyd had spent at least one night with his wife and children, the following letter ran in the newspapers:

My Dearest Eddie

> Am I asking too much of you under the circumstances *to give yourself up*? If to anyone to me *or* to the men both you and I know would give you a fair deal. I have thought this over so much in the past three days, and knowing me as your devoted wife, I'll *wait* for you no matter what the outcome may be. God willing we will have the privilege of growing old together. This is all I ask of you and Eddie remember always I love you dearly.

Yours,

Frances Boyd XXXX

B.C.R.D.[31]

The next day the Boyd children were called into the ruse and, much to the disgust of most of the general public, a radio station broadcast their pleas to their father. "We miss you, Daddy, please come home."[32]

Banks pointlessly beefed up their security systems. The Boyd Gang had robbed its last bank. Their freedom was to be shortlived this time. On September 16, in response to several citizens' reports that tramps had been seen in the area, police entered a deserted barn, just northeast of Toronto. There, tired and malnourished, out of reach of their guns, the Boyd Gang surrendered.

A speedy trial date was arranged. The Gang was held in city cells directly below the courtroom. Officer Jack Webster, now historian for the Metropolitan Toronto Police Service, remembers guarding Boyd on the day of the trial.

"I told him that as a rookie cop I had walked the beat with his father and that Tom was so proud of Ed's accomplishments overseas during the war. Boyd replied, 'he should still be proud of me, my picture's on the front page of the newspaper'."[33]

The trials were over quickly. Only Willie Jackson was pleased with the outcome. He was sentenced to 20 years in Kingston Penitentiary for his part in the hold-ups and escapes. This, he felt, would give him ample time to re-new acquaintances with his many friends at his *alma mater*.

Boyd showed no emotion, not even as he listened to the judge award him a total of eight life sentences plus 27 years in jail. The news was too much for Doreen, however; she very nearly fainted and as soon as she was able to she struggled to her husband's side. Their comforting embrace was broken up seconds later.

Once she was able to compose herself, Doreen Boyd asked the judge to return her bag of toiletries, confiscated by the police during their capture last March. The Judge agreed, although he did wonder afterward why the woman's mood had improved so quickly. He actually thought he saw a trace of what could have been a smug smile on Doreen Boyd's lips as she left the courtroom hugging a small toiletries case to her chest. He might have mused that her pleasure might have come from the visiting privileges he'd granted Doreen with her husband that afternoon. If he did he was partly right. Doreen was pleased that she'd be able to see Eddie, but she was considerably more pleased that, at last, she had her toiletries back. For there, tightly rolled inside each cardboard tampon tube, was a supply of hundred dollar bills. Eddie Boyd's wife managed to walk out of the courtroom with $6000 in stolen funds.

On December 16, 1952, just after midnight, Leonard Jackson and Steve Suchan were hanged for the murder of police officer Tong.

Doreen Boyd raised her children alone, supporting them from her wages at a menial job.

Eddie Boyd became a model prisoner and was paroled in 1962, after serving only 10 years of his sentence. His freedom that time was short-lived. Parole violations soon put him back in prison.[35] In 1965 he became eligible for parole again. This time the privilege was denied. Finally, in 1966, 52-year-old Edwin Alonzo Boyd was given a new identity and released from prison on lifetime parole.

Sadly, the years apart had extinguished Doreen and Eddie's great love for one another. Within months of being given his freedom from jail, Doreen divorced him. Both eventually re-married. Ironically, they both chose to live the balance of their lives in British Columbia.

Eddie Boyd became a pillar of his new community. Police historian Jack Webster tells an amazing story to prove that point. Some years ago Boyd's testimony was required at a hearing. The Toronto Police Service dispatched officers to the west coast to interview him. Boyd greeted the representatives of his former enemy warmly. He asked where the men would be staying while they were out west. The officers told Boyd the name of the local hotel they'd checked into. Boyd feigned disgust and extended an apparently sincere invitation for them to stay at his home instead.[36]

His new wife may have thought nothing of the offer. It would be interesting to know how the former Mrs. Boyd, Eddie's beloved "Brownie," would have handled such an arrangement.

## *Endnotes*

[1]*Toronto Telegram*, 9 September, 1952.

[2]Edwin Alonzo Boyd's official police record.

[3]Ibid.

[4]*The Boyd Gang*, Marjorie Lamb and Barry Pearson, Peter Martin and Associates, 1976, Toronto, page 13.

[5]*Toronto Telegram*, 9 September, 1952, and dialogue in the movie, *The Life and Times of Edwin Alonzo Boyd*, contradicts this version of their first meeting. The script for that film was based on interviews with Ed Boyd. The *Toronto Telegram* article is based on an interview with Doreen Boyd.

[6]*Toronto Telegram*, 9 September, 1952.

[7]*The Boyd Gang*, page 14.

[8]*Toronto Telegram*, 9 September, 1952. (It is not clear which sister Doreen Boyd is referring to.)

[9]Ibid.

[10]*Toronto Telegram*, 9 September, 1952.

[11]Tom Boyd had, by this time, remarried.

[12]*Toronto Telegram*, 9 September, 1952.

[13]*The Boyd Gang*, page 16.

[14]*Toronto Telegram*, 9 September, 1952.

[15]*The Boyd Gang*, page 19.

[16]*Toronto Telegram*, 9 September, 1952.

[17]*The Boyd Gang*, page 23.

[18]*Toronto Telegram*, 9 September, 1952.

[19]Ibid.

[20]Ibid.

[21]*The Life and Times of Edwin Alonzo Boyd* (movie).

[22]*Toronto Telegram*, 9 September, 1952.

[23]*The Life and Times of Edwin Alonzo Boyd*.

[24]*The Boyd Gang*, page 144.

[25]Ibid., page 146.

[26]*Toronto Telegram*, 15 March, 1952.

[27]Ibid., 9 September, 1952.

[28]Ibid.

[29]Ibid.

[30]Ibid.

[31]*The Boyd Gang*, page 196. (Frances was one of Doreen's middle names. The initials are those of her children, the "D" likely stood for Doreen.)

[32]Ibid., page 195.

[33]Ibid., page 196.

[34]Author's conversation with Jack Webster, September 22, 1994

[35]*The Globe and Mail*, 2 November, 1965.

[36]Author's conversation with Jack Webster, September 22, 1994.

# Bibliography

## Tom Thomson & Winnifred Trainor

Addison, Ottelyn, with Elizabeth Harwood. *Tom Thomson: The Algonquin Years.* Toronto: Ryerson Press, 1969.

Frayne, Trent. "The Rebel Painter of the Pine Woods." *Maclean's,* July 1, 1953, pp. 16-17, 30-33.

Little, William T. *The Tom Thomson Mystery.* Toronto: McGraw-Hill Ryerson, 1970.

MacGregor, Roy. *Shorelines.* Toronto: McClelland and Stewart, 1980.

———. "The Legend." *The Canadian,* October 15, 1977, pp. 3-7.

Mellen, Peter. *The Group of Seven.* Toronto: McClelland and Stewart, 1970.

Murray, Joan. *The Best of Tom Thomson.* Edmonton: Hurtig Publishers, 1986.

———. *Tom Thomson: The Last Spring.* Toronto: Dundurn Press, 1994.

Sharp, Dr. Noble. "The Canoe Lake Mystery." *Journal of the Canadian Society of Forensic Science,* Vol. III, No. 2, June 1970, pp., 34-40.

Town, Harold and David P. Silcox. *Tom Thomson: The Silence and the Storm.* Toronto: MacClelland and Stewart, 1977.

## Mary Pickford & Douglas Fairbanks

Bergan, Ronald. *The United Artists Story.* New York: Crown Publishers, 1986.

Fairbanks, Douglas. *Laugh and Live.* New York: Briton Publishing Co., 1917.

———. *Making Life Worthwhile.* New York: Briton Publishing Co., 1918.

Gomery, Douglas. *The Hollywood Studio System.* New York: St. Martins Press, 1986.

Herndon, Booton. *Mary Pickford and Douglas Fairbanks, The Most Popular Couple the World Has Known.* New York: W.W. Norton and Co., 1977.

Mordden, Ethan. *The Hollywood Studios: House Style in the Golden Age of the Movies.* New York: Alfred A. Knopf, 1988.

Morley, Sheridan. *Tales From the Hollywood Raj, The British, The Movies and Tinseltown.* New York: Viking Press, 1984.

Niver, Kemp R. *Mary Pickford, Comedienne.* New York: Biograph Co., 1969.

Norman, Barry. *The Story of Hollywood.* New York: New American Library, 1987-8.

Pashdag, John. *Hollywood USA: The Moviegoers Guide to Southern California.* San Francisco: Chronicle Books, 1984.

Pickford, Mary. *Sunshine and Shadow.* Garden City: Doubleday and Co., 1955.

———. *The Demi-Widow*. New York: The Bobbs-Merrill Co., 1935.

———. *My Rendezvous with Life*. New York: H.C. Kinsey and Co., 1935.

———. *Why Not Try God*. New York: H.C. Kinsey and Co., 1934.

Windeler, Robert. *Sweetheart, The Story of Mary Pickford*. New York: Praeger Publishers, 1974.

## *Evangeline & Gabriel*

Arsenault, Bona. *History of the Acadians*, Gaspe: Fides, 1994.

Hocking, Anthony. *Nova Scotia*. Toronto: McGraw-Hill Ryerson, 1978.

Longfellow, Henry Wadsworth. *Evangeline*. Halifax: Nimbus Publishing Ltd., 1951.

Moody, Barry. *The Acadians*. Toronto: Grolier Ltd., 1981.

Ross, Sally and Alphonse Deveau. *The Acadians of Nova Scotia: Past and Present*. Halifax: Nimbus Publishing Ltd., 1992.

## *William Lyon Mackenzie King & His Mother*

Dawson, R. MacGregor. *William Lyon Mackenzie King: A Political Biography, 1874-1923*. Toronto: University of Toronto Press, 1958.

English, John and J.O. Stubbs, eds. *Mackenzie King: Widening the Debate*. Toronto: Macmillan, 1977.

Esberey, Joy E. *Knight of the Holy Spirit: A Study of William Lyon Mackenzie King*. Toronto: University of Toronto Press, 1980.

McGregor, F.A. *The Fall & Rise of Mackenzie King, 1911-1919*. Toronto: Macmillan, 1962.

Myers, Arthur. *Ghosts of the Rich and Famous*. Chicago: Contemporary Books, 1988.

Pickersgill, J.W. and D.F. Foster. *The Mackenzie King Record: Volumes I, II, III, IV*. Toronto: University of Toronto Press, 1968, 1970.

Robertson, Heather. *Willie: A Romance, Volume I of the King Years*. Don Mills: General Publishing, 1983.

———. *More Than a Rose: Prime Ministers Wives and Other Women*. Toronto: Seal Books, 1992.

Stacey, C.P. *A Very Double Life: The Private World of Mackenzie King*. Toronto: Macmillan, 1976.

## *Francis & Alma Rattenbury*

Barrett, Anthony A. and Rhodri Windsor Liscombe. *Francis Rattenbury and British Columbia: Architecture and Challenge in the Imperial Age*. Vancouver: University of British Columbia Press, 1983.

Casswell, J.D., Q.C. *A Lance for Liberty*. London: George G. Harrap & Co. Ltd., n.d.

Havers, Sir Michael, Q.C., Peter Shankland and Anthony Barrett. *Tragedy in Three Voices: The Rattenbury Murder*. London: William Kimber, 1980.

Jesse, F. Tennyson, ed. *The Trial of Alma Victoria Rattenbury and George Percy Stoner*. London: William Hodge and Co., 1935.

Napley, Sir David. *Murder at the Villa Madeira*. London: Weidenfeld and Nicolson, 1988.

Rattigan, Terence. *Cause Celebre*. London: H. Hamilton, 1978.

Reksten, Terry. *Rattenbury*. Victoria: Sono Nis Press, 1978.

## John & Mildred Ware

*The Albertan*, July 17, 1967.

Alberta Report, January 23, 1984.

*Calgary Daily Herald*, September 12, 1905.

*Calgary Herald*, dates specified.

*Calgary Tribune*, June 28, 1893.

*Farmers Advocate*, for dates specified.

MacEwan, Grant. *John Ware's Cow Country*. City?: Western Producer Prairie Books, 1973.

Marsden, Slim. unpublished, undated document. Calgary: Glenbow Museum and Archives.

*Western Producer Magazine*, April 22, 1954.

unpublished document. Calgary: Glenbow Museum and Archives, Calgary, August, 1956.

## Louis & Marie Hebert

Arsenault, Bona. *History of the Acadians*. Quebec: Fides, 1994.

Bishop, Morris. *Champlain: The Life of Fortitude*. New York: Alfred A. Knopf, 1948.

Brown, Craig, ed. *The Illustrated History of Canada*. Toronto: Lester & Orpen Denys, 1987.

Conan, Laure. *Louis Hebert: Premier Colon du Canada*. Quebec: L'Evenement, 1912.

Couillard, Abbe Azarie. *Louis Hebert: Premier Colon Canadien et Sa Famille*. Paris: DeBrower and Co., 1913.

———. *Rapport des Fetes du IIIrd Centenaire de L'Arrivee de Louis Hebert au Canada, 1617-1917*. Montreal: La Societe Royale du Canada, 1920.

Creighton, Donald. *Dominion of the North: A History of Canada*. Toronto: Macmillan, 1962.

Deir, Elspeth, Paul Deir and Keith Hubbard. *Canada: Years of Challenge to 1814*. Toronto: Holt, Rinehart and Winston, 1981.

Garrod, Stan. *Samuel de Champlain*. Don Mills: Fitzhenry and Whiteside Ltd., 1981.

Jarvis, Julia. *Louis Hebert*. Toronto: Ryerson Press, 1929.

Kent, Louise Andrews. *He Went With Champlain*. Boston: Houghton Mifflin, 1959.

Morton, W.L. and L.F. Hannon. *This Land, These People: An Illustrated History of Canada*. Agincourt: Gage Publishing, 1977.

Wilson, Charles Morrow. *Wilderness Explorer: The Story of Samuel de Champlain.* New York: Hawthorn Books Inc., 1963.

Woodcock, George. *A Social History of Canada.* Markham: Penguin Books, 1988.

## *John Brownlee & Vivian MacMillan*

Byrne, T.C. *Alberta's Revolutionary Leaders.* Calgary: Detselig Enterprises Ltd., 1991.

Edmonton Journal, applicable dates.

Foster, Franklin Lloyd. *John Edward Brownlee: A Biography.* Edmonton: University of Alberta, 1981.

Information file, Provincial Archives of Alberta.

McDougall, D. Blake. *Premiers of the Northwest Territories and Alberta, 1897-1991.* Edmonton: Legislative Library, 1991.

Palmer, Howard, and Tamara Palmer. *Alberta: A New History.* Edmonton: Hurtig Publishers, 1990.

Photo file, Provincial Archives of Alberta.

Robertson, Heather. *Lily, A Rhapsody in Red: Vol. 2, The King Years.* Toronto: James Lorimer and Co., 1986.

## *E. Pauline Johnson & ?*

Keen, Dorothy, & Martha McKeon. "Pauline Johnson: Canada's Passionate Poet." *Chatelaine,* January and February

Devorski, Lorraine. *Pauline: The Indian Poet.* Ottawa: Canadian Library Association, 1986.

Fetherling, Douglas, ed. *The Broadview Book of Canadian Anecdotes.* Peterborough: Broadview Press, 1988.

Foster, Mrs. W. Garland. *The Mohawk Princess.* Vancouver: Lions' Gate Publishing Co., 1931.

Johnson, E. Pauline. *Legends of Vancouver.* 1911.

———. *Flint and Feather: The Complete Poems of E. Pauline Johnson (Tekahionwake).* Toronto: The Musson Book Co. Ltd., 1912.

Keller, Betty. *Pauline: A Biography of Pauline Johnson.* Toronto: Douglas & McIntyre, 1981.

McRaye, Walter. *Pauline Johnson and her Friends.* Toronto: Ryerson Press, 1947.

Scott, Jack. "The Passionate Princess." Maclean's, April 1, 1952.

## *Eddie & Doreen Boyd*

Lamb, Marjorie and Barry Pearson. *The Boyd Gang.* Toronto: Peter Martin and Associate, 1976.

*Toronto Telegram,* dates as specified.